Manage People, Not Personnel

The Harvard Business Review Book Series

Manage People, Not Personnel

Motivation and Performance Appraisal

With a Preface by
Victor H. Vroom
John G. Searle Professor
of Organization and Management
Yale University

A Harvard Business Review Book

Library of Congress Cataloging-in-Publication Data

Manage people, not personnel : motivation and performance appraisal /
    with a preface by Victor H. Vroom.
        p.   cm.—(The Harvard business review book series)
    Articles originally published in the Harvard business review.
    Includes bibliographical references.
    ISBN 0-87584-228-3
    1. Personnel management.   2. Employee motivation.   3. Employees—
Rating of.   I. Series.
    [HF5549.M2994   1990]   89-77058
    658.3'14—dc20   CIP

Note: Some articles included in this book were written before researchers, writers, and editors began to take into consideration the role of women in management. The assumption that a manager is necessarily male is regrettable. The editor and the publisher hope outdated gender assumptions will not undermine the value of those essays.

The Harvard Business Review articles and Harvard Business School Notes in this collection are available individually. For information and ordering contact Operations Department, Harvard Business School Publishing Division, Boston, MA 02163. Telephone: (617) 495-6192. Fax: (617) 495-6985.

94 93 92 91 90   5 4 3 2 1

Contents

Preface

Victor H. Vroom

This collection of readings concerns human motivation in the workplace and the continuing search for effective ways of managing it. The importance of human motivation to the practice of management has not always been recognized. In this era of global competition it is fitting that a volume be assembled to attest not only to the importance of the problem, but also to the growing body of research, theory, and experience relevant to its solution.

To this writer, it seems appropriate that this collection of readings concerning motivation and performance appraisal should come from Harvard. This great university has a long and distinguished tradition in the study of motivation in the workplace. From the Harvard Business School, under the leadership of an Australian psychologist, Elton Mayo, came the famous Hawthorne experiments at the Western Electric Company. The account of these experiments by Fritz Roethlisberger and William Dickson in a book published in 1939 called *Management and the Worker* dramatically brought attention to the role of motivation in work performance and, in the view of most scholars, launched the inquiry that this book continues.

Less commonly recognized is the fact that at about the same time, on the other side of the Charles River, a psychology professor at Harvard by the name of Henry Murray published a book called *Explorations in Personality,* in which he sought to describe the dimensions of human motivation. Among these dimensions were "needs for achievement" and "needs for affiliation," which became the organizing focus of the work of David McClelland and his colleagues, some of which is described in articles in this volume.

Murray and Mayo represented two different traditions. The former was an academic psychologist interested in the fundamental processes of motivation in individual behavior; the latter was a psychologist with a basic interest in the process of management. Each of these two persons has a different set of "descendants."

Following in the tradition of Murray were such people as Kurt Lewin, David McClelland, and Norman Maier, each of whom shared Murray's deep roots in the academy. These three psychologists carried out research in industry, but their principal purpose was to test concepts and ideas that originated in the psychological laboratory. Upholding the tradition of Mayo were scholars such as Douglas McGregor, Rensis Likert, and Warren Bennis, each of whom was dedicated to improving the practice of management and who borrowed concepts and findings of academic psychology that were useful to them.

In the early days of the quest to understand motivation in the workplace, there was little exchange between these two traditions. If Mayo knew Murray or Kurt Lewin (who was at MIT, only a few miles from Mayo), it is not clear from his writings. Similarly, there is no evidence that Murray or Lewin read and were influenced by Mayo's books.

Now, a half century later, there is much more interaction between the two groups. Disciplines such as organizational behavior and fields of professional practice such as organization development have arisen, blurring the boundaries drawn by their intellectual predecessors. This book reflects this strengthening partnership. Although each of the articles is written for the manager, they all embrace both the findings of academic psychology and the most recent findings from managerial practice.

The articles are divided into two major sections, "Motivation" and "Performance Appraisal." Wickham Skinner sets a broad foundation for both sections in "Big Hat, No Cattle." He describes the fundamental goal of human resource management as the creation of a "motivated work force" in which "people are energized and committed." This state of affairs is seen as "an organization's most effective competitive weapon" in responding to contemporary challenges.

How is this critical state of affairs to be achieved? Michael Beer and Richard E. Walton, in their note on reward systems and the role of compensation, make a distinction between extrinsic and intrinsic motivation, one commonly found in the psychological literature. Extrinsic motivation corresponds to what Lewin called "induced forces" and what is meant by the colloquial usage "the carrot and stick." Applied to the work situation, it refers to rewards and punishments, controlled by others in one's work environment, that may be linked to various aspects of performance. Money, promotions, and recognition by one's manager or coworkers are examples of sources of extrinsic motivation. Intrinsic motivation, on the other hand, stems from a person's relationship to the task itself. One is intrinsically motivated to the degree to which one derives gratification from achievement of the goal of performing a task effectively independent of the rewards one receives from others for so doing.

The articles in the part of this collection dealing with motivation provide useful perspectives for managers on both extrinsic and intrinsic motivation. R. Roosevelt Thomas, Jr., stresses the importance of managers and individual subordinates discussing the needs that each brings to the relationship. In these discussions they should work toward a psychological contract that explicitly recognizes both sets of needs. Thomas asserts the desirability of establishing reward practices so that individuals "see and believe that good performance leads to both extrinsic and intrinsic rewards."

For more than a quarter of a century Frederick Herzberg has been a vociferous proponent of intrinsic motivation. His article, "One More Time: How Do You Motivate Employees?" is a classic, first published in the *Harvard Business Review* in 1968. In this article Herzberg emphasizes the limitations of extrinsic rewards and punishments, referring to the latter by the acronym KITA (meaning "kick in the ass"). His solution is motivation through the work itself, to be achieved through job enrichment. In his retrospective commentary written almost 20 years later, Herzberg muses that the pragmatics of global competition have resurrected KITA and have decreased attention to sources of motivation that are intrinsic to people's relationship to the tasks they perform.

Harry Levinson is equally critical of the power of extrinsic sources of motivation, which he calls "the great jackass fallacy." He describes the carrot and stick approach as responsible for the formation of unions, the frequent sabotage of management's motivation efforts, and employees' suspicion that management seeks to manipulate them. Levinson is less explicit than Herzberg about the most effective means of motivating by intrinsic methods. Whereas Herzberg stresses work redesign, Levinson seemingly emphasizes leadership and power equalization.

In his article "From Control to Commitment in the Workplace," Walton echoes Herzberg's and Levinson's conviction that intrinsic motivation is the preferred answer. However, he seems to disagree strongly with Herzberg that recent trends in practice are opposed to this principle. He describes an ongoing revolution in the management of work involving a movement toward a form of organization in which workers are given broad responsibilities, encouraged to contribute, and helped to derive satisfaction from their work. His inventory of personnel policies in traditional plants (utilizing control) compared with plants of new design (utilizing commitment) is invaluable to those interested in following in the footsteps of General Foods, General Motors, Cummins Engine, and Procter & Gamble, each of which has experimented successfully with high-involvement plants. Walton's recommendations are quite similar to the steps proposed by Jay Lorsch and Haruo Takagi to retain the commitment of plateaued managers.

Rosabeth Moss Kanter's article, "The Attack on Pay," changes the focus of attention to extrinsic rewards. Here she exhorts managers to turn their employees into entrepreneurs, not by enriching their jobs or by involving them in decision making, but by paying them for performance. Employees' pay should be based less on the jobs they hold and more on the contributions they make to the bottom line.

The attentive reader cannot help but notice the vast differences between Herzberg's prescriptions about how to motivate people and those of Kanter! How can one reconcile the two different perspectives? Can both be right, as suggested by Thomas? If this is true, extrinsic and intrinsic motivation are additive and complement one another. Another possibility is that both are right *under different conditions*. This situational or contingency approach to motivation would suggest that there are kinds of jobs, work environments, or even cultures that lend themselves to motivating people by intrinsic methods and others for which extrinsic rewards may be more applicable. While reading the evidence given by the advocates of both approaches, the reader may wish to reflect on the circumstances under which each might be correct.

The contingency approach—as opposed to the idea that extrinsic and intrinsic rewards are complementary—is less troubled by a recent and growing body of evidence suggesting that, at least in the long run, extrinsic and intrinsic motivation tend to conflict or compete with one another.[1] E. L. Deci and R. M. Ryan have carried out an impressive series of studies showing that, under controlled laboratory conditions, sources of extrinsic motivation such as pay and threats of punishment tend to diminish intrinsic motivation. To put it succinctly, the "fun" that one can experience in carrying out tasks tends to be reduced when one encounters compelling extrinsic incentives for performing the task. There is a fable that conveys the spirit of the Deci and Ryan finding:

> In a little Southern town where the Klan was riding again, a Jewish tailor had the temerity to open his little shop on the main street. To drive him out of the town the Kleagle of the Klan set a gang of little ragamuffins to annoy him. Day after day they stood at the entrance of his shop. "Jew! Jew!," they hooted at him. The situation looked serious for the tailor. He took the matter so much to heart that he began to brood and spent sleepless nights over it. Finally out of desperation he evolved a plan.
>
> The following day, when the little hoodlums came to jeer at him, he came to the door and said to them, "From today on any boy who calls me 'Jew' will get a dime from me." Then he put his hand in his pocket and gave each boy a dime.
>
> Delighted with their booty, the boys came back the following day and began to shrill, "Jew! Jew!" The tailor came out smiling. He put his hand in his pocket and gave each of the boys a nickel, saying, "A dime is too much—I can only afford a nickel today." The boys went away satisfied because, after all, a nickel was money, too.
>
> However, when they returned the next day to hoot at him, the tailor gave them only a penny each.
>
> "Why do we get only a penny today?" they yelled.
>
> "That's all I can afford."
>
> "But two days ago you gave us a dime, and yesterday we got a nickel. It's not fair, mister."
>
> "Take it or leave it. That's all you're going to get!"
>
> "Do you think we're going to call you 'Jew' for one lousy penny?"
>
> "So don't!"
>
> And they didn't.[2]

In his recent book, Akio Morita, chairman of Sony, makes a similar point about the possible deleterious effects of extrinsic rewards on intrinsic motivation. He writes, "We like to give the same sort of raise to all. I think this keeps our people well motivated. This may be a Japanese trait, but I do not think so."[3] While it is not yet clear how significant such effects are in work performance in real settings, they do raise questions about the efficacy of simultaneously embracing both extrinsic and intrinsic avenues of approach to the same motivation problem.

The second half of the book deals with the subject of performance appraisal. This important subject is relevant to motivation in so far as it is a process aimed at aligning goals of managers and their direct reports. However, it is more focused, although equally controversial.

Perhaps the most famous article ever written on the subject of appraisals is "An Uneasy Look at Performance Appraisal" by Douglas McGregor, also known for coining the terms *Theory X* and *Theory Y*. McGregor is highly critical of the conventional approach to performance appraisal: in Michael Beer's terminology, the "tell and sell approach." He recommends an alternative that puts major responsibility on subordinates for establishing performance goals and for appraising themselves while progressing toward them.

McGregor's emphasis on goal setting is consistent with the findings of an impressive field experiment carried out at General Electric on the consequences of two alternative methods of appraisal. The experiment is discussed in "Split Roles in Performance Appraisal" by Herbert Meyer, Emanuel Kay, and John French. A work planning and review approach in which the manager took the role of counselor was substituted for a more traditional approach in which the manager acted as judge. A critical component of work planning and review was establishing goals and deadlines for achieving them. The investigators found that traditional appraisals had little or no effect on the subordinate's future job performance. The new work planning and review system elicited more favorable attitudes from subordinates and generated appreciable improvement in their performance.

The emphasis on holding subordinates accountable for goal attainment but maximizing individual discretion in the methods by which the goals are achieved is sometimes called management by objectives. In his article "Appraisal of *What* Performance?" Harry Levinson takes issue with this exclusive focus in appraisals on end results. In many instances, how the game is played is as important as whether the goal was achieved. According to Levinson, people need to know "the topography of the land they are expected to cross and the routes as perceived by those to whom they report." He recommends that managers use the recording of critical incidents concerning the subordinate's behavior to augment the emphasis on results. Such critical incidents can be used in feedback and coaching of the subordinate as well as in making decisions regarding compensation and promotion. Levinson delivers a different attack on MBO systems in "Management by Whose Objectives?" In this article he argues that MBO serves as an organizational control device and, in fact, increases the pressure on individuals to do their jobs. As such, he believes that its value is limited and that it is frequently self-defeating. He argues instead for considering the personal goals of the individual first in a manner reminiscent of Thomas's characterization of the psychological contract.

Beer and Robert Ruh acknowledge the effectiveness as well as the incompleteness of MBO for both coaching and promotional decisions. They describe a performance management system developed at Corning Glass. Managers rated their subordinates on behavioral scales found to be relevant to performance at Corning. Examples of scales include conflict resolution, decisiveness, and flexibility. Then, through one or more developmental interviews, the manager attempted to help subordinates see what changes in behavior were needed and how to plan for them.

Winston Oberg discusses in "Make Performance Appraisal Relevant" both MBO and critical incident methods along with other more traditional approaches to performance appraisal. His basic point is a situational or contingency one—that the method be tailored to the purpose.

The final article in the performance appraisal section, by Gellerman and Hodgson, describes the effects of a new performance appraisal system introduced at American Cyanamid. In this company, performance ratings by managers directly determine compensation levels. The major change was collapsing a ten-point rating scale (with a forced distribution among categories) into a much simpler three-point scale in which 90 percent of employees were rated in the intermediate, or "good," category. Under this relatively undifferentiated system, employees rated appraisals as substantially more fair and more related to their performance than under the finely differentiated system.

The articles in this collection represent the wide spectrum of views of leading scholars and practitioners interested in motivation and performance appraisal. Some of the diversity can be attributed to the fact that the articles have been written over a 30-year period during which much has been learned about the topics. However, it would be a mistake to assume that controversy no longer exists. The readers of this volume will be exposed to and, it is hoped, will participate in a lively debate concerning motivation and performance appraisal—issues of fundamental importance to management.

Notes

1. See E. L. Deci and R. M. Ryan, *Intrinsic Motivation and Self-Determination in Human Behavior* (New York: Plenum, 1985).
2. N. Ausubel, ed., *A Treasury of Jewish Folklore* (New York: Crown, 1976), p. 440.
3. Akio Morita, *Made in Japan: Akio Morita and Sony* (New York: Weatherhill, 1986), p. 186.

PART

I

Motivation

1
Big Hat, No Cattle: Managing Human Resources

Wickham Skinner

In the Dallas airport the other day I saw many tall, well-dressed, and impressive-looking men wearing large, immaculate Stetson cowboy hats. As I walked by one such hat-wearer, I noticed two middle-aged, sunburned men in faded blue jeans standing nearby. They eyed the same fellow, looked him up and down, and then one said quietly to the other, "Big hat, no cattle."

The same can be said of the massive efforts to improve the management of people in U.S. industry. Since World War II, calling it "human relations," "personnel management," "labor relations," and now "management of human resources," business has spent millions to make employees productive, loyal, and motivated.

First, academics, with minds opened by the Hawthorne experiments, led the movement to manage people effectively. Now, eager consultants and zealous staff experts nurture it. *Fortune* writes of personnel directors as the "new corporate heroes." Library shelves overflow with people management books, and a hundred new ones appear every year. Two hundred documented attempts are going on to improve the quality of work life (QWL), and three nationally known institutions have charters to improve productivity and QWL.

Since Hawthorne, successive waves of people-problem solutions and programs have washed and tumbled industry. In some desperation, managers have steadily invested in supervisory training, organizational behavior, interpersonal behavior, T-groups, sensitivity training, employee attitude surveys, job enrichment, flexible benefits, and expanded fringe benefits—bigger pensions, subsidized insurance, more holidays, shorter work days, four-day weeks, and canned communications packages—and now companies are attempting to revive the "work ethic" with human resource departments. Big programs, but where are the payoffs?

Not in productivity. Recent figures show a decline in employee productivity for the United States.

Not in absence of strikes.

Not in widespread amicable labor relations.

Not in the strategic position of many U.S. industries in international competition.

Not in the absence of government intervention, such as OSHA and EEO regulations.

Not in public confidence, support, and credibility in our business system or big corporations.

Not in the image of managers as a benign, trusted group in our society.

Not in the absence of hostility or class warfare.

Not in enthusiastic employee acceptance of new technology, machinery, or equipment in factories, of stripped-down offices, or of efficiency gains in the ever-expanding service industries.

Big hat, no cattle!

Human resources management seems to be mostly good intentions and whistling in the dark or averting unionization. And the results of the 1970s suggest that we may not even be holding our own. The poor management of the work force in this country is damaging the nation and our standard of living. It is making us uncompetitive with the Japanese and some other Asians, the West Germans, the Swiss, and many others.

I do not wish to exaggerate the gloomy aspects of this picture. A handful of large (and certainly many medium-sized and smaller) companies appear to have made their work forces into competitive assets. And surely modest progress has occurred nearly everywhere. For the most part, sweatshops are a thing of the past. Workplaces are better lit and ventilated and are generally safer than in the past. The atmosphere at work is less coldly formal, and decision making more participative. Managers are more aware of feelings and relationships and make fewer overt demands of employees. Fewer "bulls of the woods" charge about offices and factories. Personnel people are more professional, more companies have clearly stated grievance procedures, and house publications regularly explain how and why companies are managing themselves for their employees' benefit.

Some will argue that we've been doing many of the right things and that it is societal factors such as the "declining work ethic," the "new breed," and the "new sociology" that are eroding management's efforts. Regardless, in most companies the results of enlightened people management are simply more comfort, more relaxation, more freedom from pressure, more security, more benefits, and higher pay, not more productivity and loyalty.

What's gone wrong? Why do so few companies actually make use of the greatest competitive weapon of all—the powerful resources of motivated, energized, cooperative, trusting people?

Few managers need much convincing about the importance of people. All the managers I've talked to say, "People are our greatest asset." But they also report, "We don't know how to motivate them." "People are getting harder to manage." "Personnel departments don't give us the leadership we need." "We're just hanging in there trying to cope."

Managers have had difficulty managing human resources for four reasons:

1. Achieving wholehearted cooperation, energy, and commitment from large numbers of employees is difficult, so managers are often unrealistic in their hopes.[1]
2. Concepts concerning the management of large numbers of people often convey contradictory messages to managers.
3. Critical problems in the corporate management of personnel, such as the place of human resources management (HRM) in corporate decision making, the role of personnel staff, and a lack of sufficient human resources management know-how at top management levels, remain largely unresolved.
4. Some management assumptions concerning HRM undermine the efforts of many managers, no matter how well intentioned they may be.

Achieving Employee Commitment

Capturing the loyalty of hundreds or thousands of individuals in one business enterprise so that they direct their energies toward the goals of the company is enormously difficult. The goals of the corporation are long-range and general in nature—profit and growth. But employees usually focus on short time horizons to meet their needs in wages, salaries, working conditions, fair treatment, and promotion. Drawing a connection between these sets of goals is not easy.

Effective relationships between individuals and companies rest on employees' trust that the goals are connected. But developing trust often requires overcoming years of bad experience and many employees' belief that companies exploit people. Of every 100 employees, 5 or 10 will have been disappointed or burned by some job-related experience, which may have been beyond the company's control. Their subsequent alienation can subvert the efforts of managers and personnel officers to build morale.

Given that working in a social, industrial operation requires people to give up many freedoms and that groups acting collectively play on that loss of freedom to better their own short-term interests, that the work force is uncommitted should be no surprise.

Seen this way, the fight for a motivated work force is an uphill battle. It's rosy idealism to think that every employee is going to turn on and perform with 100% devotion to a company and its objectives. Short-term economic interests are in clear conflict. Employees see their share of the pie as being cut smaller to serve up larger profits to owners. Further, political factors such as Nader's Raiders and the anti–big-business wing of the Democratic party exploit employees' distrust of business, the corporation, and managers, whom employees often see as being out for themselves and siding with their corporate bosses against the employee.

People instinctively resent forces that manage and control them—big business, directors, the industrial establishment, the boss, the boss's boss. The antiestablishment seeds sown in the late 1960s and early 1970s are bearing fruit, and more employees than ever are unwilling to subject themselves wholly to an organization or the discipline of a trade, profession, or team.

Given these obstacles to collaboration, that cooperation occurs within the corporate world at all is miraculous.

Conflicts in Theory

Managers use many different organizational techniques to achieve collaboration and productivity. Researchers can take large credit for the multitude of concepts and tools on hand. They must also, however, accept responsibility for the fact that their different disciplines often conflict and work at cross-purposes.

For example, in most companies managers employ four different disciplines to improve employee performance and relations—human relations, labor relations, personnel administration, and industrial engineering. Since human relations itself includes at least three major schools, six fairly distinct sets of ideas and concepts can be at work in the same organization at the same time:

1. *Human relations.* Theories of *group behavior* deal with social interaction and interpersonal relationships through such tools as theories X and Y and sensitivity training. The school's precept is that because group behavior is critical to collaboration and success, groups must bestow authority and control upward.

   The *individual behavior* school of human relations focuses on individual psychology, leadership, power, authority, responsibility, and the subconscious. Its main concern is the individual's feelings and drives and how they affect the workplace.

   Organizational development goes further and focuses on the need for people to reason together about their common difficulties. Its central belief is that employees can often manage themselves better than managers can.

2. *Labor relations.* Labor laws, public policy, the economics of wages and costs, demographics and manpower management, collective bargaining, contract administration, and grievances are under the purview of labor relations. It sees politics at the plant, corporation, union, state, and national levels together with labor laws as keys to any situation. Its stance is usually adversarial and tough—sticking to contract terms, denying exceptions, avoiding precedents, and building a powerful position for bargaining.

3. *Personnel management.* Activities involved in managing large numbers of people in the aggregate—namely, recruiting, selecting, training, compensating, and developing them—are the province of personnel management. This discipline holds that if companies perform those tasks well, they will acquire a set of employees with appropriate motives, habits, and behavior; and if managers are consistent and apply policies that induce desired behavior, a good climate will result.

4. *Industrial engineering.* This school concentrates on designing jobs to fit technology and human capabilities and controlling performance with standards based on industrial engineering studies. It holds that efficiency and productivity are products of economic rewards and hard-nosed, disciplined supervision.

Each of these four schools focuses on acquiring an effective, loyal, and committed group of employees, but all work in very different ways. My concern is not that disagreement arises among these experts or that they have different approaches to the same problem. I do not think that one school is right and the others wrong, that one is better than another, or that any should be ignored. On the contrary, they all offer ideas and tools that are often very effective, though perhaps not when used at the same time.

The problem is a little like having a car that has good wheels, a shiny body, an efficient engine, excellent brakes, and a terrific hydraulic system but that won't go or that no one in the family wants to drive. Big hat, no cattle.

Each school of thought makes a contribution, a vital contribution, like the wheels and the engine, but the whole system sputters and founders and doesn't produce enough involved, energetic, and loyal workers. Usually companies do not know how to put these ingredients together in one effective corporate system, for the four schools offer managers contradictory advice.

Two things appear to be missing from the systems. One is a comprehensive unifying concept. Another is a general manager who can effectively mix and match these necessary ingredients. Unfortunately, such a person is of a rare breed.

Corporate Management of Personnel

The third set of problems holding back progress toward better people management has to do with the structure of corporations, their size, diversity, and allocation of authority.

As corporations grow in size and diversity, the difficulty of managing employee relations increases. With size come organizational layers that effectively remove top managers from the large numbers of employees at the base of the pyramid. By necessity, communication processes, which are handled via mass media broadcasts, house organs, speeches, and employee letters, become more political and less personal.

When a company grows, the connection between the corporate well-being and the needs of separate divisions and locations can break. In principle, headquarters may be willing to let the divisions deal with their local labor forces on their own, but in letting the divisions take different courses, the corporation may endanger its bargaining position with the union. And even if the company is not unionized, the personnel office might fear that one division's low-cost demands could bring in a union, be shortsighted, or give the company a bad reputation as a place to work.

Also, the Equal Employment Opportunity Act has vastly increased the need for headquarters to be in control, union or not. Yet each division has different tasks and needs, different skills and attitudes in its work force. Division A may need a labor force that is especially cost-effective, while Division B, where the strategy may call for rapid product turnover, requires employees to be adaptive.

Given these potential conflicts, experimenting with new approaches becomes riskier in large organizations than in small. Decisions become more sensitive, have longer shadows, and, understandably, executives may become more cautious and may procrastinate or pass the buck when they can.

These problems of size and diversity plague many large corporations these days. Their effects are perplexity and conflict at headquarters, frustration and irritation at divisional and plant locations, and a mishmash of personnel policies and practices that have no clear focus. Policies that swing from the corporate to the divisional point of view, with the responsibility resting in neither location, are often ineffective.

TIME IS AN ENEMY

Human resources management faces a further fundamental problem that few companies have resolved. Acquiring and developing the right talents for the business as it changes strategy, technology, and products requires more shrewd, wise, long-range planning than any other corporate endeavor. Companies can usually replace or rebuild technology, physical facilities, products, markets, or business systems in three to five years. But how long does it take to change the attitudes of 1,000 employees with an average age, let's assume, of 40 and with 10 years of seniority?

Clearly, management cannot dismiss the work force and start over again. But it often takes years to effect much genuine change, and one bad decision or unfortunate sequence of events can undo those years of slow progress.

In contrast to the nature of the HRM task, which is a function that requires long-term thinking, consistency, and staying power, short-range pressures such as budgets and annual plans force short-term reactions. Successful managers seldom stay put long enough to see their HRM investments pay off. Also, executive compensation systems seldom reward a manager for five years' investment in HRM policies and activities.

The scarcity of general managers who are as capable, confident, and experienced in the management of large numbers of people as they are in production, marketing, finance, and control is a further problem in many companies. Nonetheless, despite their inexperience, executives who reach the top must select and integrate the six different concepts and disciplines of human relations, personnel administration, and industrial engineering. They must also manage the conflicts among the interests of the corporation as a whole, the different divisions, and the separate plants and facilities.

Why do so many general managers usually lack these skills? Several factors contribute to the difficulty.

The first is that personnel work has seldom been attractive to fast-moving, younger general managers, who see the field as out of the mainstream of the business. Also, they see personnel administration as a staff function that is strictly advisory, that lacks authority and power, and that deals with small-scale, troublesome problems. A personnel job is seldom an attractive position for a manager who wants to run something independently. Because of personnel's conflict-ridden, pressured, contradictory nature, the decisions personnel managers make are touchy and cumbersome. Because they involve many other managers, they are not only time-consuming but also often frustrating.

For these reasons, few outstanding managers move into personnel work, and those in it often have problems getting out. The detail, the time required to gain expertise, the low status in the organization, and the lack of clear-cut authority can swallow up and overwhelm all but the very best in the field.

Questionable Management Premises

Finally, a few commonly held assumptions, the validity of which is increasingly doubtful, are at the root of the HRM problem.

WITH GOOD MANAGERS HRM TAKES CARE OF ITSELF

If one believes that well-intentioned managers naturally do well at HRM, the following will also seem valid:

Responsible, generous, enlightened top management will develop an effective employee group because its considerate and humane practices will inevitably trickle down and permeate the organization.

Management may share its prerogative to manage if it wishes, but philosophically employees have no right to manage.

People are fortunate to have jobs for which someone else has invested the capital.

People are adaptable to a wide variety of tasks and conditions.

Someone will turn up able and willing to do any job if the pay is right.

These premises are no longer valid. Widespread dissatisfaction with jobs despite adequate pay has been documented. More workers now see good jobs as rights. Employees demand more autonomy at work and question management's right to administrate, and indeed its competence and wisdom to manage, without participation.

PERSONNEL IS NOT VERY IMPORTANT

If the personnel department is a housekeeping function, it follows that:

It makes available services and advice that line managers can accept or reject since they have the responsibility for line operations.

The personnel department's job is to get good people and keep everybody reasonably happy.

Managers responsible for line operations can accept or reject personnel's advice as that of a "staff" department. Relegating to housekeeping or staff advice activities that directly impinge on a corporation's most vital competitive resource no longer makes sense.

Decisions affecting human resource quality should not be dealt with in a secondary, catch-up, tidy-up, reactive way. Doing so gives a lower priority to personnel activities than to production, sales, or finance; results in personnel management assignments being a sentence to oblivion; fosters second-rate, sloppy personnel activities; and removes accountability from personnel officers for setting up reactive, short-term HRM policies.

CONTROL IS ALL

If control systems are really what make an organization run well, it follows that:

By establishing careful and detailed annual forecasts and budgets and monitoring results by month, quarter, and year to meet the plans adopted, managers can effectively control and operate companies.

This premise drives out long-range thinking as well as the long lead times required to build effective human resources. The quantifiables remain, but the "soft quality" items such as training and development, appropriate compensation structures, and communication activities are expendable.

EVERY PROBLEM HAS A SOLUTION

The eternally optimistic macho belief is that if reason is applied:

When managers put good minds to work on a problem, it will yield quickly.

When good managers who will be held accountable are armed with good solutions, substantial improvements will result.

This premise accounts for many "big hats"; managers have adopted programs "to fix" poor morale or low productivity instead of getting at basic underlying causes. Short-term fixes or "programs" do not work in human resources development any better than they do in government.

Managers wishing superior human resources must get at fundamental rather than superficial symptoms; they need to accept disappointments and unexpected outcomes of solutions to complex problems, and they need the staying power to work persistently at improving the quality of human resources. These problems are massive and stubborn. When disillusionment and frustration hit, many managers react judgmentally, blaming the union or the government, the "vanishing work ethic" or "the new breed," instead of their own piecemeal, reactive approach to the management of people.

Since changing habits, skills, values, beliefs, and attitudes in a work force takes years, the lack of long-range planning in human resources is frequently disastrous. So the ultimate irony is that the personnel function—which deals with the most fundamental and central corporate competitive resource and which has the longest time horizon of any function—is left with no long-range strategy and allowed to react merely to transient pressures and events.

To develop human resources, corporate management will have to make some fundamental changes in its conventional wisdom.

Let me suggest five processes to include in a new approach:

1. Managers need to tackle the mistaken premises head-on and cast them out in favor of a new set like the following.

   If managers continually fail to listen, communicate, explain, anticipate, and in every way nurture commitment and mutual understanding, employees will inevitably become alienated. In the nature of people and organizations there is a relentless gravitational slide toward alienation.

   Managers can develop and tailor a work force to meet the particular performance needs of an organization.

   Because superior human resources create the most central, basic, and powerful strategic competitive advantage possible, human resources management should receive top priority.

   Employees are stakeholders in the enterprise. Their interest in the conditions of employment and work are as real as those of stockholders and managers. The problem is not whether to keep them involved in the management of the enterprise, but how.

   As a function, personnel has as much a right and an obligation to monitor the quality and prescribe the processes of personnel activity (selection, compensation, communication development, et cetera) as accountants do to prescribe and monitor accounting policies and procedures. The top echelon of leading companies in this respect, such as Hewlett-Packard and Dana Corporation, gives the personnel function broad license in any and all HRM activities.

2. Any company can begin to improve the management of human resources simply by doing the basics better. The most practical way to start is by performing all the routine ongoing personnel activities with extraordinary care. Research suggests that for the many reasons cited earlier, recruiting, selection, compensation, job design, training, and communications procedures are in many companies hastily and inadequately carried out.

   Worst of all is supervision—the oldest and most written about of management skills. The business schools neglect it, and economics, schedules, costs, and time pressures allow careless and inhumane practices to characterize it.

   Poor supervision is absolutely unnecessary—yet millions of workers have to put up with it. It hurts American manufacturing and service industries beyond belief. The importance of good supervision is so obvious that its rarity is astounding.

   The enormous improvements in HRM at General Motors began when managers went back to the basics of good supervision and communication. For instance, although QWL programs were behind the turnaround at Tarrytown, the fundamental changes were achieved by supervisors simply treating people with care and respect.

3. Managers need to set a seven-year time horizon for their human resources planning and operation. I pick seven years simply to make the point that it's not one, two, three, or even five. Planning in personnel administration needs at least that amount of time to survive several generations of top executives' strategy shifts, economic recessions, division and companywide crises, government policy changes, legislative revolutions, and technological advances. It takes at least seven years for managers to install, live with, improve, and reap the benefits of major change in personnel activities; to weed out unproductive skills or attitudes; and to hire a new generation. And it takes that long for employees to live through a period of history in a company that forms a new foundation of trust.

   Seen as a seven-year ongoing problem, the task of human resources management takes on a whole new cast demanding staying power as well as clear philosophy and strategy. For example, IBM's philosophy that people are valuable to the company has permeated the organization from the beginning. Similarly, at Hewlett-Packard the founders enunciated a set of standards that placed people first. To this day, these values persist with great benefit to these companies.

4. Having a seven-year horizon requires that managers develop a philosophy, some objectives, and a strategy. Since human resources strategic planning is as yet a largely unknown art and since it may take researchers years to develop competence, managers would do better to begin on their own rather than wait for the perfect approach.

   But how to begin? The combined experiences of four major U.S. corporations that have been working at HRM for a long time (Honeywell, American Hospital Supply, Dana Corporation, and Westinghouse) offer several lessons.

   A first step is to identify the *implicit* tendencies of present personnel policies and practices in terms of the skills, attitudes, and behavior they develop. Each corporate unit and division has implicit objectives in its personnel activities—to develop a work force that achieves low costs, to be flexible, or to acquire the skills for special projects, for instance. In most companies, such analysis will show that the implicit goals of the various personnel policies and activities are contradictory. Further, the uniformities in policy and practices across divisions, departments, and functions are also frequently dysfunctional in meeting the strategic needs of those separate groups.

A second useful step in human resources strategy planning is to identify by function, department, and division the desired behavioral characteristics of each employee group. These will depend on the company's or division's objectives and plans for gaining competitive advantage. That plan requires certain product, marketing, manufacturing, and financial strategies. These in turn will each have specific human resources implications. Managers need to uncover these implications and clearly specify them.

When managers juxtapose the human resources implications of their plans with those implicit in their personnel policies and activities, the need for change will emerge. From this process they can develop a human resources strategy that details by division, department, or function the human resources and specific policies and practices needed in the basic areas of human resources management. Then they can make long-term plans.

Pioneers in human resources strategy make such planning a central part of their annual plans, budgets, and long-range strategy. In other companies, however, managers commonly let HRM become a residual or an outcome of the plans rather than a key input. At best, most divisional or company managers merely project from extrapolations the numbers in various personnel categories they will need in the future.

Experience in HRM strategic planning shows that the process nearly always raises a fundamental problem: the divisions or departments of the company have different competitive strategies and often need different performance from their people. Similarly, within a division or a location, groups may need different personnel policies and activities. But can a company, for example, pay people differently in engineering than it can in purchasing or accounting? The answer is yes, but only when management discards the old uniformity rules and designs personnel policies to achieve strategically essential objectives.

5. Companies wishing to improve their HRM need to establish a long-term program to develop general managers with human resources management skills and experience. Considering the personnel department as a functional operation with strong authority and responsibility for effective human resources management practices has helped several companies to attract and keep good personnel managers.

By regarding the development of superior human resources as an essential competitive requirement that needs long-range, functional strategic plans, top managers can attract many of the best managers in the company to the HRM function. Some companies that have moved outstanding managers into personnel functions for two- to four-year periods have, after five to seven years, developed a top management group, a high proportion of which has had in-depth experience in the formulation and implementation of human resources strategy.

A group of loyal, productive employees is an organization's most effective competitive weapon. But during the last decade variations among persons available for employment appear to have greatly increased. Subtle differences in job and personal skills and in attitudes toward work and employers have made selecting an outstanding set of employees even more difficult. Mass education, which makes schooling level as a selection criterion less meaningful than it used to be, has compounded the problem. Leading companies in HRM have learned that the old adage that "people are people" is wrong: there are enormous differences between a good employee and a superb one. A small fraction of companies have learned to insist stubbornly on hiring only the very best.

These increased problems in achieving a "quality level" set of employees have made this HRM strategy, when successfully carried out, a uniquely dynamic competitive weapon. But it is more important than ever to recruit and develop a high-quality group of employees, for companies with a head start are hard to catch. Their good people attract others like themselves, while conventional organizations have to accept what is left.

Human resources planning can act as a catalyst and an operating mechanism to accelerate the building of an effective work force. Where this is accomplished, people are energized and committed and become the most powerful, fundamental corporate competitive resource of all.

Note

1. The term *large numbers* is used in this article to distinguish between the management issues concerning interpersonal and small group relationships and those relating to large groups, departments, divisions, or entire companies and institutions. My focus is on the latter, not on the former.

2
Harvard Business School Note: Reward Systems and the Role of Compensation

Michael Beer and Richard E. Walton

The design and management of reward systems present the general manager with one of the most difficult HRM (human resource management) tasks. This HRM policy area contains the greatest contradictions between the promise of theory and the reality of implementation. Consequently, organizations sometimes go through cycles of innovation and hope as reward systems are developed, followed by disillusionment as these reward systems fail to deliver.

Rewards and Employee Satisfaction

Gaining an employee's satisfaction with the rewards given is not a simple matter. Rather, it is a function of several factors that organizations must learn to manage:

1. The individual's satisfaction with rewards is, in part, related to what is expected and how much is received. Feelings of satisfaction or dissatisfaction arise when individuals compare their input—job skills, education, effort, and performance—to output—the mix of extrinsic and intrinsic rewards they receive.
2. Employee satisfaction is also affected by comparisons with other people in similar jobs and organizations. In effect, employees compare their own input/output ratio with that of others. People vary considerably in how they weigh various inputs in that comparison. They tend to weigh their strong points more heavily, such as certain

skills or a recent incident of effective performance. Individu͟
tend to overrate their own performance compared with ͟
they receive from their supervisors. The problem of unr
ratings exists partly because supervisors in most or͟
not communicate a candid evaluation of their su͟
formances to them. Such candid communicatio͟
unless done skillfully, seriously risks damag͟
The bigger dilemma, however, is that failure   ͟
municate a candid appraisal of performance makes
employees to develop a realistic view of their own ͟
thus increasing the possibility of dissatisfaction with the ͟
are receiving.

3. Employees often misperceive the rewards of others; their misper
ception can cause the employees to become dissatisfied. Evidence
shows that individuals tend to overestimate the pay of fellow workers doing similar jobs and to underestimate their performance (a
defense or self-esteem-building mechanism). Misperceptions of the
performance and rewards of others also occur because organizations
do not generally make available accurate information about the salary or performance of others.

4. Finally, overall satisfaction results from a mix of rewards rather
than from any single reward. The evidence suggests that intrinsic
rewards and extrinsic rewards are both important and that they
cannot be directly substituted for each other. Employees who are
paid well for repetitive, boring work will be dissatisfied with the
lack of intrinsic rewards, just as employees paid poorly for interesting, challenging work may be dissatisfied with extrinsic rewards.

Rewards and Motivation

From the organization's point of view, rewards are intended to
motivate certain behaviors. But under what conditions will rewards
actually motivate employees? To be useful, rewards must be seen
as timely and tied to effective performance.

One theory suggests that the following conditions are necessary
for employee motivation.[1]

1. Employees must believe effective performance (or certain specified
behavior) will lead to certain rewards. For example, attaining certain
results will lead to a bonus or approval from others.

2. Employees must feel that the rewards offered are attractive. Some
employees may desire promotions because they seek power, but

others may want a fringe benefit, such as a pension, because they are older and want retirement security.

3. Employees must believe a certain level of individual effort will lead to achieving the corporation's standards of performance.

As indicated, motivation to exert effort is triggered by the prospect of desired rewards: money, recognition, promotion, and so forth. If effort leads to performance and performance leads to desired rewards, the employee is satisfied and motivated to perform again.

As previously mentioned, rewards fall into two categories: extrinsic and intrinsic. *Extrinsic rewards* come from the organization as money, perquisites, or promotions or from supervisors and co-workers as recognition. *Intrinsic rewards* accrue from performing the task itself, and may include the satisfaction of accomplishment or a sense of influence. The process of work and the individual's response to it provide the intrinsic reward. But the organization seeking to increase intrinsic rewards must provide a work environment that allows these satisfactions to occur; therefore, more organizations are redesigning work and delegating responsibility to enhance employee involvement.

Equity and Participation

The ability of a reward system both to motivate and to satisfy depends on who influences and/or controls the system's design and implementation. Even though considerable evidence suggests that participation in decision making can lead to greater acceptance of decisions, participation in the design and administration of reward systems is rare. Such participation is time-consuming.

Perhaps a greater roadblock is that pay has been one of the last strongholds of managerial prerogatives. Concerned about employee self-interest and compensation costs, corporations do not typically allow employees to participate in pay-system design or decisions. Thus, it is not possible to test thoroughly the effects of widespread participation on acceptance of and trust in reward systems.

Compensation Systems: The Dilemmas of Practice

A body of experience, research, and theory has been developed about how money satisfies and motivates employees. Virtually every study on the importance of pay compared with other potential rewards has shown that pay is important. It consistently ranks among the top five rewards. The importance of pay and other rewards, however, is affected by many factors. Money, for example, is likely to be viewed differently at various points in one's career, because the need for money versus other rewards (status, growth, security, and so forth) changes at each stage. National culture is another important factor. American managers and employees apparently emphasize pay for individual performance more than do their European or Japanese counterparts. European and Japanese companies, however, rely more on slow promotions and seniority as well as some degree of employment security. Even within a single culture, shifting national forces may alter people's needs for money versus other rewards.

Companies have developed various compensation systems and practices to achieve pay satisfaction and motivation. In manufacturing firms, payroll costs can run as high as 40% of sales revenues, whereas in service organizations payroll costs can top 70%. General managers, therefore, take an understandable interest in payroll costs and how these dollars are spent.

The traditional view of managers and compensation specialists is that if the right system can be developed, it will solve most problems. This is not a plausible assumption, because there is no one right answer or objective solution to what or how someone should be paid. What people will accept, be motivated by, or perceive as fair is highly subjective. Pay is a matter of perceptions and values that often generate conflict.

MANAGEMENT'S INFLUENCE ON ATTITUDES TOWARD MONEY

Many organizations are caught up in a vicious cycle that they partly create. Firms often emphasize compensation levels and a belief in individual pay for performance in their recruitment and internal communications. This is likely to attract people with high needs for money as well as to heighten that need in those already employed. Thus, the meaning employees attach to money is partly shaped by management's views. If merit increases, bonuses, stock options, and perquisites are held out as valued symbols of recognition and success, employees will come to see them in this light even more than they might have perceived them at first. Having heightened money's importance as a reward, management must then respond to employees who may demand more money or better pay-for-performance systems.

Firms must establish a philosophy about rewards and the role of pay in the mix of rewards. Without such a philosophy, the compensation practices that happen to be in place, for the reasons already stated, will continue to shape employees' expectations, and those expectations will sustain the existing practices. If money has been emphasized as an important symbol of success, that emphasis will continue even though a compensation system with a slightly different emphasis might have equal motivational value with fewer administrative problems and perhaps even lower cost. Money is important, but its degree of importance is influenced by the type of compensation system and philosophy that management adopts.

PAYROLL STRATIFICATION: A ONE- OR TWO-CLASS SOCIETY?

When an organization develops different compensation systems for different levels of the organization that offer different fringe benefits, pay-for-performance rewards, and administrative procedures, it is sending a message to employees about more than just the specific behavior the compensation system is intended to reward. That message is that there are differences in the company's expectations of the commitment and role of employees at different levels and the degree to which they are full and responsible members of the organization.

There are several understandable reasons for these differences. To get around the intended effects of progressive tax laws, corporations pay managers in a form different from that of lower-level employees. Deferred compensation, stock options, and various perquisites protect executives from taxation that reduces the value of their rewards.

In the United States, all organizations must make a distinction between *exempt employees* (those who, according to the wage and hour laws, have significant decision-making responsibility, typically managers and professional employees) and *nonexempt employees* (all other regular members of the organization—typically clerical white-collar and hourly blue-collar employees). Federal law requires nonexempt employees to receive overtime pay for a workweek that exceeds 40 hours; exempt employees are, as the name implies, exempt from such legislative protection. Because of this legal requirement, organizations must maintain records of time worked by nonexempt employees, which often results in the use of time clocks. These groups are also given different payroll labels: salaried payroll for exempt employees and hourly payroll for production employees. Thus, a two-class language is created.

Federal law governing overtime pay for nonexempt employees was created in the 1930s to protect employees from exploitation by management. It can, and often does, have the unintended result of creating or reinforcing certain assumptions made by managers about their employees' commitment to the organization. It might also affect employees' perceptions of their roles in the organization and thereby alter their commitment. A two-class society is subtly reinforced within the organization.

ALL-SALARIED SYSTEM.   Some organizations have attempted to overcome this legislated division of the work force through an all-salaried compensation system. Workers traditionally paid by the hour join management in receiving a weekly or monthly salary (nonexempt employees are still paid on an hourly basis for overtime work). Several large nonunion companies (IBM and Gillette) have used this system for decades. More recently, the United Auto Workers union has encouraged America's Big Three automakers to consider it.

Although an all-salaried system cannot eliminate the legislated distinction between exempt and nonexempt employees, it can at least remove one symbolic, but nonetheless important, difference: workers join managers in having more flexibility, since time can be taken off from work with no loss in pay. Thus, workers can be given more responsibility for their hours. Such treatment, in turn, could increase their commitment and loyalty to the organization.

Some managers fear that adopting a salaried system across the board will lead to greater absenteeism, but this does not appear to have happened. However, such a system by itself will not increase commitment. Nevertheless, as part of an overall shift in corporate philosophy and style, it can play an important supporting role. Companies such as Hewlett-Packard and IBM as well as participative nontraditional plants at Procter & Gamble, Dana, TRW, and Cummins Engine have successfully used the all-salaried payroll in this way.

SYSTEMS FOR MAINTAINING EQUITY

To maintain employee satisfaction with pay, corporations have developed systems that are intended to maintain pay equity with comparable internal and external persons and groups.

The consequences of inequity in employee pay regarding the external labor markets are potentially severe for a corporation, which would be unable to attract and keep the talent required. The costs of maintaining that equity, however, are also high. Meeting all competitive wage offers obtainable by employees—the extreme form of maintaining external equity—can encourage employees to search for the highest job offers to convince management to increase their pay. This results in a market system for determining compensation much like the free-agent system in sports—a time-consuming and expensive proposition for employers that can lead to internal inequities. It can also lead an employee to a self-centered orientation toward career and pay.

Some companies, such as IBM, intentionally position their total compensation package at the high end of the market range. High total compensation does not, however, ensure that the best employees are retained. To keep them, a company must also pay its better performers more than it pays poorer performers, and the difference must be significant in the judgment of individual employees.

The potential consequences of internal pay inequity are employee dissatisfaction, withholding of effort, and lack of trust in the system. Internal inequity can result in conflict within the organization, which consumes the time and energy of managers and personnel. Maintaining high internal equity, however, can result in overpaying some people compared to the market, a competitive cost disadvantage to the organization, while underpaying others, thus destroying external equity.

There is continual tension in an organization between concerns for external and internal equity. Line personnel may be willing to sacrifice corporate internal equity to attract and keep the talent they want for their departments. Human resource personnel, with their corporate view, are forced to oppose such efforts by line managers because they perceive efforts to pay whatever is needed to attract a candidate as a threat to internal equity. Human resource personnel insist on the integrity of the job-evaluation and wage-survey systems to avoid the costly conflicts that they fear will inevitably follow if numerous exceptions to the job-evaluation system are allowed. This dilemma remains insoluble; no new system will eliminate it. The balance must be continually managed to reduce problems and maintain a pay system that yields equity and cost-effectiveness.

JOB EVALUATION.   In the United States, the typical method of determining pay levels is evaluating the worth of a job to the organization through a job-evaluation system. Most U.S. firms utilize some form of job evaluation.

Job evaluations begin by describing the various jobs within an organization. Then jobs are evaluated by considering several job factors: working conditions, necessary technical knowledge, required managerial skills, and importance to the organization of the results for which the employee is held accountable. A rating for each factor is made on a standard scale, and the total rating points can be used to rank jobs hierarchically. Next, a salary survey is taken to identify comparable jobs in other organizations and to learn what those organizations are paying for similarly rated jobs.

The salary survey and other considerations—such as legislation, job-market conditions, and the organization's willingness to pay— establish pay ranges for jobs. (The tighter the labor market, the more closely wages will be tied to the going rate. In a loose labor market, the other factors will tend to dominate.) Jobs may then be grouped into a smaller number of classifications and assigned a salary range. The level of the individual employee within his or her particular range is determined by a combination of job performance, seniority, experience, or any other combination of factors selected by the organization.

Job-evaluation plans, along with wage surveys, have been used in wage-and-salary administration for over 50 years. They have proved useful for maintaining internal and external equity.

Even if these steps are taken, however, no job-evaluation system can solve the problem of salary compression that inevitably occurs when new or experienced employees are hired. To recruit successfully in the labor market, firms must offer competitive wages, and these competitive wages sometimes create inequities (salary compression) with the salaries of employees who have been with the firm for some time. These inequities occur because corporations typically do not raise the salaries of incumbents automatically when salary surveys result in an upward movement of the salary range. To do so would be costly; not doing so also allows the firms to keep the pay of poorer performers behind the market by denying merit increases.

Some analysts argue that companies should solve inequities due to compression by regularly raising wages for everyone when salary surveys so indicate and by managing poor performers through other means. Some companies ask managers to position their subordinates within the appropriate pay range according to performance, providing larger increases for good performers over several years so they will be near the top of their range and giving poor performers lower increases or no increases to keep them at the bottom of the range.

The conflicting objectives—keeping costs down and rewarding good performers—not the job-evaluation system itself cause inequity and dissatisfaction. Of these objectives, cost effectiveness is the critical factor, because good performance can be rewarded and poor performance discouraged in other monetary and nonmonetary ways. General managers must decide if the cost of across-the-board increases is worth the benefits of more perceived internal and external equity. To solve the equity problems, they must clarify their philosophy and make choices between objectives of cost and equity, a process that is determined more by values and financial constraints than by systems.

Certain problems are associated with pay systems structured by job evaluation. Salary ranges associated with jobs limit the pay increases an individual can obtain. Thus, significant advancements in status and pay can come only through promotions. This need for promotion can cause technical people to seek promotions to management positions, even though their real skills and interests might be in technical work. If no promotions are available, individuals' needs for advancement and progress are frustrated.

Additionally, job-evaluation systems cause a certain loss of flexibility in transferring people within an organization. If that transfer is to a job with a lower pay grade, fear of lower pay and status will reduce the individual's willingness to transfer. Although companies usually "red circle" that individual's pay by making an exception and maintaining the individual's salary above the range of the new job, the perception of loss and the reality of an actual loss of pay over time makes such a transfer difficult.

To solve problems of job-evaluation systems, some companies have come up with an alternative: a person- or skill-based evaluation system. These systems promise to solve the flexibility and limited-growth problem of job evaluation, but they do not solve all the equity problems already discussed.

PERSON/SKILL EVALUATION. Person- or skill-based evaluation systems base salary on the person's abilities. Pay ranges are arranged in steps, from least skilled to most skilled. Employees come into the organization at an entry-level pay grade and move up the skill-based ladder after they have demonstrated competence at the next level. Such a system should lead to higher pay for the most skilled individuals and encourage the acquisition of new skills.

Skill-based systems are generally thought to allow more flexibility in moving people from one job to another and introducing new technology. A skill-based compensation system can also change management's orientation. Instead of limiting assignments to be consistent with job level, managers must shift their emphasis to utilize the available skills of people, since employees are being paid for those skills. Moreover, a skill-based evaluation system's greatest benefit is that it communicates to employees a concern for their development. This concern leads management to develop competence and utilize it, resulting in greater employee well-being and organizational effectiveness.

Person-based evaluation systems have been applied to technical personnel in R&D organizations and are often called technical ladders. They could be applied to other technical specialists such as lawyers, sales personnel, and accountants. Their use might encourage good specialists to stay in these roles rather than seek management jobs that pay more but for which they may not have talent. The organizations would avoid losing good technical specialists and gaining poor managers.

Skill-based pay systems have also been applied to production-level employees in the past decade. Companies such as Procter & Gamble, General Motors, and Cummins Engine have introduced plans in some of their more progressive plants that pay workers for the skills they possess rather than for the jobs they hold. The benefits of flexibility and employee growth and satisfaction, which were mentioned earlier, have been experienced in these plants.

There are some problems to be considered in a person- or skill-based approach, however. For one, many individual employees may, after several years, reach the top skill level and find themselves with no place to go. At this point, the organization might consider some type of profit-sharing scheme to encourage these employees to continue to seek ways of improving organizational effectiveness. Another problem is that a skills-evaluation program calls for a large investment in training, because pay increases depend upon the learning of new skills. Furthermore, external equity is more difficult to manage. Because each organization has its own unique configurations of jobs and skills, it is unlikely that individuals with similar skills can be found elsewhere, particularly in the same community, which is where production workers typically look for comparisons. This is less of a problem for professional employees whose jobs are more similar across companies. Because skill-based systems emphasize learning new tasks, employees may come to feel that their higher skills call for higher pay than the system provides, particularly when they compare their wages with those of workers in traditional jobs. Without effective comparisons expectations could rise, unchecked by a good reality test.

By far the most difficult problem facing a skills-evaluation plan is its administration. To make the system work properly, attention must be paid to the skill level of every employee. Some method must be devised, first, to determine how many and what new skills must be learned to receive a pay boost and, second, to determine whether or not the individual employee has, in fact, mastered those new skills. The ease with which the first point is achieved depends on how measurable or quantifiable the necessary skills are. Identification of particular skills is more easily accomplished for lower-level positions than for top management or professional positions.

Skill-based pay systems hold out some promise of improving competence in a cost-effective way and enhancing both organizational effectiveness and employee well-being. They are not solutions for all situations and depend heavily on solving the problem of measuring and assessing skills or competencies. Only an organization with a climate of trust is likely to use the system successfully. Moreover, skill-based compensation systems work only for those organizations where skilled workers are essential and where flexibility is required. They are also hard to introduce in organizations where a traditional job-evaluation system exists.

SENIORITY

Seniority has been accepted as a valid criterion for pay in some countries. Japanese companies, for instance, use seniority-based pay along with other factors, such as slow-but-steady promotion, to help achieve a desired organizational culture. In the United States, proponents of a seniority-based pay system tend to be trade unions. Distrustful of management, unions often feel that any pay-for-performance system will end up increasing paternalism, unfairness, and inequities. Thus, unions often prefer a strict seniority system. To many managers in the United States, however, seniority appears to run contrary to the country's individualistic ethos, which maintains that individual effort and merit should be rewarded above all else.

PAY FOR PERFORMANCE

Some reasons why organizations pay their employees for performance are as follows:

1. Under the right conditions, a pay-for-performance system can motivate desired behavior.
2. A pay-for-performance system can help attract and keep achievement-oriented individuals.
3. A pay-for-performance system can help to retain good performers while discouraging the poor performers.
4. In the United States, at least, many employees, both managers and workers, prefer a pay-for-performance system, although white-collar workers are significantly more supportive of the notion than blue-collar workers are.

But there is a gap, and the evidence indicates a wide gap, between the desire to devise a pay-for-performance system and the ability to make such a system work.

The most important distinction among various pay-for-performance systems is the level of aggregation at which performance is defined—individual, group, and organizationwide.[2] Several pay-for-performance systems are summarized in Exhibit I.

Historically, pay for performance has meant pay for individual performance. Piece-rate incentive systems for production employees and merit salary increases or bonus plans for salaried employees have been the dominant means of paying for performance. In the last decade, piece-rate incentive systems have dramatically declined because managers have discovered that such systems result in dysfunctional behavior, such as low cooperation, artificial limits on

Exhibit I. *Pay-for-Performance Systems*

Individual Performance	Group Performance	Organizationwide Performance
Merit system	Productivity incentive	Profit sharing
Piece rate	Cost-effectiveness	Productivity-sharing
Executive bonus		(Scanlon Plan)

production, and resistance to changing standards. Similarly, more questions are being asked about individual bonus plans for executives as top managers discover their negative effects.

Meanwhile, organizationwide incentive systems are becoming more popular, particularly because managers are finding that they foster cooperation, which leads to productivity and innovation. To succeed, however, these plans require certain conditions. A review of the key considerations for designing a pay-for-performance plan and a discussion of the problems that arise when these considerations are not observed follow.

INDIVIDUAL PAY FOR PERFORMANCE. The design of an individual pay-for-performance system requires an analysis of the task. Does the individual have control over the performance (result) that is to be measured? Is there a significant effort-to-performance relationship? For motivational reasons already discussed, such a relationship must exist. Unfortunately, many individual bonus, commission, or piece-rate incentive plans fall short in meeting this requirement. An individual may not have control over a performance result, such as sales or profit, because that result is affected by economic cycles or competitive forces beyond his or her control. Indeed, there are few outcomes in complex organizations that are not dependent on other functions or individuals, fewer still that are not subject to external factors.

Choosing an appropriate measure of performance on which to base pay is a related problem incurred by individual bonus plans. For reasons discussed earlier, effectiveness on a job can include many facets not captured by cost, units produced, or sales revenues. Failure to include all activities that are important for effectiveness can lead to negative consequences. For example, sales personnel who receive a bonus for sales volume may push unneeded products, thus damaging long-term customer relations, or they may push an unprofitable mix of products just to increase volume. These same salespeople may also take orders and make commitments that cannot be met by manufacturing. Instead, why not hold salespeople responsible for profits, a more inclusive measure of performance? The obvious problem with this measure is that sales personnel do not have control over profits.

These dilemmas are constantly encountered and have led to the use of more subjective but inclusive behavioral measures of performance. Why not observe if the salesperson or executive is performing all aspects of the job well? More merit salary increases are based on subjective judgments and so are some individual bonus plans. Subjective evaluation systems, though they can be all-inclusive if based on a thorough analysis of the job, require deep trust in management, good manager-subordinate relations, and effective interpersonal skills. Unfortunately, these conditions are not fully met in many situations, though they can be developed if judged to be sufficiently important.

GROUP AND ORGANIZATIONWIDE PAY PLANS. Organizational effectiveness depends on employee cooperation in most instances. An organization may elect to tie pay, or at least some portion of pay, indirectly to individual performance. Seeking to foster teamwork, a company may tie an incentive to some measure of group performance, or it may offer some type of profit or productivity-sharing plan for the whole plant or company.

Gains-sharing plans have been used for years and in many varieties. The real power of a gains-sharing plan comes when it is supported by a climate of participation.[3] Various structures, systems, and processes involve employees in decisions that improve the organization's performance and result in a bonus throughout the organization. The Scanlon Plan is one such example. When the plan is installed in cooperation with workers and unions, a management-labor committee is created. Then committees seek and review suggestions for reducing costs. Payout is based on improvements in the sales-to-cost ratio of the plant compared to some agreed-upon base period before the adoption of the plan.

Organizationwide incentive plans that are part of a philosophy of participation require strong labor-management cooperation in design and administration. For example, the Scanlon Plan requires a direct employee vote with 75% approval before implementation.

Without joint participation, commitment to any organizationwide incentive plan system will be low, as will its symbolic and motivational value.

Several critical decisions influence the effectiveness of a gains-sharing plan:

1. Who should participate in the plan's design and administration, and how much participation will be allowed by management and union?
2. What will be the size of the unit covered? Small units obviously offer easier identification with the organization's performance and the bonuses that result.
3. What standard will be used to judge performance? Employees, the union (if involved), and management must agree on this for strong commitment. There are inevitable disagreements.
4. How will the gains be divided? Who shares in the gains? What percentage of the gain goes to the company and what percentage to employees?

When management and employees have gone through a process of discussion and negotiation, allowing a consensus to emerge on these questions, a real change in management-employee and union relations can occur. A top-down process would not yield the same benefits. Gains-sharing approached participatively can create a fundamental change in the psychological and economic ownership of the firm. Therein lies its primary motivational and satisfactional value; however, only a management that embraces values consistent with participation can make it work.

Summary

Reward system policies should, in most instances, follow rather than lead other human resource policies. This note began by stating that the rewards policy area presents the general manager with one of the more difficult HRM tasks. There are numerous dilemmas and contradictions inherent in a reward system that make it difficult to design and administer with predictable outcomes.

How important are intrinsic rewards compared with pay and other extrinsic rewards? How much emphasis should be placed on these rewards, and what effect do policies regarding one set of rewards have on the other? Questions arise not only about what systems are most effective for maintaining internal and external pay equity but also about how employee perceptions of equity and trust can be enhanced. Questions surface about the efficacy and role of pay-for-performance systems. The process of designing the system may be as important as the design itself when it comes to compensation. How much participation and communication went into the design and the administration of the pay systems? How does that amount fit with the culture of the organization? What message has the organization given about how much influence, involvement, and development employees will receive? There is an inevitable need for a fit between the reward system and other HRM policies and corporate culture.

Notes

1. Edward E. Lawler, *Pay and Organizational Effectiveness: A Psychological View* (New York: McGraw-Hill, 1971), pp. 267–272.
2. Ibid., pp. 82–85.
3. Christopher S. Miller and Michael H. Schuster, "Gain-sharing Plan: A Comparative Analysis," *Organizational Dynamics* (Summer 1987), pp. 44–67.

3
Harvard Business School Note: Managing the Psychological Contract

R. Roosevelt Thomas, Jr.

The purpose of this note is to consider the individual-organization relationship and its implications for the manager of a functional unit (a sales force, manufacturing plant, controller's department). Since most business organizations are built on functional units, managers at this level are centrally involved in managing the interface between the work of the organization and the skills of the employee. Managers are responsible not only for insuring that the technical resources for performing tasks are available (the necessary equipment, raw materials) but also for managing the motivation of their employees. They must facilitate a relationship between employees and the firm that encourages their subordinates to expend energy willingly on organizational tasks.

The Relationship

DYNAMICS OF RECIPROCATION

In the relationship between the individual employee and the organization, each party participates *only* because of what it expects to receive in exchange for participation.[1] An individual, like an organization, constitutes a system with particular needs. These two systems enter into a joint cooperative relationship only when it

1974; revised April 1985

offers opportunities for the fulfillment of their respective needs. The organization employs the individual because his or her services are essential for the achievement of its goals; similarly, the individual contributes services only when doing so leads to the fulfillment of his or her personal needs.

THE PSYCHOLOGICAL CONTRACT

The basis of this reciprocal relationship is the psychological contract, which may be defined as the mutual expectations of the individual and the organization as articulated by its managers.[2] Both parties bring to the relationship a set of expectations of what each will give and receive. (Exhibit I provides examples of areas in which the organization and the individual are likely to have expectations.) When each party enters into the relationship, it tacitly accepts the expectations of the other. The set of both the individual's and the organization's expectations becomes the basis of the psychological contract.

The individual-organization contract is termed psychological because much of it is often unwritten and unspoken. There are several reasons why this may be so:

1. Both parties may not be entirely clear about their expectations and how they wish them to be fulfilled. They may wish to avoid defining

Exhibit I. *Examples of Expectations*

What the individual may expect to receive and the organization may expect to give:	What the individual may expect to give and the organization may expect to receive:
1. Salary	1. An honest day's work
2. Personal development opportunities	2. Loyalty to organization
3. Recognition and approval for good work	3. Initiative
4. Security through fringe benefits	4. Conformity to organizational norms
5. Friendly, supportive environment	5. Job effectiveness
6. Fair treatment	6. Flexibility and a willingness
7. Meaningful or purposeful job	to learn and to develop

Source: Adapted from John Paul Kotter, "The Psychological Contract: Managing the Joining-Up Process," *California Management Review* (Spring, 1973): p. 93.

the contract until they have a better feel for what they want. This may be one explanation of the tendency of management recruiters and applicants to define their expectations in very general terms. Frequently recruiters see themselves "buying brains" that will adapt to some as yet undefined job, while applicants want to maintain as much latitude as possible in specifying the types of jobs that interest them.

2. Employees and the organization's representative may not be aware of some of their expectations. For example, organizations frequently are not explicitly aware of how much loyalty they demand of their employees. Similarly, employees are not always aware of the extent to which social interactions on the job are important to them. The fact that the parties are unaware of these needs does not make them any less real, for if they are not fulfilled, both parties will quickly become aware of their reality.

3. Some expectations may be perceived as so natural and basic that they are taken for granted and left unstated. Two examples would be the expectations of no stealing and an honest day's work for a day's pay.

4. Connected to the above, cultural norms may inhibit verbalization. Wanting to be perceived in the "Horatio Alger" tradition of self-starters may prevent an employee from probing too deeply into what is expected of him or her; similarly, norms against violating an individual's privacy may make an organization's management cautious about expressing its expectations of loyalty on and off the job.

Though the psychological contract is largely unstated and unsupported by legal sanctions, it has a commanding quality. It represents each party's expectations for the relationship's continued existence. At any given time, there will be some relatively fulfilled and unfulfilled expectations; however, each party has a minimum acceptable level of fulfillment. If either party concludes that the fulfillment of its needs is below this minimum level, it will view the contract as having been violated.

Three options are open to the dissatisfied party: (1) attempt to renegotiate the contract, (2) continue the relationship in an alienated state, and/or (3) sever the relationship. Once one of the parties becomes dissatisfied, a signal will be sent to the other expressing a desire that the contract be renegotiated. Such signals may vary from a disgruntled attitude to a violent wildcat strike or acts of sabotage. Often, a complaining employee will attempt to enlist others in the cause. These efforts may lead to collective bargaining arrangements or even to the creation of social movements. The California lettuce workers provided an example. Unable to prevail on their own, they sought the support of society. Similarly, the federal government, the civil rights movement, and the women's liberation movement have acted to renegotiate psychological contracts between minorities and organizations. This phenomenon works both ways. Corporations may join together to form a single bargaining unit; they may also appeal for public support as contracts (both psychological and legal) come up for renegotiation. In sum, both parties may seek help as they adjust to changing relationships.

If renegotiation fails or does not take place, either discontented party may become alienated, yet continue the relationship, but at the minimum acceptable level. Alienation of employees may be seen in the restriction of output and sabotage attributed to blue-collar workers.[3] Alienation on the part of the employer may be seen in the way top managers in some companies respond to an employee who fails to accept a promotion requiring a move. Some corporations have a series of experience jobs designed to foster the development of upwardly mobile employees. Occasionally, an individual on the way up will develop a strong liking for an experience job and refuse to accept a promotion. When this happens, the developmental program is blocked. This can cause serious problems for his or her superiors, for they will have to find a replacement for the slot in the program and are left with uncertainty about the employee's commitment to the company. A consequence of the individual's refusal to move is usually a decrease in opportunities for promotion or significant salary increase.

A state of alienation may persist for years if neither party is moved to change the offending conditions. (An apocryphal quotation describes the situations: "We have too many people here who are no longer with us.") If renegotiation fails, or when alienation becomes too uncomfortable, the relationship may be severed. But in our society managers are generally reluctant to fire individuals; instead, many organizations prefer to ease people out or move them into a "corner." If these alternatives are not available, either because the individual refuses to cooperate or because the organization lacks convenient corners, then the corporation will have to face its situation. It may do this by changing the standards of what it will accept from the employee or by firing him or her.

The individual's willingness to sever the relationship is a function of his or her available alternatives, which must offer rewards at least equal to those provided by the present employer. If the individual concludes that the situation is par for the course and that alternatives do not offer significant advantages, he or she will be reluctant to quit. If the alternatives are viewed as less rewarding, the willingness to endure alienation and dissatisfaction will be strengthened. The implication here is that the capacity of the organization and the individual to endure an unsatisfactory relationship may be considerable and may depend heavily on factors in the environment. An economic downturn, for example, brings pressure to clear out the deadwood from corporate corners and, at the same time, reduces the number of alternatives available to the individual.

The psychological contract is dynamic and changes as the needs of the two parties change. For example, a company's needs may change as it moves from a small dynamic firm to a large mature one. Similarly, the individual's needs change as he or she moves through the various stages of life.

Changes in the psychological contract may also be caused by dramatic shifts in the environment. Public concern and legislation about occupational safety and health have caused many firms and their employees to rethink these aspects of their psychological contracts. And public acceptance of the women's liberation movement has encouraged more and more women to demand meaningful and challenging positions. In response to these demands and expectations, one large corporation instituted a "project mobility" program designed to facilitate the upward mobility of its women clerical workers. Again, the net effect is an alteration in the psychological contract.

NATURE OF THE INDIVIDUAL'S NEEDS

The type of psychological contract an individual is likely to find attractive depends on the needs embedded in his or her personality. For decades, management has assumed that fulfillment of important needs would motivate employees to work; however, during this period several successive views of the individual have been popular with managers. The following discussion is based primarily on Edgar Schein's concept of the "organizational man and the process of management."[4]

The *rational-economic* view of the individual, popular since the turn of the century, assumed that the individual's basic motivation was economic. Operating on a rational basis, human beings would do whatever resulted in the greatest economic gain. Individuals had feelings (emotions), however, that were largely irrational and had to be neutralized. The implied managerial strategy was one of reward and control. Workers were rewarded with economic gains and controlled so that they would not fall victim to irrational feelings.

In the 1940s and 1950s the *social-man* model was advocated. Here, the individual was motivated primarily by a desire for social contact at work and performed at work according to how well this need was met. The employee was viewed as being more responsible to social forces than to management's incentives and controls. An effective manager had to meet the social needs of employees.

In the *self-actualization model,* next to come into vogue, the individual was seen as having a hierarchy of needs: (1) survival needs, (2) social needs, (3) self-esteem needs, (4) needs for autonomy, and (5) need for self-actualization in the sense of maximum use of all his or her resources. Individuals were considered to be self-motivated and self-controlled and capable of voluntarily meshing their goals with those of the organization. Here, the role of the manager was to make the work challenging and interesting; the manager's job was to define the task so that a person who desired challenge, autonomy, and opportunity for self-discipline would find the task attractive. In exchange for good performance, the organization was to provide opportunities for self-actualizing.

Each of the above schools of thought attempted to set forth a universal model of the individual. The *complex-man* model, which seems better to capture the nature of human personality, suggests that universal approaches to the individual are much too simple and that a person is much more complex than implied in any of the above perspectives. The complex-man model recognizes that the individual may have a variety of needs (e.g., self-esteem, identity, competence, achievement affiliation, power) with a variety of strengths. This is because each individual has a history of different developmental experiences and genetic configurations.

To use this model, a manager must have a diagnostic perspective and must be sensitive to differences among employees. The complexity is reduced, however, because of the tendency of individuals with similar need patterns to be attracted to a given organizational unit. This is probably a result of both the organization's selection process and career choices by the individual. Nevertheless, it is still possible to have a mixture of significantly different individual need patterns in one multiunit organization. Take the employees of a university, for example, who may be divided into four groups: physical plant staff, clerical staff, administrators, and faculty. In a research effort this case writer found that each of these groups had similar, but yet unique, sets of needs and expectations, centered around the nature of their jobs, pay, fringe benefits, and relationships with peers.

The most important aspect of work for physical plant workers was fringe benefits; the nature of their tasks was very much secondary. The clerical staff were much more concerned with the intrinsic nature of their tasks, although fringe benefits were still significant to this group. The faculty was primarily interested in maintaining the autonomy and support necessary for effective teaching and research, while administrators expressed a need for more professionalism. The relative weights assigned to individual expectations thus varied significantly from group to group.

Implications for the Functional Manager

ROLE OF THE FUNCTIONAL UNIT MANAGER

Because most organizations are built around functional units, the manager of such a unit is frequently the person most responsible for representing the organization and implementing the psychological contract. The manager's task is that of fulfilling the organization's end of the contract and reminding individual employees of their contractual obligations. This requires that the functional manager provide an organizational design that facilitates the performance of organizational tasks, while ensuring that employees have opportunities to realize their expectations at work.

Research suggests that maintaining a psychological contract that accomplishes these ends involves achieving a fit among the nature of the unit's task, the personalities of its members, and the unit's organizational design. When such a fit exists, the unit gains effective results and the individual members gain feelings of competence that lead to a continuing motivation to perform their jobs well.

> For example, in manufacturing plants it was found that management and professional employees had relatively low tolerance for ambiguity, preferred to work more closely with colleagues,

and preferred stronger direction from their superiors. The tasks upon which they were working were short term, relatively repetitive and predictable, and highly independent. However, only in the effective plants (lower costs, more on time deliveries, high quality, etc.) did the design of the organization fit both the personalities of members and the nature of their work. In these plants there was an organizational design which provided relatively tight control and coordination, established routines for how to conduct the work, and measured short term results.

Similarly in research laboratories, scientists and managers had a higher tolerance for ambiguity, preferred to work more alone, and without close supervision. Here the task was highly uncertain with little interdependence required and results were achieved only over a long time span. Again, only in effective laboratories (more innovations contributing to company products and processes) was there an organizational design which matched these factors. In these laboratories the organization allowed a great deal of autonomy and influence for individual scientists, and placed emphasis on measuring results over the long term.[5]

As Exhibit II suggests, such a consistency among organization, task, and human variables seems to lead to a psychological transaction benefiting both the organization and the individual. This diagram also emphasizes the often neglected point that the very act of performing the job well can also be an important motivational force.

From this perspective, the functional manager concerned with maintaining a viable psychological contract with subordinates must arrange the available organizational design variables to fit the task and individual factors in the unit. The following sections review four of the principal design tools available to functional managers as they work toward a good fit and fulfillment of the psychological contract: measurement practices, rewards, structure, and selection and development.

MEASUREMENT PRACTICES

Measurement systems are multipurpose; for example, they can provide data that are useful for decision making and future planning. The use focused on here will be their role in evaluating the individual's performance, for it is in that respect they have the most direct impact on the psychological contract.

Exhibit II.   The Context of the Psychological Contract

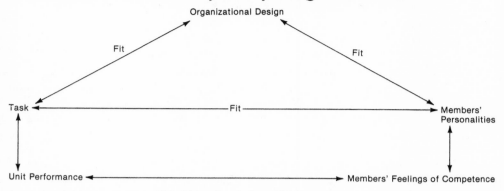

Source: Adapted from Jay Lorsch and John Morse, *Organizations and Their Members: A Contingency Approach* (New York: Harper & Row, 1974).

The unit of measurement used to evaluate performance may be any of a variety of indices. In a sales department, possibilities include volume, size of volume, increase, number of sales returns, number of visits to customers, number of new contracts, or the size of individual orders. In a manufacturing operation, quality and quantity of output, timing of output, and the size of back orders are possible units of measurement. Regardless of the measurement used, it must be congruent with task requirements and the individual's expectations and predispositions; otherwise, unit effectiveness and individual motivation will suffer. The two examples described below illustrate what may take place when an inappropriate measurement scheme is used.

1. A research laboratory in a large corporation had as its primary mission basic or pure research, as opposed to applied research. The primary unit of measurement for the lab was the completed project. Performance was evaluated informally on a quarterly basis and formally on an annual basis. At each evaluation, the emphasis was on the number of completed projects. The rationale for this measurement system was that while the corporation was interested in basic research, it also wanted ideas brought to fruition as soon as possible. The measurement system was an attempt to get around the academic inclination of scientists to drag projects out. As a result of this practice, many scientists became quite unhappy, while others designed narrowly focused projects that could be more readily com-

pleted; both behaviors were undesirable from the corporation's perspective. The dissatisfaction led to a decrease in the unit's productivity; also, the narrowly focused projects were usually applied research. Several of the top scientists left and others were threatening to do so in search of a place where research was understood.

2. A reputable eastern liberal arts college had a faculty that had done relatively little research or writing. Though the president often stressed the importance of research, research output was not used as a criterion in promotion or salary decisions. Instead, teaching effectiveness and length of service were more crucial. The college's president was puzzled as to why the faculty was not publishing more. Using the concept of fit, however, the nature of the problem was clear: the use of teaching and length of service as measurements of performance signaled that research was relatively unimportant despite the president's rhetoric. If research was truly a part of the psychological contract, or if the president wished that it be included, then it should have been reflected in measurement system.

MANAGEMENT BY OBJECTIVES.   Hoping to minimize the frequency of such misfits, many companies have turned to management by objectives (MBO) as a performance appraisal device. In theory, a properly functioning MBO system should result in measurements congruent with the task requirements and the employees' personalities.

Alva Kindall has suggested that ideally there should be five steps in the MBO process.[6] (1) The employee develops a position description and outlines areas of responsibilities and accountability. This is done in discussions with his or her immediate superior. Once agreement has been reached between the superior and subordinate on the employee's position and the results for which one is responsible and accountable, the process may proceed to step two. (2) The individual prepares a list of goals that he or she believes represent acceptable performance in the areas of responsibility. This list should be prepared in the context of the organization's objectives and include the individual's plans for self-development. (3) The subordinate seeks agreement from a superior on the list of goals. Here the superior is to act as a questioner, adviser, counselor, trainer, developer, and even "warner"; however, in no case is the supervisor to act as god or judge. (4) The individual and manager jointly determine which standards (measurements or checkpoints) will be used in evaluating the subordinate's success in attaining the objectives. (5) This is a review of the individual's results. Depending on the objectives of the manager, MBO may be used for a variety of purposes; for example, Levinson has suggested that MBO may be used for the following:

Measure and judge performance.

Relate individual performance to organizational goals.

Clarify both the job to be done and the expectations of accomplishment.

Foster the increasing competence and growth of the subordinate.

Enhance communications between superior and subordinate.

Stimulate the subordinate's motivation.

Serve as a device for organizational control and integration.

In sum, MBO may be described as a means of establishing measurements congruent with the functional unit's objectives and the individual's own expectations. Although, as Levinson points out, there have been problems in making MBO operational, this note is based on the assumption that the concept is implementable under the conditions spelled out below.[7]

MBO attempts simultaneously to signal to the individual what is desired behavior and to make provisions for the realization of individual expectations. It may be described as an effort to verbalize parts of the psychological contract and to establish measurements for evaluating the quality of its implementation. The MBO process will be useful, however, only when it fits the task requirements and individual employees' personalities; MBO is no panacea. It works best where the task is inherently rewarding, allows employee discretion and judgment, and where the employees and their superiors are predisposed to utilize such a consultative and participative process. In tasks where minimum discretion is allowed and the work is repetitive and routine, the objectives are often predetermined and little is gained by asking an employee to list the obvious. Furthermore, some employees are not comfortable with their role in an MBO program. They do not feel they should take the lead in identifying their areas of accountability and responsibility; instead, they prefer being told what to do by their superiors. Where employees hold this view, implementation of MBO would be difficult. Similarly, there are some managers who do not feel comfortable allowing their subordinates to set goals. For this group, MBO will not be a suitable tool. Where the task calls for individual judgment and discretion, and where subordinate autonomy is welcomed by subordinates and superiors, the concept of MBO would be more appropriate.

REWARDS

The rewards that managers have available as tools for implementing the psychological contract may be categorized as *intrinsic* (inherent in the job) and *extrinsic* (external to the job). Challenge, responsibility, and a sense of doing something worthwhile are examples of intrinsic rewards. Included in the extrinsic category are pay, promotional opportunities, fringe benefits, office space, and similar manifestations of status and prestige. The functional manager must develop from all reward possibilities the combination that will help bring about realization of the unit's psychological contract. Intrinsic rewards are considered later in the section on structure and job design. Pay and promotions are discussed immediately below.

PAY.   Frequently, pay is the first possibility considered by managers when thinking about rewards, yet until very recently there have been very few guidelines concerning rewards. Porter and Lawler have provided one such set of criteria for thinking about rewards in general and compensation in particular.[8] They suggest management should insure that:

1. *Rewards provided are those most desired by the employee in return for performing the job well.* This means that the pay system must be designed and administered in a manner that will allow individuals to realize their expectations. Other provisions should be made for expectations that cannot be realized through the pay system. For example, employees' expectations of friendly interactions with peers cannot be met through the pay system; instead, spatial arrangements are a more relevant means for fulfilling this expectation. Similarly, the employees' expectations of advancement as a reward for good past performance can be met only through rewarding and meaningful career paths. A critical job for managers, therefore, is that of accurately determining employees' expectations. An abundance of rewards that are not most desired by employees can result in employee dissatisfaction. The classic example of this was the reaction of paternalistic companies to unionization attempts. Having provided the employees with an abundance of material needs (company

houses, good pay, fringe benefits, etc.), the top managements of these companies were often puzzled when their employees began to press for unionization; however, they had failed to recognize and fulfill the individual's expectations of being treated like adults, not children.

2. *Superior performers are given more extrinsic rewards and are provided with more opportunities to gain intrinsic rewards than inferior performers are.* The implication here is that pay must differentiate between high and low performers and between desirable and undesirable behavior. Failure to do this will result in the communication of incorrect signals to employees. Here, a prerequisite is a measurement system capable of differentiating between high and low performers and between desirable and undesirable behavior.

3. *Reward practices lead individuals in the organization to see and believe that good performance leads to both extrinsic and intrinsic rewards.* The pay system must be understood and believed by the employees. In sum, the pay system's credibility must be maintained.

Within such broad guidelines for the design of a pay system, specific aspects will be dictated by how the manager plans to use financial compensation. For example, the manager may desire to use pay to meet only the employee's economic needs. The managerial problem would then be to set pay at a level compatible with the employees' economic expectations; also, pay differentials would be comparatively small and only marginally related to performance. In these circumstances, however, the manager must insure that the individual's remaining expectations are addressed in other ways. An example of this approach may be found in the higher grades of the civil service. A *BusinessWeek* article stated that the government's small differentials for these civil servants were criticized for not offering enough monetary incentive and rewards; however, another explanation would be that government did not view the pay system as the major reward device at the super grade level.[9] The designers of the system may have felt that at this level the major rewards were inherent in the performance of the work itself and the opportunity for public service.

A manager may wish to use pay as a means of fulfilling the competence needs of employees and as a signal of what is desired behavior. Here, pay differentials would be larger among different job levels and between high and low performers. The relationship between pay and performance would also be emphasized. In essence, the extent to which compensation is tied to performance and the differentials established among jobs must "fit" the nature of the task and employees' expectations.

In administering and designing the pay system, the manager must also be cognizant of what leads to satisfaction with pay on the part of employees. Lawler's "model of the determinants of pay satisfaction" suggests that there are several relevant variables.[10] Such satisfaction is a function of the gap between individuals' perception of what they should get and their perception of the amount of pay received. Employees' perception of what they should receive is based on their personal attributes (skill, experience, training, effort, age, seniority, company loyalty, past and present performance), their perception of what their peers are doing and receiving, their perception of their job's characteristics (level, difficulty, time span, amount of responsibility), their perception of nonmonetary rewards that will also be forthcoming, and their wage history. Similarly, employees' perception of their actual pay is determined by their wage history, their perception of the pay of their reference group, and the actual pay rate. If employees' perception of what they should receive is equal to their perception of what they actually receive, they will be satisfied. When pay falls short of their perception of what they should receive, they will be dissatisfied. Finally, when actual pay exceeds the perception of what should be received, the employee will experience feelings of guilt and inequity. The implication of Lawler's work for the design of pay schemes is straightforward: The amount of pay provided must be consistent with the perceptions of employees, or the consequences are likely to be dissatisfaction or guilt.

CAREER PATHS. A second source of extrinsic rewards to the individual employee is a meaningful career path. Here the expectation is that promotions will offer developmental opportunities and also greater opportunity to experience the job's intrinsic satisfaction as well as more money. Again, the message is the same: career paths must fit the task requirements and the individual's expectations. While career paths should offer meaningful promotional opportunities for the individual, they must also provide for organizational stability; that is, career paths should not interfere with the unit's ability to perform its tasks.

An example of career paths that did not fit task requirements was found in a consumer products company. MBAs were lured to the company's marketing department with promises of rapid promotion through the product management ranks. The company kept its commitment by moving new employees up the ladder at one- and two-year intervals. The result was great challenge for the individuals, but a great deal of confusion within the marketing function and the company. Employees moved so quickly that they did not have a chance to execute marketing plans they had developed. Consequently, it was difficult to hold any individual responsible for results. Furthermore, as a result of so much rapid movement, the marketing department's relations with other functions deteriorated. Managers in research, manufacturing, and sales complained that the frequent job changes made it impossible to know whom to contact in marketing about mutual problems, so they quit trying.

STRUCTURE

One of the principal structural concerns at the functional level is job design. Job design may be altered by modifying hierarchical agreements, providing rules, and by developing standard operating procedures. With respect to the psychological contract, the functional manager may use job design to insure that tasks requirements and/or the employees' expectations are met.

HIERARCHY, RULES, AND STANDARD OPERATING PROCEDURES. These are especially useful tools for facilitating task performance. For example, the hierarchical span of control may have an impact on the manager's ability to perform adequately. A district sales manager with a reasonable span is likely to be more capable of meaningfully supporting salespersons than a colleague with an unmanageable span of control. Similarly, rules may be used as managerial tools. Rules outlining territorial boundaries for salespersons enable the sales manager to be more efficient and effective in the utilization of personnel. Finally, standard operating procedures can be used to simplify a task by standardizing its recurring elements. In most organizations the purchasing function has been simplified through the standardization of procedures and forms.

JOB ENLARGEMENT AND ENRICHMENT. If the functional manager wishes to use job design primarily as a means of fulfilling employee expectations, he or she may sometimes find it necessary to eliminate or modify existing hierarchical arrangements, rules, and procedures. Job enlargement and job enrichment are concepts associated with the redesigning of jobs that have become too restricted concerning the employees' psychological contract.

Job enlargement is the broadening of job duties and responsibilities to eliminate as much as possible the negative characteristics of repetitive work. Job enlargement has frequently meant combining several operations in the hope of reducing repetitiveness. Unfortunately, combining several repetitive tasks often results simply in a larger repetitive task. Because of this difficulty with job enlargement, the concept of job enrichment has grown in popularity. Job enrichment is an attempt to enhance employee responsibility and autonomy through the broadening of job definitions, thus emphasizing the opportunity for individual achievement and creativity.[11] The hope has been that job enrichment would lead to improved employee morale, which, in turn, would foster greater motivation.

Reporting on his research efforts with Lorsch, Morse concluded that job enrichment is most likely to result in improved job performance when it fits both "(1) personalities of the individuals whose jobs are being designed, and (2) the technology or the task."[12] Morse suggests that the improved performance would not be due to increases in employee morale, but to increases in motivation. Where job enrichment works, it facilitates task performance and results in greater effectiveness. This improvement in effectiveness enables the individual to experience a fulfillment of competency expectations. This fulfillment then leads to a greater willingness to expend energy on the task and thus further contributes to increased effectiveness.

Certain tasks, such as assembly line activities and other work associated with large capital investments, are unavoidably repetitive and monotonous. These positions require limited judgment and allow little discretion. These tasks are not always perceived as undesirable and dull, however, because some individuals require or expect little autonomy or variety from their work. Here, job enrichment would be a violation of these individual's psychological contracts.

In summary, a functional manager may affect performance by altering the unit's structure. If performance is to be enhanced, structural changes must fit the task and the needs of the individual.

SELECTION AND DEVELOPMENT

As task requirements change, functional managers must enlist new persons to retrain existing personnel. Selection and development tools are among the functional manager's most important instruments for securing good task-individual fits.

In the context of the concepts of fit and the psychological contract, the selection process is really a matching process between the employee and the organization. In any ongoing functional unit, there is an existing psychological contract between its management and employees. The selection process must bring to the functional unit individuals who will be comfortable with the existing arrangements. For the selection process to function properly, the manager and the candidate must accurately communicate their expectations at the employment interview. This means that the manager must be skilled in articulating the expectations of the workplace and in understanding the individual's expectations and predispositions. Although a psychological interpretation of the applicant's personality is not required, the manager must be skilled in hearing and understanding all clues concerning the applicant's need structure (expectations) and personality. The manager must make a judgment as to whether or not an applicant would be able to accept the unit's existing psychological contract. A judgment must be made on the quality of the fit between management's expectations and those of the potential employee. Poor judgment here could have a negative impact on the functional unit's effectiveness. Kotter found that job satisfaction, productivity, and turnover varied with the quality of the match between the expectations of new employees and the organization—the higher the quality of the match, the greater the job satisfaction.[13]

When either task needs or the employees' expectations require changes, the functional manager has to assume responsibility for facilitating the development of subordinates. The manager must design development programs that will enable the unit's personnel to grow. A program may be highly formal and structured (e.g., academic training, the Blake-Mouton managerial grid, the Kepner-Tregoe program, or a team-building exercise), or it may be informal (e.g., the maintenance of a supportive environment, or continuous, meaningful, informal counseling with employees). The development program must fit the task requirements and the expectations of the individual. Intensive development programs in an organization with limited opportunities for advancement would likely lead to frustration, as would programs forced on individuals who have little aspiration to grow.

In this discussion of design tools, they have been viewed as a means of implementing the tacitly accepted psychological contract. It also has been repeatedly stressed that the effectiveness of design tools as implementation aids depends on their fit with the organization's task and the employees' predispositions and expectations. No one tool is a panacea for all situations. The ideas presented in this note suggest only a broad framework for thinking about these issues. The functional manager must still use discretion and judgment in selecting and using these design tools to fit a particular work situation.

Notes

1. Discussion of the psychological contract is based primarily on: Harry Levinson et al., *Management and Mental Health* (Cambridge, Mass.: Harvard University Press, 1966), pp. 22–38, and David J. Lawless, *Effective Management: A Social Psychological Approach* (Englewood Cliffs, N.J.: Prentice-Hall, 1970), pp. 144–164.
2. Levinson et al., p. 36; Lawless, p. 147.
3. See "Sabotage at Lordstown?" *Time* (February 7, 1972), p. 76.
4. Edgar Schein, *Organizational Psychology* (Englewood Cliffs, N.J.: Prentice-Hall, 1970), pp. 50–79.
5. Jay Lorsch and John Morse, *Organizations and Their Members: A Contingency Approach* (New York: Harper & Row, 1974).
6. Alva F. Kindall, *Personnel Administration: Principles and Cases* (Homewood, Ill.: Richard D. Irwin, Inc., 1969), pp. 411–415.
7. Harry Levinson, *The Great Jackass Fallacy* (Boston: Division of Research, Harvard Business School, 1973).
8. Lyman W. Porter and Edward E. Lawler III, "What Job Attitudes Tell about Motivation," *Harvard Business Review* (January–February 1968), pp. 118–126.
9. Arch Patton, "Government's Pay Disincentive," *BusinessWeek* (January 19, 1974), pp. 12–13.
10. Edward E. Lawler III, *Pay and Organizational Effectiveness: A Psychological View* (New York: McGraw-Hill, 1971), pp. 205–230.
11. John J. Morse, "A Contingency Look at Job Design," *California Management Review* (Fall 1973), p. 68.
12. Ibid., p. 69.
13. John Paul Kotter, "The Psychological Contract: Managing the Joining-Up Process," *California Management Review* (Spring 1973), p. 93.

4
One More Time: How Do You Motivate Employees?

Frederick Herzberg

How many articles, books, speeches, and workshops have pleaded plaintively, "How do I get an employee to do what I want?"

The psychology of motivation is tremendously complex, and what has been unraveled with any degree of assurance is small indeed. But the dismal ratio of knowledge to speculation has not dampened the enthusiasm for new forms of snake oil that are constantly coming on the market, many of them with academic testimonials. Doubtless this article will have no depressing impact on the market for snake oil, but since the ideas expressed in it have been tested in many corporations and other organizations, it will help—I hope—to redress the imbalance in the aforementioned ratio.

"Motivating" with KITA

In lectures to industry on the problem, I have found that the audiences are anxious for quick and practical answers, so I will begin with a straightforward, practical formula for moving people.

What is the simplest, surest, and most direct way of getting someone to do something? Ask? But if the person responds that he or

First published in the January–February 1968 issue. Republished as an HBR Classic in the September–October 1987 issue.

she does not want to do it, then that calls for psychological consultation to determine the reason for such obstinacy. Tell the person? The response shows that he or she does not understand you, and now an expert in communication methods has to be brought in to show you how to get through. Give the person a monetary incentive? I do not need to remind the reader of the complexity and difficulty involved in setting up and administering an incentive system. Show the person? This means a costly training program. We need a simple way.

Every audience contains the "direct action" manager who shouts, "Kick the person!" And this type of manager is right. The surest and least circumlocuted way of getting someone to do something is to administer a kick in the pants—to give what might be called the KITA.

There are various forms of KITA, and here are some of them:

NEGATIVE PHYSICAL KITA

This is a literal application of the term and was frequently used in the past. It has, however, three major drawbacks: (1) it is inelegant; (2) it contradicts the precious image of benevolence that most organizations cherish; and (3) since it is a physical attack, it directly stimulates the autonomic nervous system, and this often results in negative feedback—the employee may just kick you in return. These factors give rise to certain taboos against negative physical KITA.

In uncovering infinite sources of psychological vulnerabilities and the appropriate methods to play tunes on them, psychologists have come to the rescue of those who are no longer permitted to use negative physical KITA. "He took my rug away"; "I wonder what she meant by that"; "The boss is always going around me"—these symptomatic expressions of ego sores that have been rubbed raw are the result of application of:

NEGATIVE PSYCHOLOGICAL KITA

This has several advantages over negative physical KITA. First, the cruelty is not visible; the bleeding is internal and comes much later. Second, since it affects the higher cortical centers of the brain with its inhibitory powers, it reduces the possibility of physical backlash. Third, since the number of psychological pains that a person can feel is almost infinite, the direction and site possibilities of the KITA are increased many times. Fourth, the person administering the kick can manage to be above it all and let the system accomplish the dirty work. Fifth, those who practice it receive some ego satisfaction (one-upmanship), whereas they would find drawing blood abhorrent. Finally, if the employee does complain, he or she can always be accused of being paranoid; there is no tangible evidence of an actual attack.

Now, what does negative KITA accomplish? If I kick you in the rear (physically or psychologically), who is motivated? *I* am motivated; *you* move! Negative KITA does not lead to motivation, but to movement. So:

POSITIVE KITA

Let us consider motivation. If I say to you, "Do this for me or the company, and in return I will give you a reward, an incentive, more status, a promotion, all the quid pro quos that exist in the industrial organization," am I motivating you? The overwhelming opinion I receive from management people is, "Yes, this is motivation."

I have a year-old Schnauzer. When it was a small puppy and I wanted it to move, I kicked it in the rear and it moved. Now that I have finished its obedience training, I hold up a dog biscuit when I want the Schnauzer to move. In this instance, who is motivated— I or the dog? The dog wants the biscuit, but it is I who want it to move. Again, I am the one who is motivated, and the dog is the one who moves. In this instance all I did was apply KITA frontally; I exerted a pull instead of a push. When industry wishes to use such positive KITAs, it has available an incredible number and variety of dog biscuits (jelly beans for humans) to wave in front of employees to get them to jump.

Why is it that managerial audiences are quick to see that negative KITA is *not* motivation, while they are almost unanimous in their judgment that positive KITA *is* motivation. It is because negative KITA is rape, and positive KITA is seduction. But it is infinitely worse to be seduced than to be raped; the latter is an unfortunate occurrence, while the former signifies that you were a party to your own downfall. This is why positive KITA is so popular: it is a tradition; it is the American way. The organization does not have to kick you; you kick yourself.

Myths about Motivation

Why is KITA not motivation? If I kick my dog (from the front or the back), he will move. And when I want him to move again, what must I do? I must kick him again. Similarly, I can charge a person's battery, and then recharge it, and recharge it again. But it is only when one has a generator of one's own that we can talk about motivation. One then needs no outside stimulation. One *wants* to do it.

With this in mind, we can review some positive KITA personnel practices that were developed as attempts to instill "motivation":

1. **Reducing time spent at work.** This represents a marvelous way of motivating people to work—getting them off the job! We have reduced (formally and informally) the time spent on the job over the last 50 or 60 years until we are finally on the way to the "6½-day weekend." An interesting variant of this approach is the development of off-hour recreation programs. The philosophy here seems to be that those who play together, work together. The fact is that motivated people seek more hours of work, not fewer.

2. **Spiraling wages.** Have these motivated people? Yes, to seek the next wage increase. Some medievalists still can be heard to say that a good depression will get employees moving. They feel that if rising wages don't or won't do the job, reducing them will.

3. **Fringe benefits.** Industry has outdone the most welfare-minded of welfare states in dispensing cradle-to-the-grave succor. One company I know of had an informal "fringe benefit of the month club" going for a while. The cost of fringe benefits in this country has reached approximately 25% of the wage dollar, and we still cry for motivation.

   People spend less time working for more money and more security than ever before, and the trend cannot be reversed. These benefits are no longer rewards; they are rights. A 6-day week is inhuman, a 10-hour day is exploitation, extended medical coverage is a basic decency, and stock options are the salvation of American initiative. Unless the ante is continuously raised, the psychological reaction of employees is that the company is turning back the clock.

   When industry began to realize that both the economic nerve and the lazy nerve of their employees had insatiable appetites, it started to listen to the behavioral scientists who, more out of a humanist tradition than from scientific study, criticized management for not knowing how to deal with people. The next KITA easily followed.

4. **Human relations training.** Over 30 years of teaching and, in many instances, of practicing psychological approaches to handling people have resulted in costly human relations programs and, in the end, the same question: How do you motivate workers? Here, too, escalations have taken place. Thirty years ago it was necessary to request, "Please don't spit on the floor." Today the same admonition requires three "pleases" before the employee feels that a superior has demonstrated the psychologically proper attitude.

   The failure of human relations training to produce motivation led to the conclusion that supervisors or managers themselves were not psychologically true to themselves in their practice of interpersonal decency. So an advanced form of human relations KITA, sensitivity training, was unfolded.

5. **Sensitivity training.** Do you really, really understand yourself? Do you really, really, really trust other people? Do you really, really, really, really cooperate? The failure of sensitivity training is now being explained, by those who have become opportunistic exploiters of the technique, as a failure to really (five times) conduct proper sensitivity training courses.

   With the realization that there are only temporary gains from comfort and economic and interpersonal KITA, personnel managers concluded that the fault lay not in what they were doing, but in the employee's failure to appreciate what they were doing. This opened up the field of communications, a whole new area of "scientifically" sanctioned KITA.

6. **Communications.** The professor of communications was invited to join the faculty of management training programs and help in making employees understand what management was doing for them. House organs, briefing sessions, supervisory instruction on the importance of communication, and all sorts of propaganda have proliferated until today there is even an International Council of Industrial Editors. But no motivation resulted, and the obvious thought occurred that perhaps management was not hearing what the employees were saying. That led to the next KITA.

7. **Two-way communication.** Management ordered morale surveys, suggestion plans, and group participation programs. Then both employees and management were communicating and listening to each other more than ever, but without much improvement in motivation.

The behavioral scientists began to take another look at their conceptions and their data, and they took human relations one step further. A glimmer of truth was beginning to show through in the writings of the so-called higher-order-need psychologists. People, so they said, want to actualize themselves. Unfortunately, the "actualizing" psychologists got mixed up with the human relations psychologists, and a new KITA emerged.

8. **Job participation.** Though it may not have been the theoretical intention, job participation often became a "give them the big picture" approach. For example, if a man is tightening 10,000 nuts a day on an assembly line with a torque wrench, tell him he is building a Chevrolet. Another approach had the goal of giving employees a "feeling" that they are determining, in some measure, what they do on the job. The goal was to provide a *sense* of achievement rather than a substantive achievement in the task. Real achievement, of course, requires a task that makes it possible.

   But still there was no motivation. This led to the inevitable conclusion that the employees must be sick, and therefore to the next KITA.

9. **Employee counseling.** The initial use of this form of KITA in a systematic fashion can be credited to the Hawthorne experiment of the Western Electric Company during the early 1930s. At that time, it was found that the employees harbored irrational feelings that were interfering with the rational operation of the factory. Counseling in this instance was a means of letting the employees unburden themselves by talking to someone about their problems. Although the counseling techniques were primitive, the program was large indeed.

   The counseling approach suffered as a result of experiences during World War II, when the programs themselves were found to be interfering with the operation of the organizations; the counselors had forgotten their role of benevolent listeners and were attempting to do something about the problems that they heard about. Psychological counseling, however, has managed to survive the negative impact of World War II experiences and today is beginning to flourish with renewed sophistication. But, alas, many of these programs, like all the others, do not seem to have lessened the pressure of demands to find out how to motivate workers.

Since KITA results only in short-term movement, it is safe to predict that the cost of these programs will increase steadily and new varieties will be developed as old positive KITAs reach their satiation points.

Hygiene versus Motivators

Let me rephrase the perennial question this way: How do you install a generator in an employee? A brief review of my motivation-hygiene theory of job attitudes is required before theoretical and practical suggestions can be offered. The theory was first drawn from an examination of events in the lives of engineers and accountants. At least 16 other investigations, using a wide variety of populations (including some in the Communist countries), have since been completed, making the original research one of the most replicated studies in the field of job attitudes.

The findings of these studies, along with corroboration from many other investigations using different procedures, suggest that the factors involved in producing job satisfaction (and motivation) are separate and distinct from the factors that lead to job dissatisfaction. Since separate factors need to be considered, depending on whether job satisfaction or job dissatisfaction is being examined, it follows that these two feelings are not opposites of each other. The opposite of job satisfaction is not job dissatisfaction but, rather, *no* job satisfaction; and similarly, the opposite of job dissatisfaction is not job satisfaction, but *no* job dissatisfaction.

Stating the concept presents a problem in semantics, for we normally think of satisfaction and dissatisfaction as opposites—i.e., what is not satisfying must be dissatisfying, and vice versa. But when it comes to understanding the behavior of people in their jobs, more than a play on words is involved.

Two different needs of human beings are involved here. One set of needs can be thought of as stemming from humankind's animal nature—the built-in drive to avoid pain from the environment, plus all the learned drives that become conditioned to the basic biological needs. For example, hunger, a basic biological drive, makes it necessary to earn money, and then money becomes a specific drive. The other set of needs relates to that unique human characteristic, the ability to achieve and, through achievement, to experience psychological growth. The stimuli for the growth needs are tasks that induce growth; in the industrial setting, they are the job content. *Contrariwise,* the stimuli inducing pain-avoidance behavior are found in the job environment.

The growth or *motivator* factors that are intrinsic to the job are: achievement, recognition for achievement, the work itself, responsibility, and growth or advancement. The dissatisfaction-avoidance or *hygiene* (KITA) factors that are extrinsic to the job include:

Exhibit I.   Factors Affecting Job Attitudes as Reported in 12 Investigations

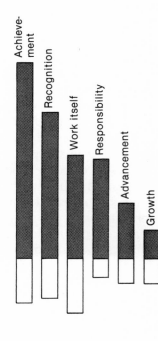

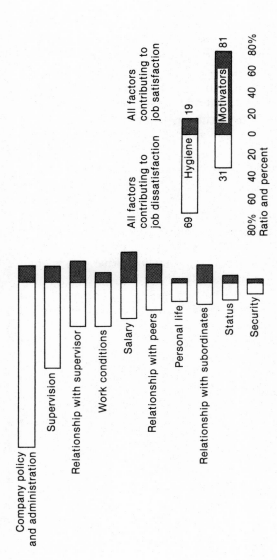

Company policy
and administration

Supervision

Relationship with supervisor

Work conditions

Salary

Relationship with peers

Personal life

Relationship with subordinates

Status

Security

All factors
contributing to
job dissatisfaction

All factors
contributing to
job satisfaction

Hygiene   19

81   Motivators

69

31

80% 60 40 20   0   20 40 60 80%
Ratio and percent

company policy and administration, supervision, interpersonal re-lationships, working conditions, salary, status, and security.

A composite of the factors that are involved in causing job sat-isfaction and job dissatisfaction, drawn from samples of 1,685 em-ployees, is shown in Exhibit I. The results indicate that motivators were the primary cause of satisfaction, and hygiene factors the primary cause of unhappiness on the job. The employees, studied in 12 different investigations, included lower level supervisors, professional women, agricultural administrators, men about to re-tire from management positions, hospital maintenance personnel, manufacturing supervisors, nurses, food handlers, military offi-cers, engineers, scientists, housekeepers, teachers, technicians, fe-male assemblers, accountants, Finnish foremen, and Hungarian engineers.

They were asked what job events had occurred in their work that had led to extreme satisfaction or extreme dissatisfaction on their part. Their responses are broken down in the exhibit into percent-ages of total "positive" job events and of total "negative" job events. (The figures total more than 100% on both the "hygiene" and "mo-tivators" sides because often at least two factors can be attributed to a single event; advancement, for instance, often accompanies assumption of responsibility.)

To illustrate, a typical response involving achievement that had a negative effect for the employee was, "I was unhappy because I didn't do the job successfully." A typical response in the small number of positive job events in the company policy and admin-istration grouping was, "I was happy because the company reor-ganized the section so that I didn't report any longer to the guy I didn't get along with."

As the lower right-hand part of the exhibit shows, of all the factors contributing to job satisfaction, 81% were motivators. And of all the factors contributing to the employees' dissatisfaction over their work, 69% involved hygiene elements.

ETERNAL TRIANGLE

There are three general philosophies of personnel management. The first is based on organizational theory, the second on industrial engineering, and the third on behavioral science.

Organizational theorists believe that human needs are either so irrational or so varied and adjustable to specific situations that the major function of personnel management is to be as pragmatic as the occasion demands. If jobs are organized in a proper manner, they reason, the result will be the most efficient job structure, and the most favorable job attitudes will follow as a matter of course.

Industrial engineers hold that humankind is mechanistically oriented and economically motivated and that human needs are best met by attuning the individual to the most efficient work process. The goal of personnel management therefore should be to concoct the most appropriate incentive system and to design the specific working conditions in a way that facilitates the most efficient use of the human machine. By structuring jobs in a manner that leads to the most efficient operation, engineers believe that they can obtain the optimal organization of work and the proper work attitudes.

Behavioral scientists focus on group sentiments, attitudes of individual employees, and the organization's social and psychological climate. This persuasion emphasizes one or more of the various hygiene and motivator needs. Its approach to personnel management is generally to emphasize some form of human relations education, in the hope of instilling healthy employee attitudes and an organizational climate that is considered to be felicitous to human values. The belief is that proper attitudes will lead to efficient job and organizational structure.

There is always a lively debate about the overall effectiveness of the approaches of organizational theorists and industrial engineers. Manifestly both have achieved much. But the nagging question for behavioral scientists has been: What is the cost in human problems that eventually cause more expense to the organization—for instance, turnover, absenteeism, errors, violation of safety rules, strikes, restriction of output, higher wages, and greater fringe benefits? On the other hand, behavioral scientists are hard put to document much manifest improvement in personnel management, using their approach.

The three philosophies can be depicted as a triangle, as is done in Exhibit II, with each persuasion claiming the apex angle. The motivation-hygiene theory claims the same angle as industrial engineering, but for opposite goals. Rather than rationalizing the work to increase efficiency, the theory suggests that work be *enriched* to bring about effective utilization of personnel. Such a systematic attempt to motivate employees by manipulating the motivator factors is just beginning.

The term *job enrichment* describes this embryonic movement. An older term, job enlargement, should be avoided because it is

Exhibit II.   *"Triangle" of Philosophies of Personnel Management*

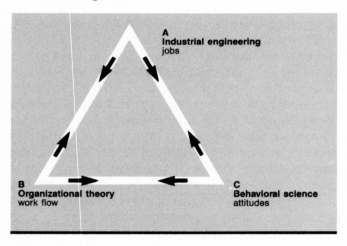

A
Industrial engineering
jobs

B
Organizational theory
work flow

C
Behavioral science
attitudes

associated with past failures stemming from a misunderstanding of the problem. Job enrichment provides the opportunity for the employee's psychological growth, while job enlargement merely makes a job structurally bigger. Since scientific job enrichment is very new, this article only suggests the principles and practical steps that have recently emerged from several successful experiments in industry.

JOB LOADING

In attempting to enrich certain jobs, management often reduces the personal contribution of employees rather than giving them opportunities for growth in their accustomed jobs. Such endeavors, which I shall call horizontal job loading (as opposed to vertical loading, or providing motivator factors), have been the problem of earlier job enlargement programs. Job loading merely enlarges the meaninglessness of the job. Some examples of this approach, and their effect, are:

Challenging the employee by increasing the amount of production expected. If each tightens 10,000 bolts a day, see if each can tighten

20,000 bolts a day. The arithmetic involved shows that multiplying zero by zero still equals zero.

Adding another meaningless task to the existing one, usually some routine clerical activity. The arithmetic here is adding zero to zero.

Rotating the assignments of a number of jobs that need to be enriched. This means washing dishes for a while, then washing silverware. The arithmetic is substituting one zero for another zero.

Removing the most difficult parts of the assignment in order to free the worker to accomplish more of the less challenging assignments. This traditional industrial engineering approach amounts to subtraction in the hope of accomplishing addition.

These are common forms of horizontal loading that frequently come up in preliminary brainstorming sessions of job enrichment. The principles of vertical loading have not all been worked out as yet, and they remain rather general, but I have furnished seven useful starting points for consideration in Exhibit III.

Exhibit III. Principles of Vertical Job Loading

Principle	Motivators involved
A. Removing some controls while retaining accountability	Responsibility and personal achievement
B. Increasing the accountability of individuals for own work	Responsibility and recognition
C. Giving a person a complete natural unit of work (module, division, area, and so on)	Responsibility, achievement, and recognition
D. Granting additional authority to an employee in his activity; job freedom	Responsibility, achievement, and recognition
E. Making periodic reports directly available to the worker himself rather than to the supervisor	Internal recognition
F. Introducing new and more difficult tasks not previously handled	Growth and learning
G. Assigning individuals specific or specialized tasks, enabling them to become experts	Responsibility, growth, and advancement

A SUCCESSFUL APPLICATION

An example from a highly successful job enrichment experiment can illustrate the distinction between horizontal and vertical loading of a job. The subjects of this study were the stockholder correspondents employed by a very large corporation. Seemingly, the task required of these carefully selected and highly trained correspondents was quite complex and challenging. But almost all indexes of performance and job attitudes were low, and exit interviewing confirmed that the challenge of the job existed merely as words.

A job enrichment project was initiated in the form of an experiment with one group, designated as an achieving unit, having its job enriched by the principles described in Exhibit III. A control group continued to do its job in the traditional way. (There were also two "uncommitted" groups of correspondents formed to measure the so-called Hawthorne Effect—that is, to gauge whether productivity and attitudes toward the job changed artificially merely because employees sensed that the company was paying more attention to them in doing something different or novel. The results for these groups were substantially the same as for the control group, and for the sake of simplicity I do not deal with them in this summary.) No changes in hygiene were introduced for either group other than those that would have been made anyway, such as normal pay increases.

The changes for the achieving unit were introduced in the first two months, averaging one per week of the seven motivators listed in Exhibit III. At the end of six months the members of the achieving unit were found to be outperforming their counterparts in the control group, and in addition indicated a marked increase in their liking for their jobs. Other results showed that the achieving group had lower absenteeism and, subsequently, a much higher rate of promotion.

Exhibit IV illustrates the changes in performance, measured in February and March, before the study period began, and at the end of each month of the study period. The shareholder service index represents quality of letters, including accuracy of information, and speed of response to stockholders' letters of inquiry. The index of a current month was averaged into the average of the two prior months, which means that improvement was harder to obtain if the indexes of the previous months were low. The "achievers" were performing less well before the six-month period started, and their

Exhibit IV. **Shareholder Service Index in**
Company Experiment
Three-month cumulative average

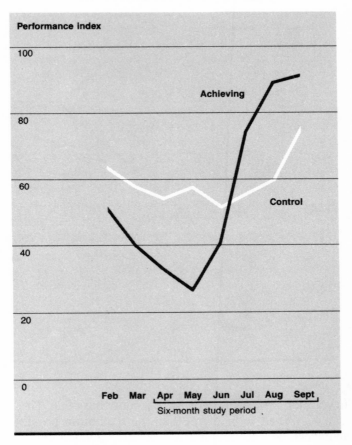

performance service index continued to decline after the introduction of the motivators, evidently because of uncertainty after their newly granted responsibilities. In the third month, however, performance improved, and soon the members of this group had reached a high level of accomplishment.

Exhibit V shows the two groups' attitudes toward their job, measured at the end of March, just before the first motivator was introduced, and again at the end of September. The correspondents were asked 16 questions, all involving motivation. A typical one was, "As you see it, how many opportunities do you feel that you

Exhibit V.   Changes in Attitudes toward Tasks in
Company Experiment
Changes in mean scores over six-month period

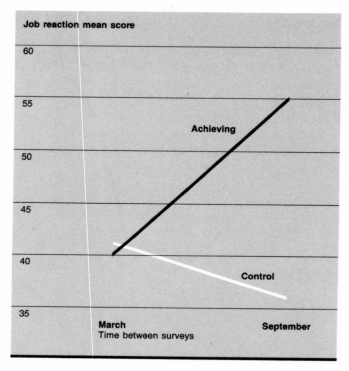

have in your job for making worthwhile contributions?" The answers were scaled from 1 to 5, with 80 as the maximum possible score. The achievers became much more positive about their job, while the attitude of the control unit remained about the same (the drop is not statistically significant).

How was the job of these correspondents restructured? Exhibit VI lists the suggestions made that were deemed to be horizontal loading, and the actual vertical loading changes that were incorporated in the job of the achieving unit. The capital letters under "Principle" after "Vertical loading" refer to the corresponding letters in Exhibit III. The reader will note that the rejected forms of horizontal loading correspond closely to the list of common manifestations I mentioned earlier.

Steps for Job Enrichment

Now that the motivator idea has been described in practice, here are the steps that managers should take in instituting the principle with their employees:

1. Select those jobs in which (a) the investment in industrial engineering does not make changes too costly, (b) attitudes are poor, (c) hygiene is becoming very costly, and (d) motivation will make a difference in performance.

2. Approach these jobs with the conviction that they can be changed. Years of tradition have led managers to believe that the content of the jobs is sacrosanct and the only scope of action that they have is in ways of stimulating people.

3. Brainstorm a list of changes that may enrich the jobs, without concern for their practicality.

4. Screen the list to eliminate suggestions that involve hygiene, rather than actual motivation.

5. Screen the list for generalities, such as "give them more responsibility," that are rarely followed in practice. This might seem obvious, but the motivator words have never left industry; the substance has just been rationalized and organized out. Words like "responsibility," "growth," "achievement," and "challenge," for example, have been elevated to the lyrics of the patriotic anthem for all organizations. It is the old problem typified by the pledge of allegiance to the flag being more important than contributions to the country—of following the form, rather than the substance.

6. Screen the list to eliminate any *horizontal* loading suggestions.

7. Avoid direct participation by the employees whose jobs are to be enriched. Ideas they have expressed previously certainly constitute a valuable source for recommended changes, but their direct involvement contaminates the process with human relations *hygiene* and, more specifically, gives them only a *sense* of making a contribution. The job is to be changed, and it is the content that will produce the motivation, not attitudes about being involved or the challenge inherent in setting up a job. That process will be over shortly, and it is what the employees will be doing from then on that will determine their motivation. A sense of participation will result only in short-term movement.

8. In the initial attempts at job enrichment, set up a controlled experiment. At least two equivalent groups should be chosen, one an experimental unit in which the motivators are systematically

Exhibit VI. *Enlargement vs. Enrichment of Correspondents' Tasks in Company Experiment*

Horizontal loading suggestions rejected	Vertical loading suggestions adopted	Principle
Firm quotas could be set for letters to be answered each day, using a rate which would be hard to reach.	Subject matter experts were appointed within each unit for other members of the unit to consult with before seeking supervisory help. (The supervisor had been answering all specialized and difficult questions.)	G
The secretaries could type the letters themselves, as well as compose them, or take on any other clerical functions.	Correspondents signed their own names on letters. (The supervisor had been signing all letters.)	B
All difficult or complex inquiries could be channeled to a few secretaries so that the remainder could achieve high rates of output. These jobs could be exchanged from time to time.	The work of the more experienced correspondents was proofread less frequently by supervisors and was done at the correspondents desks, dropping verification from 100% to 10%. (Previously, all correspondents' letters had been checked by the supervisor.)	A
The secretaries could be rotated through units, handling different customers, and then sent back to their own units.		

D

Production was discussed, but only in terms such as "a full day's work is expected." As time went on, this was no longer mentioned. (Before, the group had been constantly reminded of the number of letters that needed to be answered.)

A

Outgoing mail went directly to the mailroom without going over supervisors' desks. (The letters had always been routed through the supervisors.)

C

Correspondents were encouraged to answer letters in a more personalized way. (Reliance on the form-letter approach had been standard practice.)

B, E

Each correspondent was held personally responsible for the quality and accuracy of letters. (This responsibility had been the province of the supervisor and the verifier.)

introduced over a period of time, and the other one a control group in which no changes are made. For both groups, hygiene should be allowed to follow its natural course for the duration of the experiment. Pre- and post-installation tests of performance and job attitudes are necessary to evaluate the effectiveness of the job enrichment program. The attitude test must be limited to motivator items in order to divorce employees' views of the jobs they are given from all the surrounding hygiene feelings that they might have.

9. Be prepared for a drop in performance in the experimental group the first few weeks. The changeover to a new job may lead to a temporary reduction in efficiency.

10. Expect your first-line supervisors to experience some anxiety and hostility over the changes you are making. The anxiety comes from their fear that the changes will result in poorer performance for their unit. Hostility will arise when the employees start assuming what the supervisors regard as their own responsibility for performance. The supervisor without checking duties to perform may then be left with little to do.

After successful experiment, however, the supervisors usually discover the supervisory and managerial functions they have neglected, or which were never theirs because all their time was given over to checking the work of their subordinates. For example, in the R&D division of one large chemical company I know of, the supervisors of the laboratory assistants were theoretically responsible for their training and evaluation. These functions, however, had come to be performed in a routine, unsubstantial fashion. After the job enrichment program, during which the supervisors were not merely passive observers of the assistants' performance, the supervisors actually were devoting their time to reviewing performance and administering thorough training.

What has been called an employee-centered style of supervision will come about not through education of supervisors, but by changing the jobs that they do.

Concluding Note

Job enrichment will not be a one-time proposition, but a continuous management function. The initial changes should last for a very long period of time. There are a number of reasons for this:

The changes should bring the job up to the level of challenge commensurate with the skill that was hired.

Those who have still more ability eventually will be able to demonstrate it better and win promotion to higher level jobs.

The very nature of motivators, as opposed to hygiene factors, is that they have a much longer term effect on employees' attitudes. Perhaps the job will have to be enriched again, but this will not occur as frequently as the need for hygiene.

Not all jobs can be enriched, nor do all jobs need to be enriched. If only a small percentage of the time and money that is now devoted to hygiene, however, were given to job enrichment efforts, the return in human satisfaction and economic gain would be one of the largest dividends that industry and society have ever reaped through their efforts at better personnel management.

The argument for job enrichment can be summed up quite simply: if you have employees on a job, use them. If you can't use them on the job, get rid of them, either via automation or by selecting someone with lesser ability. If you can't use them and you can't get rid of them, you will have a motivation problem.

Appendix

Retrospective Commentary

I wrote this article at the height of the attention on improving employee performance through various (contrived) psychological approaches to human relations. I tried to redress industrial social scientists' overconcern about how to treat workers to the neglect of how to design the work itself.

The first part of the article distinguishes between motivation and movement, a distinction that most writing on motivation misses. Movement is a function of fear of punishment or failure to get extrinsic rewards. It is the typical procedure used in animal training and its counterpart, behavioral modification techniques for humans. Motivation is a function of growth from getting intrinsic rewards out of interesting and challenging work.

While the immediate behavioral results from movement and motivation appear alike, their dynamics, which produce vastly different long-term consequences, are different. Movement requires constant reinforcement and stresses short-term results. To get a reaction, management must constantly enhance the extrinsic rewards for movement.

Figure A.   *How the Hygiene-Motivator Factors Affect Job Attitudes in Six Countries*

Percentage

All factors contributing to job dissatisfaction

All factors contributing to job satisfaction

100%   80   60   40   20   0   20   40   60   80   100%

Japan   8   92   61   39

India   34   66   70   30

South Africa   20   86   72   28

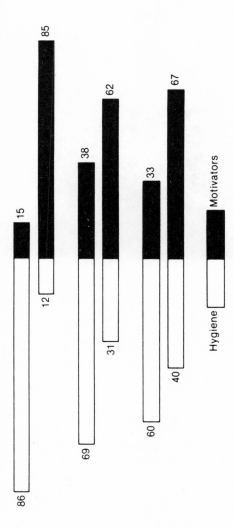

Figure B.   Sensory Ingredients of Job Enrichment

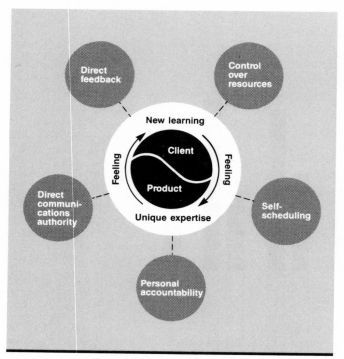

If I get a bonus of $1,000 one year and $500 the next, I am getting extra rewards both years, but psychologically I have taken a $500 salary cut.

Motivation is based on growth needs. It is an internal engine, and its benefits show up over a long period of time. Because the ultimate reward in motivation is personal growth, people don't need to be rewarded incrementally. I write a book—a big accomplishment. Then I write an article—a lesser accomplishment, but nevertheless an addition to my personal growth.

For this article, I invented the acronym KITA (kick in the ass) to describe the movement technique. The inelegance of the term offended those who consider good treatment a motivating strategy, regardless of the nature of the work itself. In this plain language I tried to spotlight the animal approach to dealing with human beings that characterizes so much of our behavioral science intervention.

The article's popularity stems in great part from readers' recognition that KITA underlies the assumed benevolence of personnel practices. If I were writing "One More Time" in 1987, I would emphasize the important, positive role of organizational behaviorists more than I did in 1968. We can certainly learn to get along better on the job. Reduced workplace tension through congenial relations is a necessary ingredient of a pleasant environment.

The second part of the article describes my motivation-hygiene theory. It suggests that environmental factors (hygienes) can at best create no dissatisfaction on the job, and their absence creates dissatisfaction. In contrast, what makes people happy on the job and motivates them are the job content factors (motivators). The controversy surrounding these concepts continues to this day.

While the original 12 studies were mostly American (they also included Finnish supervisors and Hungarian engineers), the results have been replicated throughout the world. A sampling of recent foreign investigations, which the reader can compare with the first American studies detailed in Exhibit I in "One More Time," appears in Figure A. The similarity of the profiles is worth noting.

The 1970s was the decade of job enrichment (discussed in the third part of the article), sometimes called job design or redesign by opponents of the motivation-hygiene theory. Since the first trial-and-error

Figure C.   Client Relationships in an Air Force Function

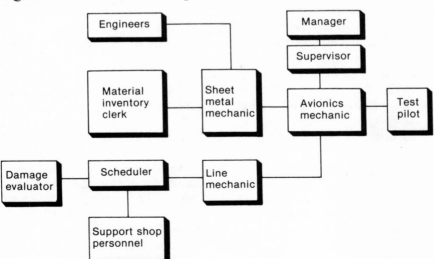

studies at AT&T, experience has produced refinements of the proce-dures for job enrichment and the goals for achieving it. I like to illustrate them in the wheel shown in Figure B.

This diagram reflects my conviction that the present-day abstraction of work has shut out feelings from the job content. Finance, for example, has become the focus of attention in most businesses, and nothing is more abstract and devoid of feeling. Part of the blame can be laid to electronic communication, which promotes detachment and abstrac-tion. Job enrichment grows out of knowing your product and your client with feeling, not just intellectually.

With reference to the motivator ingredients discussed in the 1968 article, "recognition for achievement" translates into "direct feedback" in Figure B. The wheel in Figure B shows this feedback to come chiefly from the client and product of the work itself, not from the supervisor (except in the case of new hires). The motivator factor "responsibility" translates into a number of ingredients: self-scheduling, authority to communicate, control of resources, and accountability. Finally, the motivator factors "advancement" and "growth" translate into the central dynamic of new learning leading to unique expertise. The feeling of satisfaction is also indicated as a dynamic of learning from clients and products.

The key to job enrichment is nurture of a client relationship rather than a functional or hierarchical relationship. Let me illustrate with a diagram of relationships in an airplane overhaul project carried out for the U.S. Air Force (Figure C). The avionics mechanic's external client is the test pilot, and although he reports to his supervisor, his super-visor serves him. The sheet metal mechanic and the line mechanic serve the avionics mechanic. And so on back into the system.

By backing into the system, you can identify who serves whom—not who reports to whom—which is critical in trying to enrich jobs. You identify the external client, then the core jobs, or internal client jobs, serving that client. You first enrich the core jobs with the ingredients shown in Figure B and then enrich the jobs that serve these internal clients.

During the 1970s, critics predicted that job enrichment would reduce the number of employees. Ironically, the restructuring and downsizing of U.S. companies during the 1980s have often serendipitously pro-duced job enrichment. With fewer employees performing the same tasks, some job enrichment was inevitable. But the greater efficiency of enriched jobs ultimately leads to a competitive edge and more jobs.

Today, we seem to be losing ground to KITA. It's all the bottom line, as the expression goes. The work ethic and the quality of worklife movement have succumbed to the pragmatics of worldwide competition and the escalation of management direction by the abstract fields of finance and marketing—as opposed to production and sales, where palpable knowledge of clients and products resides. These abstract fields are more conducive to movement than to motivation. I find the new entrants in the world of work on the whole a passionless lot intent on serving financial indexes rather than clients and products. Motivation encompasses passion; movement is sterile.

To return to "One More Time": I don't think I would write it much differently today, though I would include the knowledge gained from recent job enrichment experiments. The distinction between movement and motivation is still true, and motivation-hygiene theory is still a framework with which to evaluate actions. Job enrichment remains the key to designing work that motivates employees.

5
Asinine Attitudes toward Motivation

Harry Levinson

In spite of the corporate efforts to promote smooth management-employee relations, events like these continue to happen:

> The top management of a large manufacturing company discovers that some of its line employees have embezzled a five-figure sum while their supervisors stood by unperturbed. The executives are dumbfounded. They had thought that the supervisors were loyal, and that they themselves were thoughtful and kindly.

> An airline purchases a fleet of hydraulic lift trucks for placing food aboard aircraft at a large New York terminal. Although these trucks cost hundreds of thousands of dollars, they sit disabled on the airport apron. Maintenance employees and technicians occasionally glance at them contemptuously as they go about their work in sullen anger. Management is dismayed that these employees seem unresponsive to its cost-reduction efforts.

> Large companies, seeking new products, acquire smaller companies. Almost invariably, the successful managements of the acquired companies are soon gone and no new products are forthcoming. The larger organizations only increase their size and managerial burdens, and the hoped-for advantages evaporate. While this happens repeatedly, executives do not seem to learn from such failures.

When these events are looked at psychologically, their underlying causes become evident.

In the *first case,* the manufacturer renegotiated its labor contract every two years. Obviously, the appropriate person to do so was the vice president in charge of labor relations. But the people who carried out the contract and knew the employees best were the first-level supervisors; no one asked them what should be in the contract and what problems they had in implementing it. By its actions, management communicated to the supervisors that they did not matter much.

Furthermore, the union let grievances pile up just before the contract came up for renewal every two years, knowing full well that, to get a contract, management would settle the grievances in the union's favor. But the supervisors were the ones who bore the brunt of the grievances, since they carried out the terms of the contract. When management gave in, the supervisors felt that they had been undercut. In effect, these people were being told that they were stupid, that they had nothing useful to contribute to policy making, and that their job was to do as they were told. So they stood by during the stealing—if management did not care about them, why should they care about management?

In the *second case,* the issue for the airlines was much the same. A purchasing officer had bought the trucks, complete with sophisticated electronic controls. What was more natural than the purchasing officer doing the buying and getting the best? But he failed to check with the mechanics and technicians who kept the trucks operating. After all, what did they know about buying, and who asks technicians anyway?

Had he asked them, he would have learned that sophisticated electronic controls were fine for Los Angeles and Phoenix, where the weather was dry and mild, but that they failed repeatedly in New York, where the trucks were exposed to variable and sometimes harsh weather. No matter how hard the technicians worked, they could not keep the trucks functioning. Like the supervisors in the previous example, they felt that they were being exploited and contemptuously treated. Ultimately, they gave up trying to keep the trucks going. Seeing how much money the company had wasted on the trucks, they had little incentive to economize in their own small ways.

In the *third case,* what happens most frequently in merger failures is that the parent (note the use of that word) company promises the newly acquired company that there will be no changes. But changes are soon forthcoming, and the first of these is likely to be in the area of accounting control systems. Obviously, controls are necessary, and, just as obviously, many small companies do not have sophisticated controls. But they tend to be flexibly innovative for that specific reason. When controls become the central thrust of management, creative people who need flexibility leave, and the parent company is left with a corporate shell. The communication to the acquired company is that it is stupid and unsophisticated and therefore the parent must control it more rigidly.

Each of the foregoing problems would be dismissed in most organizations simply as a "failure in communications." Many psychologists would advocate dealing with such difficulties by participative management. Yet beneath that glib "explanation," and unresponsive to that ready "remedy," lies a fundamental unconscious management attitude that is responsible for most contemporary management-labor problems and for what is now being called a "crisis in motivation." I call this attitude the great jackass fallacy.

Later in this article, I shall describe the fallacy in detail and offer some suggestions for correcting it. But first let us explore in more depth the motivational crisis that it has precipitated.

Motivational Miasma

The crisis takes many forms, and its effects are easy to spot. Here are just a few examples:

Companies are repeatedly reorganized on the advice of management consultants, but to little avail in the long run.

New managerial devices, such as the four-day workweek and putting hourly people on salary, are loudly touted for their effect on employee motivation and morale, but the old problems soon reappear.

Efforts to enrich jobs by giving employees more responsibility show encouraging results, but these disappear when employees seek to influence company policy and then are turned down by management.

Business and nonprofit organizations alike are burdened by job encumbrances that result from union-management compromises.

Increasing numbers of middle managers, engineers, teachers, and hospital personnel turn toward unionization.

Many people in managerial ranks resign in favor of new jobs that pay less but offer greater individual freedom and initiative.

Most executives with whom I come in contact cannot understand why people do not respond to their efforts to sustain effective organizations, why people seemingly do not want to work, and why people want to leave apparently good organizations. Executives faced with these problems are often confused, angry, and hostile to their own people. The terms of office of chief executives, particularly those in educational and governmental administration, become shorter as the managerial frustrations increase.

The crisis in motivation has long been evident to students of organization, and they have offered problem-plagued executives a wide range of theories to cope with it. Suffice it to say that, by this time, thousands of executives are familiar with these theories. Many have taken part in managerial grid training, group dynamics laboratories, seminars on the psychology of management, and a wide range of other forms of training. Some have run the full gamut of training experiences; others have embraced a variety of panaceas offered by quacks.

DISAPPOINTING REMEDIES

The results of the aforementioned theories have not been impressive. While some companies have put them into practice with a degree of success, most have either given up their efforts as too simplistic for the complexity of organizational phenomena or have simply failed in their attempts.

There are, of course, many reasons why the remedies have failed. For one thing, executives often feel unqualified to apply the concepts. And in that feeling they are frequently right. Managers who have had little or no previous exposure to the behavioral sciences, let alone any formal training in this area, can get only the barest introductory knowledge in a brief training program. An executive would not expect a person to be able to design a complex building after a week-long training program in architecture; yet both the executive and the people who train him often expect that he will be a different person after he attends a one-week sensitivity-training laboratory.

Furthermore, it is one thing to learn to become more aware of one's own feelings; it is quite another to do something different about managing them, let alone about managing those forces that affect the feelings of other people. If everyone who had experienced psychotherapy were by that fact an expert therapist, there would be no shortage of such healers. Experience is not enough; training in a conceptual framework and supervised skill practice is also required. Many executives who have expected more of themselves and of such training have therefore been disillusioned, despite the benefits that have often resulted from even such brief experiences.

Would longer training help? Not much. Unlike marketing executives who implement marketing programs, and experts who install financial control systems, behavioral scientists (with the exception of certain kinds of psychotherapists) are not themselves expert in *doing*. While many know about the theories, and some of them practice what is called organizational development, they do not themselves change organizations. Instead they usually help people to think through alternative action possibilities and overcome communications blocks to working out their own solutions. Since most behavioral scientists are not skilled in changing organizations, then, they are not in a position to teach executives how to change them.

POWER AND FEAR. Another reason why solutions to motivation problems do not work is that many executives are fearful of losing control of their organizations. The new theories have confronted executives with the need to distribute power in their organizations, which in turn raises questions about their authority and right to manage.

A recent study of 400 top executives in Europe indicates that they feel menaced by these new theories.[1] Most see themselves in the middle of an unsettling transition in management styles. They report that they can no longer use the authority of position; instead, they must gain their position by competition with subordinates and defend that position each step of the way. Of those interviewed, 61% spontaneously indicated that their primary problem is personnel management. Almost all of these executives have leadership problems.

Many businessmen are threatened when they must stimulate people to participate in making organizational decisions and invite people to express themselves more freely. When an executive's whole life thrust has been to obtain a position of power and control, he finds it particularly threatening to witness his power eroding as older methods of control and motivation become less effective.

Coupled with the fear of losing control is the fact that a disproportionate number of executives are characteristically insensitive to feelings. Some people, for example, pursue executive careers to obtain power over others as a way of compensating for real or fancied personal inadequacies, or as a reaction to an unconscious sense of helplessness. They are neurotically driven, and their single-minded, perpetual pursuit of control blinds them to their own subtle feelings and those of others.

Furthermore, many executives have engineering, scientific, legal, or financial backgrounds. Each of these fields places a heavy emphasis on cognitive rationality and measurable or verifiable facts. People who enter them usually are trained from childhood to suppress their feelings, to maintain a competitive, aggressive, non-emotional front. They are taught to be highly logical, and they seek to impose that kind of rationality on organizations.

As a result, they simply do not understand the power of people's feelings, and all too often they are incapable of sensing such feelings in everyday practice without considerable help. They are like tone-deaf people who, attending an opera, can understand the lyrics but cannot hear the music. Such executives are typified by a company president who was a participant in a seminar on psychological aspects of management. Halfway through the first lecture, he broke in to say, "You have already told me more about this subject than I want to know." Although he stayed to the end of the program, he simply could not grasp what was being taught.

All of these reasons, coupled with the inadequacies of contemporary motivational theory itself, explain much of the gap between theory and practice. In time, with new knowledge and better training experiences, most of the gap may be overcome. But the fact remains that much more effort could be applied now. This brings us to that unconscious assumption about motivation to which I referred earlier, one held particularly by executives in all types of organizations and reinforced by organizational theories and structures.

Fact and Fallacy

Frequently, I have asked executives this question: What is the dominant philosophy of motivation in American management? Almost invariably, they quickly agree that it is the carrot-and-stick philosophy, reward and punishment. Then I ask them to close their eyes for a moment, and to form a picture in their mind's eye with a carrot at one end and a stick at the other. When they have done so, I then ask them to describe the central image in that picture. Most frequently they respond that the central figure is a jackass.

If the first image that comes to mind when one thinks "carrot-and-stick" is a jackass, then obviously the unconscious assumption behind the reward-punishment model is that one is dealing with jackasses who must be manipulated and controlled. Thus, unconsciously, the boss is the manipulator and controller, and the subordinate is the jackass.

The characteristics of a jackass are stubbornness, stupidity, willfulness, and unwillingness to go where someone is driving him. These, by interesting coincidence, are also the characteristics of the unmotivated employee. Thus it becomes vividly clear that the underlying assumption that managers make about motivation leads to a self-fulfilling prophecy. People inevitably respond to the carrot-and-stick by trying to get more of the carrot while protecting themselves against the stick. This predictable phenomenon has led to the formation of unions, the frequent sabotage of management's motivation efforts, and the characteristic employee suspicion of management's motivational (manipulative) techniques.

Employees obviously sense the carrot-and-stick conception behind management's attitudes and just as obviously respond with appropriate self-defending measures to the communications built around those attitudes. Of course, there is much talk about the need to improve communication in organizations. All too often, however, the problem is not that communication is inadequate but, rather, that it is already too explicit in the wrong way. When employees sense that they are being viewed as jackasses, they will automatically see management's messages as manipulative, and they will resist them, no matter how clear the type or how pretty the pictures.

PERPETUAL POWER GAP

Since the turn of the century, numerous different philosophies of management have appeared, each emphasizing a different dimension of the management task and each advocating a new set of techniques. Although these philosophies differ from each other in many respects, all are based on reward-punishment psychology.

For example, most of the contemporary psychological conceptions of motivation take a reward-punishment psychology for granted; they advocate trust and openness among employees and managers, but at the same time they acknowledge that the more powerful have a natural right to manipulate the less powerful.

As long as anyone in a leadership role operates with such a reward-punishment attitude toward motivation, he is implicitly assuming that he has (or should have) control over others and that they are in a jackass position with respect to him. This attitude is inevitably one of condescending contempt whose most blatant mask is paternalism. The result is a continuing battle between those who seek to wield power and those who are subject to it. The consequences of this battle are increased inefficiency, lowered productivity, heightened absenteeism, theft, and sometimes outright sabotage.

BUREAUCRATIC BADLANDS

The problems resulting from the jackass fallacy are compounded further by bureaucratic organizational structures. Such structures are based on a military model that assumes complete control of the organization by those at the top. In pure form, it is a rigid hierarchy, complete with detailed job descriptions and fixed, measurable objectives.

The bureaucratic structure requires everyone at every level to be dependent on those at higher levels. Hiring, firing, promotion, demotion, reassignment, and similar actions are the prerogatives of superiors who can make decisions unilaterally. In short, one's fate is decided by a distant "they" who are beyond one's influence and control.

Under such circumstances, the subordinate person becomes increasingly defensive. He must protect himself against being manipulated and against the feeling of helplessness that inevitably accompanies dependency. Rank-and-file employees have long done so by unionization; managerial and professional employees are beginning to follow suit, and this trend will continue to grow.

While the bureaucratic structure, with its heavy emphasis on internal competition for power and position, is often touted as a device for achievement, it is actually a system for defeat. Fewer people move up the pyramidal hierarchy at each step. This leaves a residual group of failures, often euphemistically called "career people," who thereafter are passed over for future promotions because they have not succeeded in the competition for managerial positions.

Most of these people feel resentful and defeated. Often they have been manipulated or judged arbitrarily. They are no longer motivated by competitive spirit, because the carrots and the sticks mean less. There is little need, in their eyes, to learn more; they simply do as they are told. They usually stay until retirement unless they are among the "deadwood" that is cleaned out when a new management takes over.

Executives new to a company or a higher-level job like to think of themselves as being effective in cleaning out such deadwood or trimming the excess managerial fat. Some take to that task with great vigor. Unfortunately, the consequences are more negative than enthusiastic executives like to recognize. In one large company, for example, management hoped that the forty-year-olds would respond with unbridled enthusiasm when the fifty-year-olds were cleaned out. But the younger men failed to respond, because they saw that what was happening to the older men would be their likely fate ten years hence.

Bureaucratic structure, with its implicit power-struggle orientation, increases infighting, empire building, rivalry, and a sense of futility. It tends to magnify latent feelings that the organization is a hostile environment that people can do little to change, and it bolsters the jackass fallacy. Little wonder that many young people do not want to get caught up in such situations! Since 90% of those who work do so in organizations, most young people, too, must do so. But they would rather be in organizations that provide them an opportunity to demonstrate their competence and proficiency than in organizations that test their ability to run a managerial maze successfully.

A FORMIDABLE CHALLENGE

The great jackass fallacy and the bureaucratic organization structure present major obstacles to organizational survival. They are essentially self-defeating if what an executive wants from employees is spontaneity, dedication, commitment, affiliation, and adaptive innovation.

As I have already indicated, many executives try to cope with the pathology of the system by introducing such new techniques as group dynamics and job enrichment. These are simply patches on the body politic of an organization. There is no way to integrate them effectively. When people are asked to express their feelings more freely and to take on greater responsibility, they soon come into conflict with power centers and power figures in a system geared to the acquisition of power. The latter soon cry, "Business is not a democracy," and disillusionment sets in once again, both on the part of managers who tried the new techniques and on the part of subordinates who were subjected to them.

Unless the fundamental assumptions of management (and behavioral scientists) about motivation are changed, and unless the organizational structure is altered to match these changed assumptions, the underlying jackass fallacy will remain visible to those who are subjected to it. Despite whatever practices the organization implements, people will avoid, evade, escape, deny, and reject both the jackass fallacy and the military-style hierarchy.

If the executive grasps the import of what I am saying, shudders uncomfortably, and wants to do something about the problem, what are his alternatives? Is he forever doomed to play with psychological gimmicks? Is he himself so much a victim of his assumptions that he cannot change them? I do not think that he necessarily is. There are constructive actions that he can take.

The First Steps

Anyone who supervises someone else should look carefully at the assumptions he is making about motivation. He must assess the degree to which carrot-and-stick assumptions influence his own attitudes. For example, an executive might argue that if he tried to be nice to people, the stick would be softened. But even then he would merely be exhibiting paternalistic kindness. As long as his assumptions about people remain unchanged, his "being nice" is only a disguised form of carrot-and-stick that seeks to increase loyalty by creating guilt in those who are the recipients of his managerial largesse. His first priority should be to change his way of thinking about people.

After honestly and frankly facing up to one's own assumptions about what makes people tick, the next step is to look at one's organizational structure. Most organizations are constructed to fit a hierarchical model. People assume that the hierarchical organizational structure is to organizations as the spine is to human beings, that it is both a necessity and a given. As a matter of fact, it is neither a necessity nor a given.

I am arguing not against the distribution of power and control, but, rather, that this distribution need not take one particular form. Every executive should ask himself: "Is my operation organized to achieve a hierarchical structure or is it structured to accomplish the task it must do?" If it is organized more to fit the model than to fit the task, he should begin exploring more appropriate organization models.[2] To do otherwise is to invite trouble—if it has not already started.

Conclusion

It is time for business leaders to enter a phase of more serious thinking about leadership and organizational concepts. They must do so on behalf of their own organizations as well as on behalf of society. The issue I have been discussing is critically important for society as a whole, because society increasingly is made up of organizations. The less effectively organizations carry out the work of society, the greater the cost in money and in social paralysis. The latter leads to the kind of demoralization already evident in organizations as well as in problems of transportation, health care delivery, education, and welfare.

Furthermore, we are in the midst of a worldwide social revolution, the central thrust of which is the demand of all people to have a voice in their own fate. Business leaders, many of whom have international interests and see the multiple facets of this thrust in a wide range of countries, should be in the forefront of understanding and guiding these social changes into productive channels. By applying new principles of motivation to their own organizations, they are in a position not only to sustain the vitality of those organizations but, more important, to keep them adaptive to changing circumstances.

In addition, the progressive changes that executives institute in their own organizations can then become the models for other institutional forms in a given culture. Not the least of the advantages of being on the frontier is that executives and corporations avoid the onus of being continuously compelled by angry or apathetic employees to change in ways which may be destructive to both the business and the people involved.

But leading is more than a matter of pronouncing clichés. Leading involves an understanding of motivation. It is to this understanding that business leaders must now dedicate themselves. And the way to start is by countering the great jackass fallacy in their own organizations.

Notes

1. Frederick Harmon, "European Top Managers Struggle for Survival," *European Business* (Winter 1971), p. 14.
2. Paul R. Lawrence and Jay W. Lorsch, *Organization and Environment: Managing Differentiation and Integration* (Boston: Division of Research, Harvard Business School, 1967).

6
From Control to Commitment in the Workplace

Richard E. Walton

The larger shape of institutional change is always difficult to recognize when one stands right in the middle of it. Today, throughout American industry, a significant change is under way in long-established approaches to the organization and management of work. Although this shift in attitude and practice takes a wide variety of company-specific forms, its larger shape—its overall pattern—is already visible if one knows where and how to look.

Consider, for example, the marked differences between two plants in the chemical products division of a major U.S. corporation. They make similar products and employ similar technologies, but that is virtually all they have in common.

The first, organized by businesses with an identifiable product or product line, divides its employees into self-supervising 10- to 15-person work teams that are collectively responsible for a set of related tasks. Each team member has the training to perform many or all of the tasks for which the team is accountable, and pay reflects the level of mastery of required skills. These teams have received assurances that management will go to extra lengths to provide continued employment in any economic downturn. The teams have also been thoroughly briefed on such issues as market share, product costs, and their implications for the business.

Not surprisingly, this plant is a top performer economically and rates well on all measures of employee satisfaction, absenteeism, turnover, and safety. With its employees actively engaged in identifying and solving problems, it operates with fewer levels of management and fewer specialized departments than do its sister plants. It is also one of the principal suppliers of management talent for these other plants and for the division manufacturing staff.

In the second plant, each employee is responsible for a fixed job and is required to perform up to the minimum standard defined for that job. Peer pressure keeps new employees from exceeding the minimum standards and from taking other initiatives that go beyond basic job requirements. Supervisors, who manage daily assignments and monitor performance, have long since given up hope for anything more than compliance with standards, finding sufficient difficulty in getting their people to perform adequately most of the time. In fact, they and their workers try to prevent the industrial engineering department, which is under pressure from top plant management to improve operations, from using changes in methods to "jack up" standards.

A recent management campaign to document an "airtight case" against employees who have excessive absenteeism or sub-par performance mirrors employees' low morale and high distrust of management. A constant stream of formal grievances, violations of plant rules, harassment of supervisors, wildcat walkouts, and even sabotage has prevented the plant from reaching its productivity and quality goals and has absorbed a disproportionate amount of division staff time. Dealings with the union are characterized by contract negotiations on economic matters and skirmishes over issues of management control.

No responsible manager, of course, would ever wish to encourage the kind of situation at this second plant, yet the determination to understand its deeper causes and to attack them at their root does not come easily. Established modes of doing things have an inertia all their own. Such an effort is, however, in process all across the industrial landscape. And with that effort comes the possibility of a revolution in industrial relations every bit as great as that occasioned by the rise of mass production the better part of a century ago. The challenge is clear to those managers willing to see it—and the potential benefits, enormous.

Approaches to Work-force Management

What explains the extraordinary differences between the plants just described? Is it that the first is new (built in 1976) and the other old? Yes and no. Not all new plants enjoy so fruitful an approach to work organization; not all older plants have such intractable problems. Is it that one plant is unionized and the other not? Again, yes and no. The presence of a union may institutionalize conflict and lackluster performance, but it seldom causes them.

At issue here is not so much age or unionization but two radically different strategies for managing a company's or a factory's work force, two incompatible views of what managers can reasonably expect of workers and of the kind of partnership they can share with them. For simplicity, I will speak of these profound differences as reflecting the choice between a strategy based on imposing *control* and a strategy based on eliciting *commitment*.

THE "CONTROL" STRATEGY

The traditional—or control-oriented—approach to work-force management took shape during the early part of this century in response to the division of work into small, fixed jobs for which individuals could be held accountable. The actual definition of jobs, as of acceptable standards of performance, rested on "lowest common denominator" assumptions about workers' skill and motivation. To monitor and control effort of this assumed caliber, management organized its own responsibilities into a hierarchy of specialized roles buttressed by a top-down allocation of authority and by status symbols attached to positions in the hierarchy.

For workers, compensation followed the rubric of "a fair day's pay for a fair day's work" because precise evaluations were possible when individual job requirements were so carefully prescribed. Most managers had little doubt that labor was best thought of as a variable cost, although some exceptional companies guaranteed job security to head off unionization attempts.

In the traditional approach, there was generally little policy definition with regard to employee voice unless the work force was unionized, in which case damage control strategies predominated. With no union, management relied on an open-door policy, attitude surveys, and similar devices to learn about employees' concerns. If the work force was unionized, then management bargained terms of employment and established an appeal mechanism. These activities fell to labor relations specialists, who operated independently from line management and whose very existence assumed the inevitability and even the appropriateness of an adversarial relationship between workers and managers. Indeed, to those who saw management's exclusive obligation to be to a company's shareowners and the ownership of property to be the ultimate source of both obligation and prerogative, the claims of employees were constraints, nothing more.

At the heart of this traditional model is the wish to establish order, exercise control, and achieve efficiency in the application of the work force. Although it has distant antecedents in the bureaucracies of both church and military, the model's real father is Frederick W. Taylor, the turn-of-the-century "father of scientific management," whose views about the proper organization of work have long influenced management practice as well as the reactive policies of the U.S. labor movement.

Recently, however, changing expectations among workers have prompted a growing disillusionment with the apparatus of control. At the same time, of course, an intensified challenge from abroad has made the competitive obsolescence of this strategy clear. A model that assumes low employee commitment and that is designed to produce reliable if not outstanding performance simply cannot match the standards of excellence set by world-class competitors. Especially in a high-wage country like the United States, market success depends on a superior level of performance, a level that, in turn, requires the deep commitment, not merely the obedience— if you could obtain it—of workers. And as painful experience shows, this commitment cannot flourish in a workplace dominated by the familiar model of control.

THE "COMMITMENT" STRATEGY

Since the early 1970s, companies have experimented at the plant level with a radically different work-force strategy. The more visible pioneers—among them, General Foods at Topeka, Kansas; General Motors at Brookhaven, Mississippi; Cummins Engine at Jamestown, New York; and Procter & Gamble at Lima, Ohio—have begun to show how great and productive the contribution of a truly committed work force can be. For a time, all new plants of this sort were nonunion, but by 1980 the success of efforts undertaken jointly with unions—GM's cooperation with the UAW at the Cadillac plant in Livonia, Michigan, for example—was impressive enough to encourage managers of both new and existing facilities to rethink their approach to the work force.

Stimulated in part by the dramatic turnaround at GM's Tarrytown assembly plant in the mid-1970s, local managers and union officials are increasingly talking about common interests, working to develop mutual trust, and agreeing to sponsor quality-of-work-life (QWL) or employee involvement (EI) activities. Although most of these ventures have been initiated at the local level, major exceptions include the joint effort between the Communication Workers of America and AT&T to promote QWL throughout the Bell System and the UAW-Ford EI program centrally directed by Donald Ephlin of the UAW and Peter Pestillo of Ford. In the nonunion sphere, the spirit of these new initiatives is evident in the decision by workers of Delta Airlines to show their commitment to the company by collecting money to buy a new plane.

More recently, a growing number of manufacturing companies has begun to remove levels of plant hierarchy, increase managers' spans of control, integrate quality and production activities at lower organizational levels, combine production and maintenance operations, and open up new career possibilities for workers. Some corporations have even begun to chart organizational renewal for the entire company. Cummins Engine, for example, has ambitiously committed itself to inform employees about the business, to encourage participation by everyone, and to create jobs that involve greater responsibility and more flexibility.

In this new commitment-based approach to the work force, jobs are designed to be broader than before, to combine planning and implementation, and to include efforts to upgrade operations, not just maintain them. Individual responsibilities are expected to change as conditions change, and teams, not individuals, often are the organizational units accountable for performance. With management hierarchies relatively flat and differences in status minimized, control and lateral coordination depend on shared goals, and expertise rather than formal position determines influence.

People Express, to cite one example, started up with its management hierarchy limited to three levels, organized its work force into three- or four-person groups, and created positions with exceptionally broad scope. Every full-time employee is a "manager": flight managers are pilots who also perform dispatching and safety checks; maintenance managers are technicians with other staff responsibilities; customer service managers take care of ticketing, security clearance, passenger boarding, and in-flight service. Everyone, including the officers, is expected to rotate among functions to boost all workers' understanding of the business and to promote personal development.

Under the commitment strategy, performance expectations are high and serve not to define minimum standards but to provide "stretch objectives," emphasize continuous improvement, and reflect the requirements of the marketplace. Accordingly, compensation policies reflect less the old formulas of job evaluation than the heightened importance of group achievement, the expanded scope of individual contribution, and the growing concern for such questions of "equity" as gain sharing, stock ownership, and profit sharing. This principle of economic sharing is not new. It has long played a role in Dana Corporation, which has many unionized plants, and is a fundamental part of the strategy of People Express, which has no union. Today, Ford sees it as an important part of the company's transition to a commitment strategy.

Equally important to the commitment strategy is the challenge of giving employees some assurance of security, perhaps by offering them priority in training and retraining as old jobs are eliminated and new ones created. Guaranteeing employees access to due process and providing them the means to be heard on such issues as production methods, problem solving, and human resource policies and practices is also a challenge. In unionized settings, the additional tasks include making relations less adversarial, broadening the agenda for joint problem solving and planning, and facilitating employee consultation.

Underlying all these policies is a management philosophy, often embodied in a published statement, that acknowledges the legitimate claims of a company's multiple stakeholders—owners, employees, customers, and the public. At the center of this philosophy is a belief that eliciting employee commitment will lead to enhanced performance. The evidence shows this belief to be well grounded. In the absence of genuine commitment, however, new management policies designed for a committed work force may well leave a company distinctly more vulnerable than would older policies based on the control approach. The advantages—and risks—are considerable.

The Costs of Commitment

Because the potential leverage of a commitment-oriented strategy on performance is so great, the natural temptation is to assume the universal applicability of that strategy. Some environments, however, especially those requiring intricate teamwork, problem solving, organizational learning, and self-monitoring, are better suited than others to the commitment model. Indeed, the pioneers of the deep commitment strategy—a fertilizer plant in Norway, a refinery in the United Kingdom, a paper mill in Pennsylvania, a pet-food processing plant in Kansas—were all based on continuous process technologies and were all capital- and raw-material-intensive. All provided high economic leverage to improvements in workers' skills and attitudes, and all could offer considerable job challenge.

Is the converse true? Is the control strategy appropriate whenever—as with convicts breaking rocks with sledgehammers in a prison yard—work can be completely prescribed, remains static, and calls for individual, not group, effort? In practice, managers have long answered yes. Mass production, epitomized by the assembly line, has for years been thought suitable for old-fashioned control.

But not any longer. Many mass producers, not least the automakers, have recently been trying to reconceive the structure of work and to give employees a significant role in solving problems and improving methods. Why? For many reasons, including to boost in-plant quality, lower warranty costs, cut waste, raise machine utilization and total capacity with the same plant and equipment, reduce operating and support personnel, reduce turnover and absenteeism, and speed up implementation of change. In addition, some managers place direct value on the fact that the commitment policies promote the development of human skills and individual self-esteem.

The benefits, economic and human, of worker commitment extend not only to continuous-process industries but to traditional manufacturing industries as well. What, though, are the costs? To achieve these gains, managers have had to invest extra effort, develop new skills and relationships, cope with higher levels of ambiguity and uncertainty, and experience the pain and discomfort associated with changing habits and attitudes. Some of their skills have become obsolete, and some of their careers have been casualties of change. Union officials, too, have had to face the dislocation and discomfort that inevitably follow any upheaval in attitudes and skills. For their part, workers have inherited more responsibility and, along with it, greater uncertainty and a more open-ended possibility of failure.

Part of the difficulty in assessing these costs is the fact that so many of the following problems inherent to the commitment strategy remain to be solved.

EMPLOYMENT ASSURANCES

As managers in heavy industry confront economic realities that make such assurances less feasible and as their counterparts in fiercely competitive high-technology areas are forced to rethink early guarantees of employment security, pointed questions await.

Will managers give lifetime assurances to the few, those who reach, say, 15 years' seniority, or will they adopt a general no-layoff policy? Will they demonstrate by policies and practices that employment security, though by no means absolute, is a higher priority item than it was under the control approach? Will they accept greater responsibility for outplacement?

COMPENSATION

In one sense, the more productive employees under the commitment approach deserve to receive better pay for their better efforts, but how can managers balance this claim on resources with the harsh reality that domestic pay rates have risen to levels that render many of our industries uncompetitive internationally? Already, in such industries as trucking and airlines, new domestic competitors have placed companies that maintain prevailing wage rates at a significant disadvantage. Experience shows, however, that wage freezes and concession bargaining create obstacles to commitment, and new approaches to compensation are difficult to develop at a time when management cannot raise the overall level of pay.

Which approach is really suitable to the commitment model is unclear. Traditional job classifications place limits on the discretion of supervisors and encourage workers' sense of job ownership. Can pay systems based on employees' skill levels, which have long been used in engineering and skilled crafts, prove widely effective? Can these systems make up in greater mastery, positive motivation, and work-force flexibility what they give away in higher average wages?

In capital-intensive businesses, where total payroll accounts for a small percentage of costs, economics favor the move toward pay progression based on deeper and broader mastery. Still, conceptual problems remain with measuring skills, achieving consistency in pay decisions, allocating opportunities for learning new skills, trading off breadth and flexibility against depth, and handling the effects of "topping out" in a system that rewards and encourages personal growth.

There are also practical difficulties. Existing plants cannot, for example, convert to a skill-based structure overnight because of the vested interests of employees in the higher classifications. Similarly, formal profit- or gain-sharing plans like the Scanlon Plan (which shares gains in productivity as measured by improvements in the ratio of payroll to the sales value of production) cannot always operate. At the plant level, formulas that are responsive to what employees can influence, that are not unduly influenced by factors beyond their control, and that are readily understood, are not easy to devise. Small stand-alone businesses with a mature technology and stable markets tend to find the task least troublesome, but they are not the only ones trying to implement the commitment approach.

Yet another problem, very much at issue in the Hyatt-Clark bearing plant, which employees purchased from General Motors in 1981, is the relationship between compensation decisions affecting salaried managers and professionals, on the one hand, and hourly workers, on the other. When they formed the company, workers took a 25% pay cut to make their bearings competitive, but the managers maintained and, in certain instances increased, their own salaries in order to help the company attract and retain critical talent. A manager's ability to elicit and preserve commitment, however, is sensitive to issues of equity, as became evident once again when GM and Ford announced huge executive bonuses in the spring of 1984 while keeping hourly wages capped.

TECHNOLOGY

Computer-based technology can reinforce the control model or facilitate movement to the commitment model. Applications can narrow the scope of jobs or broaden them, emphasize the individual nature of tasks or promote the work of groups, centralize or decentralize the making of decisions, and create performance measures that emphasize learning or hierarchical control.

To date, the effects of this technology on control and commitment have been largely unintentional and unexpected. Even in organizations otherwise pursuing a commitment strategy, managers have rarely appreciated that the side effects of technology are not somehow "given" in the nature of things or that they can be actively managed. In fact, computer-based technology may be the least deterministic, most flexible technology to enter the workplace since the industrial revolution. As it becomes less hardware-dependent and more software-intensive and as the cost of computer power declines, the variety of ways to meet business requirements expands, each with a different set of human implications. Management has yet to identify the potential role of technology policy in the commitment strategy, and it has yet to invent concepts and methods to realize that potential.

SUPERVISORS

The commitment model requires first-line supervisors to facilitate rather than direct the work force, to impart rather than merely practice their technical and administrative expertise, and to help workers develop the ability to manage themselves. In practice, supervisors are to delegate away most of their traditional functions—often without having received adequate training and support for their new team-building tasks or having their own needs for voice, dignity, and fulfillment recognized.

These dilemmas are even visible in the new titles many supervisors carry—"team advisers" or "team consultants," for example—most of which imply that supervisors are not in the chain of command, although they are expected to be directive if necessary and assume functions delegated to the work force if they are not being performed. Part of the confusion here is the failure to distinguish the behavioral style required of supervisors from the basic responsibilities assigned them. Their ideal style may be advisory, but their responsibilities are to achieve certain human and economic outcomes. With experience, however, as first-line managers become more comfortable with the notion of delegating what subordinates are ready and able to perform, the problem will diminish.

Other difficulties are less tractable. The new breed of supervisors must have a level of interpersonal skill and conceptual ability often lacking in the present supervisory work force. Some companies have tried to address this lack by using the position as an entry point to management for college graduates. This approach may succeed where the work force has already acquired the necessary technical expertise, but it blocks a route of advancement for workers and sharpens the dividing line between management and other employees. Moreover, unless the company intends to open up higher level positions for these college-educated supervisors, they may well grow impatient with the shift work of first-line supervision.

Even when new supervisory roles are filled—and filled successfully—from the ranks, dilemmas remain. With teams developed and functions delegated, to what new challenges do they turn to utilize fully their own capabilities? Do those capabilities match the demands of the other managerial work they might take on? If fewer and fewer supervisors are required as their individual span of control extends to a second and a third work team, what promotional opportunities exist for the rest? Where do they go?

UNION-MANAGEMENT RELATIONS

Some companies, as they move from control to commitment, seek to decertify their unions and, at the same time, strengthen their employees' bond to the company. Others—like GM, Ford, Jones & Laughlin, and AT&T—pursue cooperation with their unions, believing that they need their active support. Management's interest in cooperation intensified in the late 1970s, as improved work-force effectiveness could not by itself close the competitive gap in many industries and wage concessions became necessary. Based on their own analysis of competitive conditions, unions sometimes agreed to these concessions but expanded their influence over matters previously subject to management control.

These developments open up new questions. Where companies are trying to preserve the nonunion status of some plants and yet promote collaborative union relations in others, will unions increasingly force the company to choose? After General Motors saw the potential of its joint QWL program with the UAW, it signed a neutrality clause (in 1976) and then an understanding about automatic recognition in new plants (in 1979). If forced to choose, what will

Exhibit. **Work-force Strategies**

	Control	Transitional	Commitment
Job design principles	Individual attention limited to performing individual jobs.	Scope of individual responsibility extended to upgrading system performance, via participative problem-solving groups in QWL, EI, and quality circle programs.	Individual responsibility extended to upgrading system performance.
	Job design deskills and fragments work and separates doing and thinking.	No change in traditional job design or accountability.	Job design enhances content of work, emphasizes whole task, and combines doing and thinking.
	Accountability focused on individual.		Frequent use of teams as basic accountable unit.
	Fixed job definition.		Flexible definition of duties, contingent on changing conditions.

	Control	Transitional	Commitment
Performance expectations	Measured standards define minimum performance. Stability seen as desirable.		Emphasis placed on higher, "stretch objectives," which tend to be dynamic and oriented to the marketplace.
Management organization: structure, systems, and style	Structure tends to be layered, with top-down controls.	No basic changes in approaches to structure, control, or authority.	Flat organization structure with mutual influence systems.
	Coordination and control rely on rules and procedures.		Coordination and control based more on shared goals, values, and traditions.
	More emphasis on prerogatives and positional authority.		Management emphasis on problem solving and relevant information and expertise.
	Status symbols distributed to reinforce hierarchy.	A few visible symbols change.	Minimum status differentials to deemphasize inherent hierarchy.

Exhibit.   *Work-force Strategies* (continued)

Compensation policies	Variable pay where feasible to provide individual incentive.	Typically no basic changes in compensation concepts.		Variable rewards to create equity and to reinforce group achievements: gain sharing, profit sharing.
		Individual pay geared to job evaluation.		Individual pay linked to skills and mastery.
		In downturn, cuts concentrated on hourly payroll.	Equality of sacrifice among employee groups.	Equality of sacrifice.
Employment assurances	Employees regarded as variable costs.	Assurances that participation will not result in loss of job.		Assurances that participation will not result in loss of job.
		Extra effort to avoid layoffs.		High commitment to avoid or assist in reemployment.
				Priority for training and retaining existing work force.

Employee voice policies	Employee input allowed on relatively narrow agenda. Attendant risks emphasized. Methods include open-door policy, attitude surveys, grievance procedures, and collective bargaining in some organizations.	Addition of limited, ad hoc consultation mechanisms. No change in corporate governance.	Employee participation encouraged on wide range of issues. Attendant benefits emphasized. New concepts of corporate governance.
	Business information distributed on strictly defined "need to know" basis.	Additional sharing of information.	Business data shared widely.
Labor-management relations	Adversarial labor relations; emphasis on interest conflict.	Thawing of adversarial attitudes; joint sponsorship of QWL or EI; emphasis on common fate.	Mutuality in labor relations; joint planning and problem solving on expanded agenda.
			Unions, management, and workers redefine their respective roles.

other managements do? Further, where union and management have collaborated in promoting QWL, how can the union prevent management from using the program to appeal directly to the workers about issues, such as wage concessions, that are subject to collective bargaining?

And if, in the spirit of mutuality, both sides agree to expand their joint agenda, what new risks will they face? Do union officials have the expertise to deal effectively with new agenda items like investment, pricing, and technology? To support QWL activities, they already have had to expand their skills and commit substantial resources at a time when shrinking employment has reduced their membership and thus their finances.

The Transitional Stage

Although some organizations have adopted a comprehensive version of the commitment approach, most initially take on a more limited set of changes, which I refer to as a "transitional" stage or approach. The challenge here is to modify expectations, to make credible the leaders' stated intentions for further movement, and to support the initial changes in behavior. These transitional efforts can achieve a temporary equilibrium, provided they are viewed as part of a movement toward a comprehensive commitment strategy.

The cornerstone of the transitional stage is the voluntary participation of employees in problem-solving groups like quality circles. In unionized organizations, union-management dialogue leading to a jointly sponsored program is a condition for this type of employee involvement, which must then be supported by additional training and communication and by a shift in management style. Managers must also seek ways to consult employees about changes that affect them and to assure them that management will make every effort to avoid, defer, or minimize layoffs from higher productivity. When volume-related layoffs or concessions on pay are unavoidable, the principle of "equality of sacrifice" must apply to all employee groups, not just the hourly work force.

As a rule, during the early stages of transformation, few immediate changes can occur in the basic design of jobs, the compensation system, or the management system itself. It is easy, of course, to attempt to change too much too soon. A more common error, especially in established organizations, is to make only "token" changes that never reach a critical mass. All too often managers try a succession of technique-oriented changes one by one: job enrichment, sensitivity training, management by objectives, group brainstorming, quality circles, and so on. Whatever the benefits of these techniques, their value to the organization will rapidly decay if the management philosophy—and practice—does not shift accordingly.

A different type of error—"overreaching"—may occur in newly established organizations based on commitment principles. In one new plant, managers allowed too much peer influence in pay decisions; in another, they underplayed the role of first-line supervisors as a link in the chain of command; in a third, they overemphasized learning of new skills and flexibility at the expense of mastery in critical operations. These design errors by themselves are not fatal, but the organization must be able to make mid-course corrections.

Rate of Transformation

How rapidly is the transformation in work-force strategy, summarized in the Exhibit, occurring? Hard data are difficult to come by, but certain trends are clear. In 1970, only a few plants in the United States were systematically revising their approach to the work force. By 1975, hundreds of plants were involved. Today, I estimate that at least a thousand plants are in the process of making a comprehensive change and that many times that number are somewhere in the transitional stage.

In the early 1970s, plant managers tended to sponsor what efforts there were. Today, company presidents are formulating the plans. Not long ago, the initiatives were experimental; now they are policy. Early change focused on the blue-collar work force and on those clerical operations that most closely resemble the factory. Although clerical change has lagged somewhat—because the control model has not produced such overt employee disaffection, and because management has been slow to recognize the importance of quality and productivity improvement—there are signs of a quickened pace of change in clerical operations.

Only a small fraction of U.S. workplaces today can boast of a comprehensive commitment strategy, but the rate of transformation continues to accelerate, and the move toward commitment via some explicit transitional stage extends to a still larger number of plants and offices. This transformation may be fueled by economic necessity, but other factors are shaping and pacing it—individual leadership in management and labor, philosophical choices, organizational competence in managing change, and cumulative learning from change itself.

7
Keeping Managers off the Shelf

Jay W. Lorsch and Haruo Takagi

We may not call it lifetime employment, but still the vast majority of managers in large U.S. companies stay with one employer throughout their careers, and most of them spend the last 10 to 20 years plateaued. The hard truth is that while many managers at a plateau are still productive, many are not. Consider the following contrasting cases.

At 53, Ralph Franklin finds coming to work a drag. The best part of the week is the Friday lunch with his underwriting buddies from other departments. He's worried, though, about the extent to which the lunches have become boozy occasions. He knows they aren't good for either his health or his reputation in the insurance company, where he is a vice president.

But why care about the company anymore? While he's just gotten his 25-year pin and carries the lofty title of regional underwriting vice president, nobody who matters wants his opinions or ideas—despite the underwriting problems galore that he could solve. As long as he gets his job done to minimal standards, no one asks for his advice.

Harold Wyman is a vice president and regional sales manager for an investment firm, a position he's held for the past 11 years. At 51, he is involved in the day-to-day direction of 15 salespeople. In addition, he sees himself as an important member of the regional office's management team. He talks frequently with the partner in charge of tactics and strategy. Along with other sales managers, he also recruits, selects, and trains new sales personnel. Harold particularly enjoys the contact with these bright young people and their contagious enthusiasm. He smiles when remembering a conversation he overheard between two trainees who said that Harold's excitement and commitment inspired them.

Obviously, most top executives want managers like Harold who are committed and very motivated, but instead they see many who feel the frustrations and bitterness that Ralph expresses. Just how many potential Ralphs are there? A large number. At IBM, for instance, 80% to 90% of the managers are long-term employees. At General Electric, the problem's dimensions are huge. Of 83,000 GE managers and professionals, more than 11,000 have been with the company more than 30 years, almost 26,000 have been there more than 20 years, and more than 48,000, 10-plus. Thus about a third of these employees are in the second halves of their careers. Also, as the baby boomers age, more and more managers will reach the point of no progress.

After a brief flirtation, perhaps, with another career or employer, most people who become managers enter a company in their twenties and stay until they retire. Even in a company like Bethlehem Steel, which has experienced a big restructuring in recent years, the proportion of "lifetime" managerial employees is still high—about 80%.

Of course, especially in the United States, some managers and professionals leave voluntarily for greener pastures, but they are a small minority. Others—also a small number—are asked to leave because of poor performance. Regardless, the general broad adherence to long-term employment leads inevitably to many executives reaching a plateau. As employees progress up the organization, the structure narrows, limiting opportunities for advancement.

It is not exaggerating, therefore, to say that at some point in the latter halves of their careers most managers, like those at GE, will be plateaued; they will not be promoted again. This happens to both the Harolds and the Ralphs. But reaching a plateau doesn't have to mean retiring on the job.

Too often plateaued managers who have quit emotionally are regarded by senior executives as pariahs who need to be eliminated. What these administrators forget is that these long-service employees may form the cores of their organizations that produce the day-to-day results. Instead of considering how to eliminate such people, top executives must address different questions. How can they keep them turned on, excited, and motivated in the second halves of their careers? Can anything be done earlier to avoid their getting turned off?

The issues we cover here are first, what causes a career to derail, and second, what can top management do to ensure that it develops more Harolds than Ralphs?

First, let's look at a study of a Japanese company that helps us see why some plateaued managers stay committed while others merely go through the motions.[1]

Committed or Turned Off

The Tokyo-based manufacturing company hired its future managerial employees directly out of universities with the understanding that they would stay with the company until retirement. The 30 engineering managers who were the focus of the study entered the company in "annual classes" between 1957 and 1966. They were selected for study both because they were typical of the company's managers and because by 1982, the date of the research, they had moved through three career stages: early (21 to 30 years old), middle (31 to 40 years old), and plateaued (41 years old and up).

By 1982, these managers had from 16 to 25 years of service and had evolved into two distinct groups with very different attitudes toward their jobs and the company. Some managers were exceptionally committed to their work and the company's future. They were actively involved in and enthusiastic about the organization. A department manager's comment is typical:

"I have developed my career with this company through performing mostly tasks that contribute to the company. I have always been aware of the significance my performance had on the corporate results, and my efforts have led to successful product lines in this division. My way of thinking and my actions coincide exactly with the values of the company."

In contrast, the second group of managers was passive. Although not extremely dissatisfied with their lot, they expressed no particular interest or enthusiasm for either their work or the company. Here is a typical comment:

"When I look back over what I have been doing in the laboratory, I don't find I have any technological specialty that has given me self-confidence and career identity. I have conducted many technolog-ically different research and development projects, and all of them have been undemonstratable and minor. I am satisfied with my current status and salary level, and there is no new job I want to do."

What causes these differences in attitude? Since the chances of further advancement for managers in both groups was practically nil, an important part of the answer must lie in the things they had experienced during the early and middle stages of their careers.

BEING IN THE MAINSTREAM

The most important difference between the committed and pas-sive managers was whether their early job assignments were con-nected to the mainstream of the company's activities. A committed manager recalls his beginning experiences as an engineer:

"I was first placed in a product division. A year later, I was transferred to the laboratory in order to join an important new product development project, in which I took charge of the devel-opment of an electric component. I had created its basic idea when I was in the division.

"I reported my progress directly to the top manager of the lab-oratory any time I felt necessary. I reported to the division general manager every week; I have to consider costs, investments, and so on in addition to technologies. I was developing an important com-ponent that would create profit for the company."

A turned-off manager describes his earliest experience this way:

"The product improvement I was working on was minor to the division, and I worried that I would not make a visible contribution. I envied my friends who joined the company at the same time as I did and whose jobs were the development of the main products of the division."

As they progressed from being engineers to section managers, the employees found that working on mainstream activities became even more essential to feeling committed. A department manager remembers his experience:

"The laboratory's top manager assigned me to a joint project with several product divisions to develop a new electrical device. At that time, the company was implementing a strategy to compete with the major leaders in the market. The new device was expected to be a key competitive product.

"At last, we developed the new device. Customers really appreciated the product. It turned the expected profit contribution figure I forecast at the beginning of the project into a reality. I felt that I was creating the future of the company."

Contrast this with the experience one of the unmotivated managers reports:

"My task as a laboratory section manager was leading projects that measured electrical characteristics of materials and products that were developed in other parts of the laboratory. The purpose of these projects was simply to filter out materials and products with imperfections but not to improve them. In essence, I was cleaning up technological troubles made by other people.

"My interest in these projects quickly decreased. In fact, the technological problems I dealt with were often very difficult, and the original engineers could not have handled them.

"I continued the job simply because that was my assignment, but I was using only physical energy to do it."

A significant determinant of the enthusiastic managers' commitment to the company in the later stage of their careers is their early job experiences. In a Japanese company where financial rewards are entirely based on seniority, and career advancement largely so, it is not surprising that the most salient feature for these managers was their job assignments.

But there is more to it: these assignments also answered their needs at each career stage. When they joined the company, all the recruits were well trained technically, and like young people everywhere, they were anxious to use and develop their abilities. Those who had the chance to do so early on felt important to the organization and, consequently, felt good about both themselves and the company.

Most significant, as they entered the middle stages of their careers, as section managers in their thirties, if they had held challenging positions earlier, they were confident of their technical abilities and were ready for new hurdles. For those who wound up committed, what they called "mainstream assignments" provided the challenges. As the term *mainstream* suggests, both in terms of their work and their relationships, they were at the heart of the organization.

Their passive colleagues had had different experiences. During the early stages of their careers, they had not had such satisfying assignments. They had not been evaluated as less competent than their peers, but chance matchings of people to available assignments had not gone in their favor. They felt left out—on the periphery of things. They responded by coming to work and doing what was expected, but they lacked enthusiasm and commitment. That they were not more openly critical of their lot and of the company is probably a reflection of the Japanese culture; employees are expected to be loyal to and not complain about their employers.

Importance of Being Candid

What do the Japanese managers' experiences tell us about Harold and Ralph? One must, of course, first recognize important differences between Japanese and U.S. human resource practices. In most U.S. companies, salary increases and promotions are ostensibly related to performance, whereas in Japan, as we've seen, they aren't. Also, U.S. managerial and professional employees, unlike those in Japan, are supposed to receive annual performance reviews. At first glance, such differences might seem to diminish the important roles that job assignment and the accompanying sense of worth played at the Japanese company. But closer examination indicates that the key to turning on U.S. managers is the same: give them a mainstream role. We want to return to Ralph and Harold's contrasting experiences to illustrate the point.

Ralph's history in the insurance company provides insight into how his unhappy feelings developed. At age 27, having been to college and served in the army, he joined the company. By age 34, he had moved up the ranks of underwriters to become a branch underwriting manager. And there he stayed for ten years. After five years in the branch, he had asked several senior officers about his chances of becoming a branch manager. Like his own branch manager in performance review sessions, however, they were evasive. Nobody said he wasn't going to get the job, but no one offered much encouragement. Finally, when he was 44, Ralph became a regional underwriting manager; a few years later he was given the added title of vice president. All the way along he had been given regular salary increases.

Unfortunately for both Ralph and the company, the regional underwriting vice president position was out of the mainstream. Nobody planned it that way. Senior management had expected that Ralph and several others with similar experiences could play a central role in setting national underwriting policy and developing younger professionals. But as the market developed and the company's organization evolved, it turned out that the main action was in the branches. Ralph and his colleagues were on the periphery. Unkindly, those in the field referred to them as "dinosaurs."

In interviewing plateaued U.S. managers like Ralph, we have learned that they are a lot like their Japanese counterparts. They feel they've been treated fairly financially and have got high enough formal titles. But they miss a sense of importance, of being in a position that counts. On the shelf, they become passive and uninterested and make a contribution to the company that is far below their potential.

The importance of his mainstream jobs is evident in Harold's commitment as a regional sales vice president. After completing his navy service during the Korean War, Harold joined the firm in his first full-time job as a securities salesperson in New York. In the early years, he enjoyed not only the work but also the high income. He occasionally wondered what it might be like to work for another company, but he never was seriously tempted even to look around.

At 35, Harold was made a vice president and put in charge of a small specialty sales group in New Jersey. He held this job for six years. During this period, he learned that he was good at leading others and he enjoyed the added responsibility. In fact, the group did so well that Harold began to dream that he might some day become a partner. Since only one of the firm's 65 partners had come from the selling side, this achievement would have been remarkable. Harold's toughest time at the firm came when he failed to make partner. When he was 40, he still had secret hopes, even though his then boss as well as several other partners were very frank in telling him that he was unlikely to make it. When he was asked to take his present job, he knew that any hope he still retained was totally unrealistic.

As disappointed as he had been at the time, he now retains several positive memories of that period, the strongest being that several partners, including the division manager, had taken the time to explain the partnership decision to him. In the process, they had emphasized his importance in the regional office to the success of the firm. In retrospect, he realizes that this support was not smoke but the way they really felt. And he knows from their comments and from the way he has been treated in general that he has been a strong contributor to the firm's success.

As he looks to the future, Harold really wants more of the same. It is exciting to come in to work, to build the business, and to see the younger people develop. In fact, his only nagging concern is whether he will be able to tolerate retirement.

Two points are striking about Harold and Ralph's situations. While each had climbed as high as he could up the organizational hierarchy, one felt unused and unwanted while the other felt important and committed. Like the committed Japanese managers, Harold was still in the mainstream, which kept him turned on. Further, his bosses, unlike Ralph's, while still emphasizing his potential contribution to the firm, had told him about his limited future prospects; their candor had helped him to get through his disappointment without bitterness.

Keeping the Torch Lit

It is unrealistic to expect that all plateaued managers can be kept motivated. Because of their superiors' failure to be candid in their evaluations, some will be foundering in the wrong positions. Others may have had their spirits so damped by past grievances, real or imagined, that nothing can reignite them.

We assume, however, that most executives whose careers have stopped have the ability to carry out their responsibilities and have had a satisfactory performance record. While they may not be candidates for higher management, they have been and are completely satisfactory in their contributions. They are neither psychological nor ability misfits.

Clearly, early career experiences have a big impact on how managers view both themselves and the company before they reach the plateau. While many early events can affect such perspectives, two are critical: the first is candor about a person's career prospects. The second important factor is challenging job assignments.

Some of the actions we recommend here are geared to preventing managers from turning off in early career stages, including the time during which they learn they have plateaued. Others are intended to keep managers committed and involved after they have reached the plateau.

TELL THE TRUTH

The need for candor starts at the very beginning when company recruiters tell prospective managers on university campuses about their career possibilities. Moreover, if someone is in a sideline po-sition for a while, he or she must know why and realize it will only be for a short time. Understandably, in their enthusiasm to convince fledgling managers about the merits of their companies, recruiters create unrealistic expectations about how far most of them will go.

These expectations form a kind of psychological contract and stay with people for many years. If the "contract" is broken, the company may lose the person's trust. Supervisors, of course, also shape a young person's aspirations.

In one company we know of, a manager brought three bright young stars into a division and promised them that they would have lots of resources for working on special projects. As time went by, the newcomers found that they were handling more and more of the division's routine functions. When their boss eventually retired, his replacement disavowed any commitment to special projects and the three stars stopped shining. Eventually two of them left.

All too often senior managers are unwilling to give subordinates clear and honest feedback about their performance and prospects. As Ralph's reactions demonstrate, failure to get such data can lead to feelings of unfair treatment.

Even worse, we have observed many managers who, long after their superiors have passed them over, still believe they will ad-vance. As they gradually recognize that advancement is unlikely, they become embittered and resentful because no one has leveled with them. Contrast such situations with Harold's. Although dis-appointed at not being named a partner, because his own boss and other partners had frankly explained why and had emphasized his continued importance to the firm, Harold felt that he'd had fair treatment.

It is especially important for top managers to be candid with employees at the midpoints of their careers, a time when people are also dealing with other mid-life issues like their own mortality, the increasing independence of children, and so forth. Although senior executives can't deal with all these issues, they can and should help subordinates face up to the reality that their careers are leveling off.

In one case, the general manager of a small division in a large consumer products company was feeling restless. After 28 years of service and a history of rapid career progress, he began to worry that he would not be made a corporate vice president of a larger division. His frustration and disappointment ultimately led him to approach an executive search firm, which eventually turned up an attractive offer in another company. Feeling very ambivalent about whether to accept, he went to the group vice president who was his boss to tell him of the dilemma.

His boss remembers it this way:

"I was scared to death when I realized what the situation was. I didn't want to lose him. But I was terrified to tell him that he wouldn't make vice president here because we had concluded that he couldn't handle a bigger job even though he was doing well in his current one. I finally screwed up my courage and told him. We then talked at length about the pros and cons of the offer, but what we both didn't realize at the time was that my candor with him had solved his dilemma.

"I learned this the next day when he called and asked if I'd join his wife and him for dinner. They both thanked me for calling a spade a spade and explained that he wanted to stay in the company. Once he understood how I and others saw him, he realized he felt so much a part of our company that he didn't want to leave, and he understood that his search for alternatives was out of frustration with not knowing where he stood."

Candor helps people face and accept the reality that they are not going to advance farther, but the results are not usually so dramatic. As a rule, senior executives need to be persistent during a period of several months and patient in giving the subordinate time to accept the facts.

Also, such frankness is not easy to come by. Senior managements find it difficult to derail employees. No one likes to make definitive judgments about another person's prospects. As Harry Levinson has pointed out, people feel guilty about communicating such appraisals.[2] Also, as in the last case, many top executives are afraid that subordinates will respond to such honesty by leaving. Some may go, of course, but the greater danger is that lack of candor will lead managers to lose their motivation to contribute even though they're still on board.

It's much easier to be open with people at critical points in their careers if you've had sound relationships with them from the beginning. Senior executives need to have routine, frank conversations with their subordinates about performance, prospects, and the expectations on both sides. If the two people maintain such a dialogue over several years, sufficient mutual trust is likely to grow so that when difficult things need to be said, they will be easier for the boss to deliver and for the subordinate to accept. Such a relationship can be an important preventive against the loss of a manager's commitment.

CHALLENGE WITH GOOD JOBS

To understand more clearly why challenges are so important, consider what we know about the psychological states of employees as they reach their forties and fifties. Since they have by then accepted the idea that they won't advance farther, the challenge for them will have to come from their current work. This means they will want to use the skills and expertise that they have developed throughout their careers.

Besides, if they've spent 15 to 20 challenging mainstream years with their companies, they identify closely with them. And it's when people identify with their organizations that they care about the development of the next generations of professionals and managers.[3] It is one way they can deal with what Erik Erikson has labeled the generativity issue—that is, "What will I leave behind for the next generation?"

With this perspective, three broad guidelines seem useful:

Continue to provide meaningful work. While this is the same thing that we suggested for the early career stages, it now involves a different emphasis. For one thing, it is important to provide assignments where the person can apply professional or technical skills as well as managerial talents. Ralph would have been much more engaged if he could have used his underwriting skills. Similarly, the passive Japanese managers would have felt more committed if their accumulated engineering knowledge had been put to use. The problem is that in many companies it's the management jobs that provide the hierarchical status and the involvement in mainstream activities.

We suggest that senior executives recognize and reward the professional contributions plateaued managers have made. For example, one big aerospace company uses older engineering managers as consultants to its engineering groups.

A way to offer new challenges, albeit not necessarily more important tasks, is to rotate jobs at the same level.[4] For example, a district sales manager who moves to a new territory gets a fresh set of customers to understand and new subordinates to lead and develop. The challenge of learning and dealing with a new situation can make the same responsibilities more exciting. Whatever management considers for providing meaningful work, the guiding principle must be finding ways to enable experienced employees to use their skills and knowledge to contribute.

Encourage involvement in decisions and activities. Here we have in mind two things. First, give managers as much autonomy as possible to carry out their responsibilities. Allow them to make decisions using their accumulated experience and knowledge. Be unobtrusive with the controls you place on their activities.

Second, find ways to use managers' experience and knowledge in ways that go beyond their jobs. Serving on task forces or committees is one example. Perhaps you're considering building a new facility. Why not let plateaued managers serve on the planning group? Their experience and wisdom may be useful, and participation will build their feeling of commitment. At one commercial bank, executives who have stopped progressing in their careers work with other employees and outside directors on a corporate responsibility committee. But the particular task is not the critical factor. What is important is that senior management search for innovative ways to enable experienced executives to make a real contribution to the organization.

Foster teaching and coaching. Because older executives identify with the company and are concerned about the next generation, they can serve as teachers and coaches of new professionals and managers. The benefits to the development of the younger people are obvious. But more important to our concerns, such roles meet important psychological needs of plateaued managers. Contributing in this way makes them feel necessary to the future of the company to which they have devoted so much of themselves.

Notes

1. Haruo Takagi, *The Flaw in Japanese Management* (Ann Arbor, Mich.: UMI Research Press, 1985).

2. Harry Levinson, "Appraisal of *What* Performance?" *Harvard Business Review* (July–August 1976), p. 30.

3. Daniel J. Levinson et al., *The Seasons of a Man's Life* (New York: Alfred A. Knopf, 1978).

4. See Gordon E. Forward, "Wide-open Management at Chaparral Steel," *Harvard Business Review* (May–June 1986), p. 96.

8
Power Is the
Great Motivator

David C. McClelland and David H. Burnham

What makes or motivates a good manager? The question is so enormous in scope that anyone trying to answer it has difficulty knowing where to begin. Some people might say that a good manager is one who is successful; and by now most business researchers and businesspeople themselves know what motivates people who successfully run their own small businesses. The key to their success has turned out to be what psychologists call "the need for achievement," the desire to do something better or more efficiently than it has been done before. Any number of books and articles summarize research studies explaining how the achievement motive is necessary for people to attain success on their own.[1]

But what has achievement motivation got to do with good management? There is no reason on theoretical grounds why a person who has a strong need to be more efficient should make a good manager. While it sounds as if everyone ought to have the need to achieve, in fact, as psychologists define and measure achievement motivation, it leads people to behave in very special ways that do not necessarily lead to good management.

For one thing, because they focus on personal improvement, on doing things better by themselves, achievement-motivated people want to do things themselves. For another, they want concrete short-term feedback on their performance so that they can tell how well they are doing. Yet a manager, particularly one of or in a large

March–April 1976

Authors' note: All the case material in this article is disguised.

complex organization cannot perform all the tasks necessary for success by him- or herself. Managers must manage others so that they will do things for the organization. Also, feedback on subordinates' performance may be a lot vaguer and more delayed than it would be if they were doing everything themselves.

The manager's job seems to call more for people who can influence others than for those who do things better on their own. In motivational terms, then, we might expect the successful manager to have a greater "need for power" than need to achieve. But there must be other qualities beside the need for power that go into the makeup of a good manager. Just what these qualities are and how they interrelate is the subject of this article.

To measure the motivations of managers, good and bad, we studied a number of individual managers from different large U.S. corporations who were participating in management workshops designed to improve their managerial effectiveness.

The general conclusion of these studies is that the top manager of a company must possess a high need for power: that is, a concern for influencing people. However, this need must be disciplined and controlled so that it is directed toward the benefit of the institution as a whole and not toward the manager's personal aggrandizement. Moreover, top managers' need for power ought to be greater than their need for being liked by people.

Now let us look at what these ideas mean in the context of real individuals in real situations and see what comprises the profile of the good manager. Finally, we will look at the workshops themselves to determine how they go about changing behavior.

Measuring Managerial Effectiveness

First off, what does it mean when we say that a good manager has a greater need for "power" than for "achievement"? To get a more concrete idea, let us consider the case of Ken Briggs, a sales manager in a large U.S. corporation who joined one of our managerial workshops. Some six or seven years ago, Ken Briggs was promoted to a managerial position at corporate headquarters, where he had responsibility for salespeople who service his company's largest accounts.

In filling out his questionnaire at the workshop, Ken showed that he correctly perceived what his job required of him: namely, that he should influence others' success more than achieve new goals himself or socialize with his subordinates. However, when asked with other members of the workshop to write a story depicting a managerial situation, Ken unwittingly revealed through his fiction that he did not share those concerns. Indeed, he discovered that his need for achievement was very high—in fact over the 90th percentile—and his need for power was very low, in about the 15th percentile. Ken's high need to achieve was no surprise—after all, he had been a very successful salesman—but obviously his motivation to influence others was much less than his job required. Ken was a little disturbed but thought that perhaps the measuring instruments were not too accurate and that the gap between the ideal and his score was not as great as it seemed.

Then came the real shocker. Ken's subordinates confirmed what his stories revealed: he was a poor manager, having little positive impact on those who worked for him. Ken's subordinates felt that they had little responsibility delegated to them, that he never rewarded but only criticized them, and that the office was not well organized, but confused and chaotic. On all three of these scales, his office rated in the 10th to 15th percentile relative to national norms.

As Ken talked the results over privately with a workshop leader, he became more and more upset. He finally agreed, however, that the results of the survey confirmed feelings he had been afraid to admit to himself or others. For years, he had been miserable in his managerial role. He now knew the reason: he simply did not want to nor had he been able to influence or manage others. As he thought back, he realized that he had failed every time he had tried to influence his staff, and he felt worse than ever.

Ken had responded to failure by setting very high standards—his office scored in the 98th percentile on this scale—and by trying to do most things himself, which was close to impossible; his own activity and lack of delegation consequently left his staff demoralized. Ken's experience is typical of those who have a strong need to achieve but low power motivation. They may become very successful salespeople and, as a consequence, may be promoted into managerial jobs for which they, ironically, are unsuited.

If achievement motivation does not make a good manager, what motive does? It is not enough to suspect that power motivation may be important; one needs hard evidence that people who are better managers than Ken Briggs do in fact possess stronger power mo-

Exhibit I.   Correlation between Morale Score and Sales Performance for a Large U.S. Corporation

Average percentage gain in sales by district from 1972 to 1973

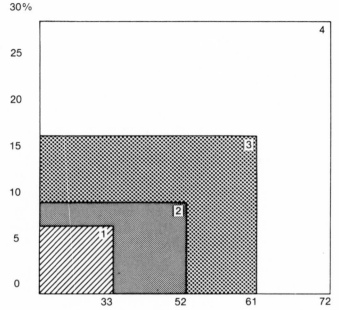

Morale score (perceived organizational clarity plus team spirit)

1 = 6 districts   2 = 4 districts   3 = 4 districts   4 = 2 districts

tivation and perhaps score higher in other characteristics as well. But how does one decide who is the better manager?

Real-world performance measures are hard to come by if one is trying to rate managerial effectiveness in production, marketing, finance, or research and development. In trying to determine who the better managers were in Ken Briggs's company, we did not want to rely only on the opinions of their superiors. For a variety of reasons, superiors' judgments of their subordinates' real-world performance may be inaccurate. In the absence of some standard measure of performance, we decided that the next best index of managers' effectiveness would be the climate they create in the office, reflected in the morale of subordinates.

Almost by definition, a good manager is one who, among other things, helps subordinates feel strong and responsible, who rewards them properly for good performance, and who sees that things are organized in such a way that subordinates feel they know what they should be doing. Above all, managers should foster among subordinates a strong sense of team spirit, of pride in working as part of a particular team. If a manager creates and encourages this spirit, the subordinates certainly should perform better.

In the company Ken Briggs works for, we have direct evidence of a connection between morale and performance in the one area where performance measures are easy to come by—namely, sales. In April 1973, at least three employees from this company's 16 sales districts filled out questionnaires that rated their office for organizational clarity and team spirit. Their scores were averaged and totaled to give an overall morale score for each office. The percentage gains or losses in sales for each district in 1973 were compared with those for 1972. The difference in sales figures by district ranged from a gain of nearly 30% to a loss of 8%, with a median gain of around 14%. Exhibit I shows the average gain in sales performance plotted against the increasing averages in morale scores.

In Exhibit I we can see that the relationship between sales and morale is surprisingly close. The six districts with the lowest morale early in the year showed an average sales gain of only around 7% by year's end (although there was wide variation within this group), whereas the two districts with the highest morale showed an average gain of 28%. When morale scores rise above the 50th percentile in terms of national norms, they seem to lead to better sales performance. In Ken Briggs's company, at least, high morale at the beginning is a good index of how well the sales division actually performed in the coming year.

And it seems very likely that the manager who can create high morale among salespeople can also do the same for employees in other areas (production, design, and so on), leading to better performance. Given that high morale in an office indicates that there is a good manager present, what general characteristics does he or she possess?

A NEED FOR POWER

In examining the motive scores of over 50 managers of both high and low morale units in all sections of the same large company, we found that most of the managers—over 70%—were high in power motivation compared with men in general. This finding confirms the fact that power motivation is important for management. (Remember that as we use the term *power motivation,* it refers not to dictatorial behavior, but to a desire to have impact, to be strong and influential.) The better managers, as judged by the morale of those working for them, tended to score even higher in power motivation. But the most important determining factor of high morale turned out not to be how their power motivation compared to their need to achieve but whether it was higher than their need to be liked. This relationship existed for 80% of the better sales managers as compared with only 10% of the poorer managers. And the same held true for other managers in nearly all parts of the company.

In the research, product development, and operations divisions, 73% of the better managers had a stronger need for power than a need to be liked (or what we term "affiliation motive") as compared with only 22% of the poorer managers. Why should this be so? Sociologists have long argued that, for a bureaucracy to function effectively, those who manage it must be universalistic in applying rules. That is, if they make exceptions for the particular needs of individuals, the whole system will break down.

The manager with a high need for being liked is precisely the one who wants to stay on good terms with everybody, and, therefore, is the one most likely to make exceptions in terms of particular needs. If an employee asks for time off to stay home with a sick spouse to help look after the kids, the affiliative manager, feeling sorry for the person, agrees almost without thinking.

When President Ford remarked in pardoning ex-President Nixon that he had "suffered enough," he was responding as an affiliative manager would, because he was empathizing primarily with Nixon's needs and feelings. Sociological theory and our data both argue, however, that the person whose need for affiliation is high does not make a good manager. This kind of person creates poor morale because he or she does not understand that other people in the office will tend to regard exceptions to the rules as unfair to themselves, just as many U.S. citizens felt it was unfair to let Richard Nixon off and punish others less involved than he was in the Watergate scandal.

SOCIALIZED POWER

But so far our findings are a little alarming. Do they suggest that the good manager is one who cares for power and is not at all concerned about the needs of other people? Not quite, for the good manager has other characteristics that must still be taken into account.

Above all, the good manager's power motivation is not oriented toward personal aggrandizement but toward the institution that he or she serves. In another major research study, we found that the signs of controlled action or inhibition that appear when a person exercises his or her imagination in writing stories tell a great deal about the kind of power that person needs.[2] We discovered that, if a high power motive score is balanced by high inhibition, stories about power tend to be altruistic. That is, the heroes in the story exercise power on behalf of someone else. This is the "socialized" face of power as distinguished from the concern for personal power, which is characteristic of individuals whose stories are loaded with power imagery but that show no sign of inhibition or self-control. In our earlier study, we found ample evidence that these latter individuals exercise their power impulsively. They are more rude to other people, they drink too much, they try to exploit others sexually, and they collect symbols of personal prestige such as fancy cars or big offices.

Individuals high in power and in control, on the other hand, are more institution-minded; they tend to get elected to more offices, to control their drinking, and to want to serve others. Not surprisingly, we found in the workshops that the better managers in the corporation also tend to score high on both power and inhibition.

Profile of a Good Manager

Let us recapitulate what we have discussed so far and have illustrated with data from one company. The better managers we studied are high in power motivation, low in affiliation motivation, and high in inhibition. They care about institutional power and use it to stimulate their employees to be more productive. Now let us compare them with affiliative managers—those in whom the need for affiliation is higher than the need for power—and with the personal power managers—those in whom the need for power is higher than for affiliation but whose inhibition score is low.

In the sales division of our illustrative company, there were managers who matched the three types fairly closely. Exhibit II shows how their subordinates rated the offices they worked in on responsibility, organizational clarity, and team spirit. There are scores

Exhibit II.   Average Scores on Selected Climate Dimensions by Subordinates of Managers with Different Motive Profiles

Percentile ranking of average scores (national norms)

0	10	20	30	40	50	60

Sense of responsibility

Organizational clarity

Team spirit

Scores for at least three subordinates of:

☐ Affiliative managers (affiliation greater than power, high inhibition)

▨ Personal power managers (power greater than affiliation, low inhibition)

▓ Institutional managers (power greater than affiliation, high inhibition)

from at least three subordinates for each manager, and several managers are represented for each type, so that the averages shown in the exhibit are quite stable. Note that the manager who is concerned about being liked by people tends to have subordinates who feel that they have very little personal responsibility, that organizational procedures are not clear, and that they have little pride in their work group.

In short, as we expected, affiliative managers make so many ad hominem and ad hoc decisions that they almost totally abandon orderly procedures. Their disregard for procedure leaves employees feeling weak, irresponsible, and without a sense of what might happen next, of where they stand in relation to their manager, or even of what they ought to be doing. In this company, the group of affiliative managers portrayed in Exhibit II were below the 30th percentile in morale scores.

The managers who are motivated by a need for personal power are somewhat more effective. They are able to create a greater sense of responsibility in their divisions and, above all, a greater team spirit. They can be thought of as managerial equivalents of successful tank commanders such as General Patton, whose own daring inspired admiration in his troops. But notice how in Exhibit II these men are still only in the 40th percentile in the amount of organizational clarity they create, as compared to the high power, low affiliation, high inhibition managers, whom we shall term "institutional."

Managers motivated by personal power are not disciplined enough to be good institutional builders, and often their subordinates are loyal to them as individuals rather than to the institution they both serve. When a personal power manager leaves, disorganization often follows. His subordinates' strong group spirit, which the manager has personally inspired, deflates. The subordinates do not know what to do for themselves.

Of the managerial types, "institutional" managers are the most successful in creating an effective work climate. Exhibit II shows that their subordinates feel that they have more responsibility. Also, these managers create high morale because they produce the greatest sense of organizational clarity and team spirit. If such a manager leaves, he or she can be more readily replaced by another manager, because the employees have been encouraged to be loyal to the institution rather than to a particular person.

MANAGERIAL STYLES

Since it seems undeniable from Exhibit II that either kind of power orientation creates better morale in subordinates than a "people" orientation, we must consider that a concern for power is essential to good management. Our findings seem to fly in the face of a long and influential tradition of organizational psychology, which insists that authoritarian management is what is wrong with most businesses in this country. Let us say frankly that we think the bogeyman of authoritarianism has in fact been wrongly used to downplay the importance of power in management. After all, management is an influence game. Some proponents of democratic management seem to have forgotten this fact, urging managers to be primarily concerned with people's human needs rather than with helping them to get things done.

But a good deal of the apparent conflict between our findings and those of other behavioral scientists in this area arises from the fact that we are talking about *motives,* and behaviorists are often talking about *actions.* What we are saying is that managers must be interested in playing the influence game in a controlled way. That does not necessarily mean that they are or should be authoritarian in action. On the contrary, it appears that power-motivated managers make their subordinates feel strong rather than weak. The true authoritarian in action would have the reverse effect, making people feel weak and powerless.

Thus another important ingredient in the profile of a manager is his or her managerial style. In the illustrative company, 63% of the better managers (those whose subordinates had higher morale) scored higher on the democratic or coaching styles of management as compared with only 22% of the poorer managers, a statistically significant difference. By contrast, the latter scored higher on authoritarian or coercive management styles. Since the better managers were also higher in power motivation, it seems that, in action, they express their power motivation in a democratic way, which is more likely to be effective.

To see how motivation and style interact, let us consider the case of George Prentice, a manager in the sales division of another company. George had exactly the right motive combination to be an institutional manager. He was high in the need for power, low in the need for affiliation, and high in inhibition. He exercised his power in a controlled, organized way. His stories reflected this fact. In one, for instance, he wrote, "The men sitting around the table were feeling pretty good; they had just finished plans for reorganizing the company; the company has been beset with a number of organizational problems. This group, headed by a hard-driving, brilliant young executive, has completely reorganized the company structurally with new jobs and responsibilities. . . ."

This described how George himself was perceived by the company, and shortly after the workshop he was promoted to vice president in charge of all sales.

But George was also known to his colleagues as a monster, a tough guy who would "walk over his grandmother" if she stood in the way of his advancement. He had the right motive combination and, in fact, was more interested in institutional growth than in personal power, but his managerial style was all wrong. Taking his cue from some of the top executives in the corporation, he told people what they had to do and threatened them with dire consequences if they didn't do it.

When George was confronted with his authoritarianism in a workshop, he recognized that this style was counterproductive—in fact, in another part of the study we found that it was associated with low morale—and he subsequently changed to acting more like a coach, which was the scale on which he scored the lowest initially. George saw more clearly that his job was not to force other people to do things but to help them to figure out ways of getting their job done better for the company.

THE INSTITUTIONAL MANAGER

One reason why it was easy for George Prentice to change his managerial style was that in his imaginative stories he was already having thoughts about helping others, characteristic of people with the institution-building motivational pattern. In further examining institution builders' thoughts and actions, we found they have four major characteristics:

1. They are more organization-minded; that is, they tend to join more organizations and to feel responsible for building up these organizations. Furthermore, they believe strongly in the importance of centralized authority.
2. They report that they like to work. This finding is particularly interesting, because our research on achievement motivation has led many commentators to argue that achievement motivation promotes the "Protestant work ethic." Almost the precise opposite is true. People who have a high need to achieve like to get out of work by becoming more efficient. They would like to see the same result obtained in less time or with less effort. But managers who have a need for institutional power actually seem to like the discipline of work. It satisfies their need for getting things done in an orderly way.
3. They seem quite willing to sacrifice some of their own self-interest for the welfare of the organization they serve. For example, they are more willing to make contributions to charities.

4. They have a keen sense of justice. It is almost as if they feel that if people work hard and sacrifice for the good of the organization, they should and will get a just reward for their efforts.

It is easy to see how each of these four concerns helps a person become a good manager, concerned about what the institution can achieve.

MATURITY.   Before we go on to look at how the workshops can help managers to improve their managerial style and recognize their own motivations, let us consider one more fact we discovered in studying the better managers at George Prentice's company. They were more mature. Mature people can be most simply described as less egotistic. Somehow their positive self-image is not at stake in what they are doing. They are less defensive, more willing to seek advice from experts, and have a longer-range view. They accumulate fewer personal possessions and seem older and wiser. It is as if they have awakened to the fact that they are not going to live forever and have lost some of the feeling that their own personal future is all that important.

Many U.S. businesspeople fear this kind of maturity. They suspect that it will make them less hard driving, less expansion-minded, and less committed to organizational effectiveness. Our data do not support their fears. These fears are exactly the ones George Prentice had before he went to the workshop. Afterward he was a more effective manager, not despite his loss of some of the sense of his own importance, but because of it. The reason is simple: his subordinates believed afterward that he genuinely was more concerned about the company than about himself. Where once they respected his confidence but feared him, they now trust him. Once he supported their image of him as a "big man" by talking about the new Porsche and the new Honda he had bought; when we saw him recently he said, almost as an aside, "I don't buy things anymore."

Changing Managerial Style

George Prentice was able to change his managerial style after learning more about himself in a workshop. But does self-knowledge generally improve managerial behavior?

Some people might ask, "What good does it do to know, if I am a manager, that I should have a strong power motive, not too great a concern about being liked, a sense of discipline, a high level of maturity, and a coaching managerial style? What can I do about it?" The answer is that workshops for managers that give information to them in a supportive setting enable them to change.

Consider the results shown in Exhibit III, where "before" and "after" scores are compared. Once again we use the responses of subordinates to give some measure of the effectiveness of managers. To judge by their subordinates' responses, the managers were clearly more effective afterward. The subordinates felt that they were given more responsibility, that they received more rewards, that the organizational procedures were clearer, and that morale was higher. These differences are all statistically significant.

But what do these differences mean in human terms? How did the managers change? Sometimes they decided they should get into another line of work. This happened to Ken Briggs, for example,

Exhibit III. *Average Scores on Selected Climate Dimensions by over 50 Salespeople before and after Their Managers Were Trained*

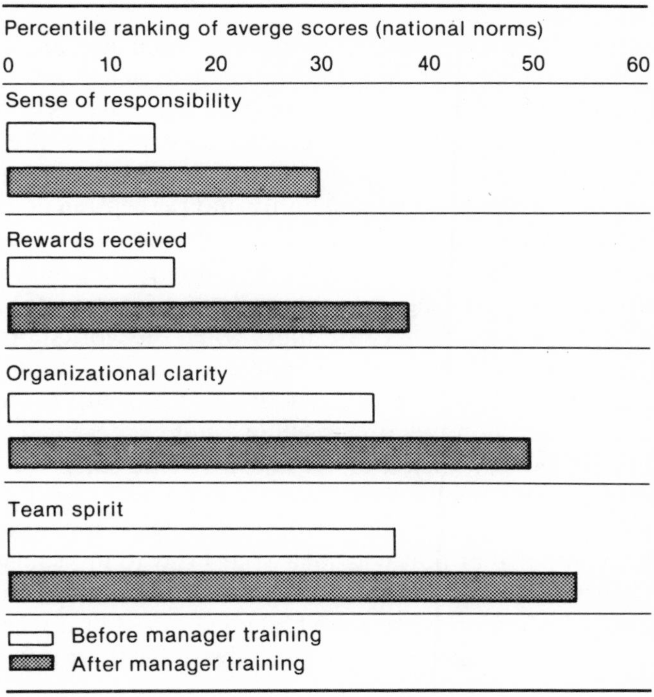

Percentile ranking of averge scores (national norms)

0   10   20   30   40   50   60

Sense of responsibility

Rewards received

Organizational clarity

Team spirit

☐ Before manager training
▨ After manager training

who found that the reason why he was doing so poorly as a manager was because he had almost no interest in influencing others. He understood how he would have to change if he were to do well in his present job, but in the end decided, with the help of management, that he would prefer to work back into his first love, sales.

Ken Briggs moved into "remaindering," to help retail outlets for his company's products get rid of last year's stock so that they could take on each year's new styles. He is very successful in this new role; he has cut costs, increased dollar volume, and in time has worked himself into an independent role selling some of the old stock on his own in a way that is quite satisfactory to the business. And he does not have to manage anybody anymore.

In George Prentice's case, less change was needed. He was obviously a very competent person with the right motive profile for a top managerial position. When he was promoted, he performed even more successfully than before because he realized the need to become more positive in his approach and less coercive in his managerial style.

But what about people who do not want to change their jobs and discover that they do not have the right motive profile to be managers?

The case of Charlie Blake is instructive. Charlie was as low in power motivation as Ken Briggs, his need to achieve was about average, and his affiliation motivation was above average. Thus he had the affiliative manager profile, and, as expected, the morale among his subordinates was very low. When Charlie learned that his subordinates' sense of responsibility and perception of a reward system were in the 10th percentile and that team spirit was in the 30th, he was shocked. When shown a film depicting three managerial climates, Charlie said he preferred what turned out to be the authoritarian climate. He became angry when the workshop trainer and other members in the group pointed out the limitations of this managerial style. He became obstructive in the group process and objected strenuously to what was being taught.

In an interview conducted much later, Charlie said, "I blew my cool. When I started yelling at you for being all wrong, I got even madder when you pointed out that, according to my style questionnaire, you bet that that was just what I did to my salespeople. Down underneath I knew something must be wrong. The sales performance for my division wasn't so good. Most of it was due to me anyway and not to my salespeople. Obviously their reports that they felt very little responsibility was delegated to them and that I didn't reward them at all had to mean something. So I finally decided to sit down and try to figure what I could do about it. I knew I had to start being a manager instead of trying to do everything myself and blowing my cool at others because they didn't do what I thought they should. In the end, after I calmed down on the way back from the workshop, I realized that it is not so bad to make a mistake; it's bad not to learn from it."

After the course, Charlie put his plans into effect. Six months later, his subordinates were asked to rate him again. He attended a second workshop to study these results and reported, "On the way home I was very nervous. I knew I had been working with those people and not selling so much myself, but I was very much afraid of what they were going to say about how things were going in the office. When I found out that the team spirit and some of those other low scores had jumped from around the 30th to the 55th percentile, I was so delighted and relieved that I couldn't say anything all day long."

When he was asked how he acted differently from before, he said, "In previous years when the corporate headquarters said we had to make 110% of our original goal, I had called the salespeople in and said, in effect, 'This is ridiculous; we are not going to make it, but you know perfectly well what will happen if we don't. So get out there and work your tail off.' The result was that I worked twenty hours a day and they did nothing.

"This time I approached it differently. I told them three things. First, they were going to have to do some sacrificing for the company. Second, working harder is not going to do much good because we are already working about as hard as we can. What will be required are special deals and promotions. You are going to have to figure out some new angles if we are to make it. Third, I'm going to back you up. I'm going to set a realistic goal with each of you. If you make that goal but don't make the company goal, I'll see to it that you are not punished. But if you do make the company goal, I'll see to it that you will get some kind of special rewards."

When the salespeople challenged Charlie, saying he did not have enough influence to give them rewards, rather than becoming angry Charlie promised rewards that were in his power to give—such as longer vacations.

Note that Charlie has now begun to behave in a number of ways that we found to be characteristic of the good institutional manager.

He is, above all, higher in power motivation, the desire to influence his salespeople, and lower in his tendency to try to do everything himself. He asks the salespeople to sacrifice for the company. He does not defensively chew them out when they challenge him but tries to figure out what their needs are so that he can influence them. He realizes that his job is more one of strengthening and supporting his subordinates than of criticizing them. And he is keenly interested in giving them just rewards for their efforts.

The changes in his approach to his job have certainly paid off. The sales figures for his office in 1973 were up more than 16% over 1972 and up still further in 1974 over 1973. In 1973 his gain over the previous year ranked seventh in the nation; in 1974 it ranked third. And he wasn't the only one in his company to change managerial styles. Overall sales at his company were up substantially in 1973 as compared with 1972, an increase that played a large part in turning the overall company performance around from a $15 million loss in 1972 to a $3 million profit in 1973. The company continued to improve its performance in 1974 with an 11% further gain in sales and a 38% increase in profits.

Of course not everyone can be reached by a workshop. Henry Carter managed a sales office for a company that had very low morale (around the 20th percentile) before he went for training. When morale was checked some six months later, it had not improved. Overall sales gain subsequently reflected this fact, since it was only 2% above the previous year's figures.

Oddly enough, Henry's problem was that he was so well liked by everybody that he felt little pressure to change. Always the life of the party, he is particularly popular because he supplies other managers with special hard-to-get brands of cigars and wines at a discount. He uses his close ties with everyone to bolster his position in the company, even though it is known that his office does not perform well compared with others.

His great interpersonal skills became evident at the workshop when he did very poorly at one of the business games. When the discussion turned to why he had done so badly and whether he acted that way on the job, two prestigious participants immediately sprang to his defense, explaining away Henry's failure by arguing that the way he did things was often a real help to others and the company. As a result, Henry did not have to cope with such questions at all. He had so successfully developed his role as a likable, helpful friend to everyone in management that, even though his salespeople performed badly, he did not feel under any pressure to change.

Checks and Balances

What have we learned from Ken Briggs, George Prentice, Charlie Blake, and Henry Carter? Principally, we have discovered what motive combination makes an effective manager. We have also seen that change is possible if a person has the right combination of qualities.

Oddly enough, the good manager in a large company does not have a high need for achievement, as we define and measure that motive, although there must be plenty of that motive somewhere in the organization. The top managers shown here have a high need for power and an interest in influencing others, both greater than their interest in being liked by people. The manager's concern for power should be socialized—controlled so that the institution as a whole, not only the individual, benefits. People and nations with this motive profile are empire builders; they tend to create high morale and to expand the organizations they head.

But there is also danger in this motive profile; empire building can lead to imperialism and authoritarianism in companies and in countries.

The same motive pattern that produces good power management can also lead a company or a country to try to dominate others, ostensibly in the interests of organizational expansion. Thus it is not surprising that big business has had to be regulated from time to time by federal agencies. And it is most likely that international agencies will perform the same regulative function for empire-building countries.

For an individual, the regulative function is performed by two characteristics that are part of the profile of the very best managers—a greater emotional maturity, where there is little egotism, and a democratic, coaching managerial style. If an institutional power motivation is checked by maturity, it does not lead to an aggressive, egotistic expansiveness.

For countries, this checking means that they can control their destinies beyond their borders without being aggressive and hostile. For individuals, it means they can control their subordinates and influence others around them without resorting to coercion or to an authoritarian management style. Real disinterested statesmanship has a vital role to play at the top of both countries and companies.

Summarized in this way, what we have found out through empirical and statistical investigations may just sound like good common sense. But the improvement over common sense is that now the characteristics of the good manager are objectively known. Managers of corporations can select those who are likely to be good managers and train those already in managerial positions to be more effective with more confidence.

Notes

1. For instance, see David C. McClelland, *The Achieving Society* (New York: Van Nostrand, 1961) and (with David Winter) *Motivating Economic Achievement* (New York: Free Press, 1969).
2. David C. McClelland, William N. Davis, Rudolf Kalin, and Erie Warner, *The Drinking Man* (New York: The Free Press, 1972).

9
The Attack
on Pay

Rosabeth Moss Kanter

Status, not contribution, has traditionally been the basis for the numbers on employees' paychecks. Pay has reflected where jobs rank in the corporate hierarchy—not what comes out of them.

Today this system is under attack. More and more senior executives are trying to turn their employees into entrepreneurs—people who earn a direct return on the value they help create, often in exchange for putting their pay at risk. In the process, changes are coming into play that will have revolutionary consequences for companies and their employees. To see what I have in mind, consider these actual examples:

To control costs and stimulate improvements, a leading financial services company converts its information systems department into a venture that sells its services both inside and outside the corporation. In its first year, the department runs at a big profit and employees begin to wonder why they can't get a chunk of the profits they have generated instead of just a fixed salary defined by rank.

In exchange for wage concessions, a manufacturer offers employees an ownership stake. Employee representatives begin to think about total company profitability and start asking why so many managers are on the payroll and why they are paid so much.

March–April 1987

Author's note: I thank Barry Stein, Cynthia Ingols, Paul Loranger, Carolyn Russell, Wendy Brown, and D. Quinn Mills for their valuable contributions.

To encourage initiative in reaching performance targets, a city government offers large salary increases to managers who can show major departmental improvements. After a few years, the amount in managers' paychecks bears little relationship to their levels in the organization.

In traditional compensation plans, each job comes with a pay level that stays about the same regardless of how well the job is performed or what the real organizational value of that performance is. Pay scales reflect such estimated characteristics as decision-making responsibility, importance to the organization, and number of subordinates. If there is a merit component, it is usually very small. The surest way—often the only way—to increase one's pay is to change employers or get promoted. A mountain of tradition and industrial relations practice has built up to support this way of calculating pay.

Proponents of this system customarily assert that the market ultimately determines pay, just as it determines the price of everything else that buyers wish to acquire. Compensation systems cannot be unfair or inappropriate, therefore, because they are incapable of causing anything. Actually, however, because it is so difficult to link people's compensation directly to their contributions, all the market really does is allow us to assume that people occupying equal positions tend to be paid equally and that people with similar experience and education tend to be worth about the same. So while the market works in macroeconomic terms, the process at a microeconomic level is circular: we know what people are worth because that's what they cost in the job market; but we also know that what people cost in the market is just what they're worth.

Given logic like this, it's not hard to see why such strange bedfellows as feminist activists and entrepreneurially minded managers both attack this traditional system as a manifestation of the paternalistic benefits offered across the board by Father Corporation. "We've got corporate socialism, not corporate capitalism," charged the manager of new ventures for a large industrial company. "We're so focused on consistent treatment internally that we destroy enterprise in the process."

These old arrangements are no longer supportable. For economic, social, and organizational reasons, the fundamental bases for determining pay are under attack. And while popular attention has focused on comparable worth—equalizing pay for those doing comparable work—the most important trend has been the loosening relationship between job assignment and pay level.

Four separate but closely related concerns are driving employers to rethink the meaning of worth and look beyond job assignments in determining pay—equity, cost, productivity, and the rewards of entrepreneurship.

It's Not Fair!

Every year, routine company surveys show fewer employees willing to say that traditional pay practices are fair. In particular, top management compensation has been assailed as unjustifiably high, especially when executives get large bonuses while their companies suffer financial losses or are just recovering from them.

Despite economic data showing an association between executive compensation and company performance, many professionals still argue that the amounts are excessive and reflect high status rather than good performance. Likewise, the existence of layers on layers of highly paid managers no longer seems entirely fair. Employees question why executives should be able to capture returns others actually produce. And they are beginning to resent compensation plans like the one in a leading well-run bank that gives managers bonuses of up to 30% of their pay for excellent branch performance, while branch employees get only a 6% to an 8% annual increase.

If executives get bonuses for raising profits, many urge, so should the workers who contribute to those profits. Indeed, this is the theory behind profit sharing in general. Such programs, and there are several widely used variants, have in common the very appealing and well-accepted notion that all employees—not just management—should share in the gains from enhanced performance.

Profit sharing is ordinarily a straightforward arrangement in which a fraction of the net profits from some period of operation are distributed to employees. The distribution may be either immediate or deferred, and the plan may not include all employees.

The plan at Lincoln Electric, the world's largest manufacturer of arc-welding products, is particularly generous. Every year, Lincoln pays out 6% of net income in common stock dividends—the "wages of capital." The board determines another sum to be set aside as seed money for investment in the future. The balance, paid to all employees, ranges from 20% of wages and salary, already competitive, to more than 120%. The company has remained profitable even in the face of sales declines in the 1981–1983 recession, to the benefit of employees as well as stockholders.

Overall, probably about a half million companies have some form of profit sharing, if both deferred and cash payouts are included. In private enterprises other than those categorized as small businesses, government statistics show that by 1983 19% of all production employees, 27% of all technical and clerical employees, and 23% of all professional and administrative employees were covered by profit-sharing agreements.

The variant known as gain sharing takes profit sharing one giant step farther by attempting, usually with some elaborate formula, to calculate the contributions of specific groups of employees whose contingent pay depends on those varying results. Although the basis for calculation varies from one gain-sharing plan to another, the plans have two principles in common: first, the payout reflects the contribution of groups rather than individuals (on the theory that teams and collective effort are what count), and second, the rewards to be shared and the plan for their distribution are based on objective, measurable characteristics (so that everyone can see what is owed and when it is owed).

According to experts, several thousand companies have gain-sharing programs of some sort. These programs already involve millions of workers and seem to be growing in popularity. The Scanlon Plan, probably the oldest, best-known, and most elaborate gain-sharing system, usually distributes 75% of gains to employees and 25% to the company. In addition, this plan is organized around complex mechanisms and procedures that spell out how employees at various levels are to participate, not only in control of the process but also in opportunities to help improve performance and thereby their own shares. At Herman Miller, Inc., gain sharing is described not simply as a compensation system but rather as a way of life for the company.

Group or all-employee bonuses, especially when linked to fairly specific indicators, provide another way to share some of the benefits of good performance more equitably. But evidence shows that their potential far exceeds their use. Although group performance bonuses are continuing to grow, top executives are much more likely to capture a portion of the benefits of increased profitability than employees are. In a recent Conference Board study of 491 companies, 58% had top executive bonus plans but only 11% had profit-sharing plans, 8% all-employee bonuses, 3% group productivity incentives, and fewer than 1% group cost-control incentives.

Performance-related compensation plans generally ignore employees other than top management and, to a lesser extent, some middle managers. And even in incentive-conscious high-technology companies, gain sharing is rare. While more than half the high-tech companies included in a recent Hay Associates compensation survey had cash or stock awards for individuals, only 6% had gain-sharing or group profit-sharing programs. Concerns about equity—including those framed in terms of comparable worth—are not altogether misplaced therefore.

Companies have long been concerned with one fundamental fairness issue—the relative compensation of employees in general. Now, however, they face two new issues that are complex, hard to resolve, and rapidly getting worse. The first, evident in the debate over gain sharing and profit sharing, sets up what employees get against what the organization gets from their efforts. The second, evident in the debate over comparable worth, is how groups in an organization fare in relation to each other. At the very least, these issues call for better measurement systems or new principles on which various constituencies can agree.

Let Them Eat Dividends

Facing challenges from competitors, companies in every field are seeking ways to reduce fixed labor costs. One sure way is to peg pay to performance—the company's as well as the individual's. Merit awards, bonuses, and profit-sharing plans hold out the promise of extra earnings for those who truly contribute. But it is their cost-reduction potential that really makes executives' eyes sparkle with dollar signs.

Making pay float to reflect company performance is the cornerstone of MIT economist Martin L. Weitzman's proposal for a "share economy." If many companies can be induced to share profits or revenues with their employees, Weitzman argues, then the cure for stagflation would be at hand. Among other things, companies would have an incentive to create jobs because more workers would be paid only in proportion to what they have brought in.[1]

For organizations struggling to compete, these macroeconomic implications are a lot less tantalizing than the more immediate benefits to be gained by asking workers to take their lumps from business cycles—or, employees would add, poor management decisions—along with their companies. Moreover, a similar logic clearly accounts for some of the appeal of employee ownership, especially to companies in industries where deregulation has created enormous cost competitiveness.

According to one recent book about employee ownership, *Taking Stock: Employee Ownership at Work,* at least 6 major airlines and 15 trucking companies have adopted employee ownership plans in response to deregulation.[2] Overall, the authors estimate that some 11 million employees in 8,000-plus businesses now own at least 15% of the companies employing them.

While many companies have found employee ownership attractive primarily as a financing scheme, there is little doubt that, properly designed and managed, it can positively affect corporate success. Take Western Air Lines as an illustration. After losing $200 million over four years, this company created the Western Partnership by trading a 32.4% ownership stake, a meaningful profit-sharing plan, and four seats on the board of directors for wage cuts and productivity improvements of 22.5% to 30%. In 1985 Western distributed more than $10 million to its 10,000 employees—$100 each in cash and the rest in employees' accounts. Now employees are making about $75 million on Western's sale to Delta.

Such schemes have obvious advantages over another highly visible alternative for fixed-labor-cost reduction—two-tier wage systems, which bring in new hires at a lower scale than current employees. Most of us can see the obvious inequity in paying two groups differently for doing exactly the same job. But pay pegged to actual performance? Earnings tied to company profits? What could be more fair?

The clear problems—that lower-paid employees cannot afford income swings as readily as the more highly paid and that employee efforts are not always directly related to company profitability—do not seem to deter the advocates. The fixed part of the paycheck is already shrinking in many American companies. Even the bonus is being used to supplement these efforts, especially among manufacturing companies. A recent study by the Bureau of National Affairs reveals that one-shot bonus payments, replacing general pay increases, were called for in almost 20% of all 1985 union contract settlements outside the construction industry, up from a mere 6% in 1984. Similarly, 20% of the 564 companies in Hewitt Associates'

1986 compensation survey gave one-time bonuses to white-collar workers, up from 7% in 1985.

These one-time payments do not raise base pay, nor do they affect overtime calculations. In fact, just the opposite occurs: they reduce the cost of labor. More than two-thirds of the bonus provisions the BNA studied were accompanied by wage freezes or decreases.

Bucks for Behavior

The cost attack is one straightforward way for companies to become more competitive, at least in the short run. In the long run, however, pay variations or rewards, contingent on specific and measurable achievements of individuals at every level, are likely to be even more effective in stimulating employee enterprise and channeling behavior. What better way could there be, proponents argue, to help employees recognize what is most useful and to guide their efforts appropriately?

Merrill Lynch's compensation system for its 10,400 brokers, introduced in February 1986, is a good example. To encourage brokers to spend more time with larger, more active customers, the firm has cut commissions for most small trades and discounts and rewards the accumulation of assets under its management. The pay system was developed in direct response to new products like the firm's Cash Management Account because the old system wasn't adequate to reward performance in new and growing areas management wanted to stress.

Commissions and bonuses for sales personnel are standard practice in most industries, of course. What seem to be changing are the amounts people can earn (for example, more than double one's salary at General Electric Medical Systems' Sales and Service Division), the number of people who can earn them, and the variety of productivity bonuses, especially in highly competitive new industries.

PSICOR is a small Michigan company supplying equipment and professionals (called perfusionists) for open-heart surgery. Perfusionists are in great demand and frequently change employers, so founder Michael Dunaway searched for a way to give them immediate rewards because the standard 10% increase at the end of the year was too remote.

First he tried random bonuses of $100 to $500 for superior performance, but tracking proved difficult. Then in 1982 he hit on the idea of continuous raises—increases in every paycheck—calculated to add up to at least a 5% annual raise over base salary, with up to 8% more in a lump sum at year-end based on overall performance. Employee response was positive, but the accounting department was soon drowning in paperwork.

PSICOR's latest system combines quarterly raises of up to 5% a year, based solely on performance, with a series of additional bonuses to reward specific activities: higher caseloads, out-of-town assignments, professional certification, and the like. Turnover is less than 2% and drops to less than ½% for those employed two years or more.

Of course, some companies are going in exactly the opposite direction—for seemingly good reason. As an ex-director of sales compensation for IBM confessed, "We used to give bonuses and awards for every imaginable action by the sales force. But the more complex it got, the more difficult it was to administer, and the results were not convincing. When we began to ask ourselves why Digital Equipment had salespeople, who are tough competitors, on straight salary, we decided perhaps we'd gone overboard a bit."

Even in commercial real estate leasing, long a highly performance-oriented business, one major and very effective Boston company—Leggat, McCall & Werner, Inc.—has for years had its brokers on salary.

Nevertheless, the tide is moving in the other direction—toward more varied individual compensation based on people's own efforts. This trend reaches its fullest expression, however, not in pay-for-performance systems like those just described but in the scramble to devise ways to reward people in organizations for acting as if they were running their own businesses.

A Piece of the Action

The prospect of running a part of a large corporation as though it were an independent business is one of the hottest old-ideas-refurbished in American industry. Many companies are encouraging potential entrepreneurs to remain within the corporate fold by paying them like owners when they develop new businesses. And even very traditional organizations are looking carefully at the possibility of setting up new ventures with a piece of the action for the entrepreneurs. "If one of our employees came along with a proposition, I'm not sure how anxious we'd be to do it," one bank executive said. "But ten years ago, we wouldn't have listened at all. We'd have said, 'You've got rocks in your head.' "

Most of the new entrepreneurial schemes pay people base salaries, generally equivalent to those of their former job levels, and ask them to put part of their compensation at risk, with their ownership percentage determined by their willingness to invest. This investment then substitutes for any other bonuses, perks, profit sharing, or special incentives they might have been able to earn in their former jobs. Sometimes the returns are based solely on percentages of the profits from their ventures; sometimes the returns come in the form of phantom stock pegged to the companies' public stock prices. Potential entrepreneurs cannot get as rich under this system as they could if they were full owners of independent businesses who shared ownership with other venture capitalists. But they are also taking much less risk.

AT&T's new venture development process, begun just before divestiture, illustrates how large corporations are trying to capture entrepreneurship. Currently seven venture units are in operation, each sponsored by one of AT&T's lines of business. One started in 1983, three in 1984, and three more in 1985. The largest is now up to 90 employees.

William P. Stritzler, the AT&T executive responsible for overseeing this process, offers venture participants three compensation alternatives corresponding to three levels of risk.

Option one allows venture participants to stick with the standard corporate compensation and benefits plan and to keep the salaries associated with their previous jobs. Not surprisingly, none of the seven has chosen this option.

Under option two, participants agree to freeze their salaries at the levels of their last jobs and to forgo other contingent compensation until the venture begins to generate a positive cash flow and the AT&T investment is paid back (or, with the concurrence of the venture board, until the business passes certain milestones). At that point, venture participants can get one-time bonuses equal to a maximum of 150% of their salaries. Five of the seven venture teams have selected this option.

The third option, chosen by two self-confident bands of risk takers, comes closest to simulating the independent entrepreneur's situation. Participants can contribute to the venture's capitalization through paycheck deductions until the venture begins to make money and generate a positive cash flow. Investments are limited only by the requirement that salaries remain above the minimum wage—to avoid legal problems and prevent people from using personal funds. In exchange, participants can gain up to eight times their total investment.

To date, participants have put in from 12% to 25% of their salaries, and one of the two ventures has already paid several bonuses at a rate just below the maximum. The other, a computer-graphics-board venture housed outside Indianapolis, could return $890,000 to its 11 employee-investors in the near future.

The numbers show just how attractive AT&T employees find this program: ideas for new ventures began coming in before the program was announced, and in the planning year alone, 300 potential entrepreneurs developed proposals. Perhaps 2,000 ideas have been offered since, netting a venture formation rate of about 1 from every 250 ideas. People from every management level have been funded, including a first-line supervisor and a fifth-level manager (at AT&T, roughly equivalent to those just below officer rank), and in principle, management is even willing to offer this option to nonmanagers.

Entrepreneurial incentives are especially prevalent at high-technology companies—not surprising, given the importance and mobility of innovators. For example, a 1983 random sample of 105 Boston-area companies employing scientists and engineers compared the high-tech enterprises, dependent on R&D for product development, with their more traditional, established counterparts. The high-tech companies paid lower base salaries on average but offered more financial incentives, such as cash bonuses, stock options, and profit-sharing plans.[3]

The entrepreneurial paycheck is on the rise wherever management thinks that people could do as well or better if they were in business for themselves—in high tech and no-tech alike. Au Bon Pain, a Boston-based chain of bakeries and restaurants, with $30 million in revenue from 40 stores nationwide, is launching a partnership program that will turn over a big piece of the action to store managers. Under the plan, annual revenues exceeding $170,000 per store will be shared fifty-fifty with the partners.

If business developers and revenue growers are getting a chance to share in the returns, will inventors in the same companies be far behind? Probably not. The inventors' rights challenge is another nudge in the direction of entrepreneurial rewards.

Traditional practice has rewarded salaried inventors with small bonuses (often $500 to $1,000) for each patent received and some nonmonetary incentives to encourage their next inventions. Recognition ranges from special awards and promotion to master status entailing the use of special laboratories, freedom of project choice, sabbaticals, and the like. Cash awards are often given, but they are generally not tied to product returns. For outstanding innovation, IBM, for example, offers awards (which can be $10,000 or more) and invention achievement ($2,400 and up).

Increasingly, however, we are seeing strong competitive and legal pressures to reward employed inventors as if they were entrepreneurs by tying their compensation to the market value of their output. They too want a piece of the action and a direct return on their contributions.

The Challenge to Hierarchy

If pay practices continue to move toward contribution as the basis for earnings, as I believe they will, the change will unleash a set of forces that could transform work relationships as we know them now. To illustrate, let's look at what happens when organizations take modest steps to make pay more entrepreneurial.

In 1981, the city of Long Beach, California, established a pay-for-performance system for its management as part of a new budgeting process designed to upgrade the city government's performance against quantifiable fiscal and service delivery targets. Under the new system, managers can gain or lose up to 20% of their base salaries, so the pay of two managers at the same level can vary by up to $40,000. Job category and position in the hierarchy are far weaker determinants of earnings. In fact, at least two people are now paid more than the city manager.

While the impact of a system like this on productivity and entrepreneurship is noticeable, its effect on work relationships is more subtle. People don't wear their paychecks over their name badges in the office, after all. But word does get around, and some organizations are having to face the problem of envy head-on. In two different companies with new-venture units that offer equity participation, the units are being attacked as unfair and poorly conceived. The attackers are aggrieved that venture participants can earn so much money for seemingly modest or even trivial contributions to the corporation overall, while those who keep the mainstream businesses going must accept salary ceilings and insignificant bonuses.

In companies that establish new-enterprise units, this clash between two different systems is self-inflicted. But sometimes the
conflict comes as an unwelcome by-product of a company's efforts
to expand into new businesses via acquisition. On buying a brokerage firm, a leading bank found that it had also acquired a very
different compensation system: a generous commission arrangement means that employees often earn twice their salary in bonuses
and, once in a while, five times. In 1985, six people made as much
in salary and commissions as the chairman did in his base salary,
or roughly $500,000 each. These people all made much more than
their managers and their managers' managers and virtually everyone else in the corporation except the top three or four officers, a
situation that would have been impossible a few years ago.

Now such discrepancies cannot be prevented or kept quiet. "People in the trade know perfectly well what's happening," the bank's
senior administration executive told me. "They know the formula,
they see the proxy statements, and they are busy checking out the
systems by which we and everybody else compensate these people."

To avoid the equivalent of an employee run on the bank—with
everyone trying to transfer to the brokerage operation—the corporation has felt forced to establish performance bonuses for branch
managers and some piece-rate systems for clerical workers, though
these are not nearly as generous as the managers' extra earning
opportunities.

This system, though it solves some problems, creates others. The
executive responsible recognizes that although these new income-
earning opportunities are pegged to individual performance, people
do not work in isolation. Branch managers' results really depend
on how well their employees perform, and so do the results of nearly
everyone else except those in sales (and even there a team effort
can make a difference). Yet, instead of teamwork, the bank's practices may encourage competition, the hoarding of good leads, and
the withholding of good ideas until one person can claim the credit.
"We talk about teamwork at training sessions," this executive said,
"and then we destroy it in the compensation system."

Team-based pay raises its own questions, however, and generates
its own set of prickly issues. There is the "free rider" problem, in
which a few nonperforming members of the group benefit from the
actions of the productive members. And problems can arise when
people resent being dependent on team members, especially those
with very different organizational status.

There are also pressure problems. Gain-sharing plans, in particular, can create very high peer pressure to do well, since the pay of all depends on everyone's efforts. Theodore Cohn, a compensation expert, likes to talk about the Dutch company, Philips, in which twice-yearly bonuses can run up to 40% of base pay. "Managers say that a paper clip never hits the floor—a hand will be there to catch it," Cohn recounts. "If a husband dies, the wake is at night so that no one misses work. If someone goes on vacation, somebody else is shown how to do the job. There is practically no turnover."

Similarly, Cohn claims that at Lincoln Electric, where performance-related pay is twice the average factory wage, peer pressure can be so high that the first two years of employment are called purgatory.[4]

Another kind of pressure also emerges from equity-ownership and profit-sharing systems—the pressure to open the books, to disclose managerial salaries, and to justify pay differentials. Concerns like these bubble up when employees who may never have thought much about other people's pay suddenly realize that "their" money is at stake.

These concerns and questions of distributional equity are all part of making the system more fair as well as more effective. Perhaps the biggest issue, and the one most disturbing to traditionalists, is what happens to the chain of command when it does not match the progression of pay. If subordinates can out-earn their bosses, hierarchy begins to crumble.

Social psychologists have shown that authority relationships depend on a degree of inequality. If the distance between boss and subordinate declines, so does automatic deference and respect. The key word here is *automatic*. Superiors can still gain respect through their competence and fair treatment of subordinates. But power shifts as relationships become more equal.

Once the measures of good performance are both clearly established and clearly achieved, a subordinate no longer needs the goodwill of the boss quite so much. Proven achievement reflected in earnings higher than the boss's produces security, which produces risk taking, which produces speaking up and pushing back. As a result, the relationship between boss and subordinate changes from one based on authority to one based on mutual respect.

This change has positive implications for superiors as well as subordinates. For example, if a subordinate can earn more than the boss and still stay in place, then one of the incentives to compete for the boss's job is removed. Gone, too, is the tension that can build when an ambitious subordinate covets the boss's job and will do anything to get it. In short, if some of the *authority* of hierarchy is eliminated, so is some of the *hostility*.

In most traditional organizations, however, the idea of earning more than the boss seems insupportable and, to some people, clearly inequitable. There are, of course, organizational precedents for situations in which people in lower-ranked jobs are paid more than those above. Field sales personnel paid on commission can often earn more than their managers; star scientists in R&D laboratories may earn more than the administrators nominally placed over them; and hourly workers can make more than their supervisors through overtime pay or union-negotiated wage settlements. But these situations are usually uncommon, or they're accepted because they're part of a dual-career ladder or the price of moving up in rank into management.

To get a feeling for the kinds of difficulties pay imbalances can create in hierarchical organizations, let's look at a less extreme case in which the gap between adjacent pay levels diminishes but does not disappear. This is called pay compression, and it bothers executives who believe in maintaining hierarchy.

In response to an American Management Association survey of 613 organizations, of which 134 were corporations with more than $1 billion in sales, 76% reported problems with compression.[5] Yet only a few percentage points divide the organizations expressing concern from those that do not. For example, the average earnings difference between first-line production supervisors and the highest-paid production workers was 15.5% for organizations reporting compression problems, and only a little higher, 20%, for those not reporting such problems. In the maintenance area, the difference was even less—a 15.1% average earnings difference for those who said they had a problem versus 18.2% for those who said they did not. Furthermore, for a large number of companies claiming a compression problem, the difference between levels is actually greater than their official guidelines stipulate.

What is most striking to me, however, is how great the gap between adjacent levels still is—at least 15% difference in pay. Indeed, it is hard to avoid the conclusion that the executives concerned about compression are responding not to actual problems but to a perceived threat and the fear that hierarchy will crumble because of new pay practices.

What organizations say they will and won't do to solve compression problems supports this interpretation. While 67.4% of those concerned agree that an instant-bonus program would help, 70.1% say their companies would never institute one. And while 47.9% say that profit sharing for all salaried supervisors would help, 64.7% say that their companies would never do that either. In fact, the solutions least likely to be acceptable were precisely those that would change the hierarchy most—for example, reducing the number of job classifications, establishing fewer wage levels, and granting overtime compensation for supervisors (in effect, equalizing their status with that of hourly workers). On the other hand, the most favored solutions involved aids to upward mobility like training and rapid advancement that would keep the *structure* of the hierarchy intact while helping individuals move within it.

Innovative Thoughts

The attacks on pay I've identified all push in the same direction. Indeed, they overlap and reinforce each other as, for example, a decision to reward individual contributors makes otherwise latent concerns about equity much more visible and live. Without options, private concerns can look like utopian dreams. Once those dreams begin to appear plausible, however, what was "the way things have to be" becomes instead a deliberate withholding of fair treatment.

By creating new forms for identifying, recognizing, and ultimately permitting contributions, the attack on pay goes beyond pay to color relationships throughout an organization. In the process, the iron cage of bureaucracy is being rattled in ways that will eventually change the nature, and the meaning, of hierarchy in ways we cannot yet imagine.

Wise executives, however, can prepare themselves and their companies for the revolutionary changes ahead. The shift toward contribution-based pay makes sense on grounds of equity, cost, productivity, and enterprise. And there are ways to manage that shift effectively. Here are some options to consider:

Think strategically and systematically about the organizational implications of every change in compensation practices. If a venture unit offers an equity stake to participants, should a performance-based bonus with similar earning potential be offered to managers of mainstream businesses? If gain sharing is implemented on the shop floor, should it be extended to white-collar groups?

Move toward reducing the fixed portion of pay and increasing the variable portion. Give business unit managers more discretion in distributing the variable pool, and make it a larger, more meaningful amount. Or allow more people to invest a portion of their salary in return for a greater share of the proceeds attributed to their own efforts later on.

Manage the jealousy and conflict inherent in the more widely variable pay of nominal peers by making standards clear, giving everyone similar opportunities for growth in earnings, and reserving a portion of the earnings of stars or star sectors for distribution to others who have played a role in the success. Balance individual and group incentives in ways appropriate to the work unit and its tasks.

Analyze—and, if necessary, rethink—the relationship between pay and value to the organization. Keep in mind that organizational levels defined for purposes of coordination do not necessarily reflect contributions to performance goals, and decouple pay from status or rank. And finally, be prepared to justify pay decisions in terms of clear contributions—and to offer these justifications more often, to more stakeholder groups.

Notes

1. Martin L. Weitzman, *The Share Economy: Conquering Stagflation* (Cambridge, Mass.: Harvard University Press, 1984).
2. Michael Quarrey, Joseph Blasi, and Corey Rosen, *Taking Stock: Employee Ownership at Work* (Cambridge, Mass.: Ballinger, 1986).
3. Jay R. Schuster, *Management Compensation in High Technology Companies: Assuring Corporate Excellence* (Lexington, Mass.: Lexington Books, 1984).
4. Theodore H. Cohn, "Incentive Compensation in Smaller Companies," *Proceedings of the Annual Conference of the American Compensation Association* (Scottsdale, Ariz.: ACA, 1984), pp. 1–7.
5. James W. Steele, *Paying for Performance and Position* (New York: AMA Membership Publishing Division, 1982).

PART
II
Performance Appraisal

1
An Uneasy Look at
Performance Appraisal

Douglas McGregor

Performance appraisal within management ranks has become standard practice in many companies during the past 20 years and is currently being adopted by many others, often as an important feature of management development programs. The more the method is used, the more uneasy I grow over the unstated assumptions that lie behind it. Moreover, with some searching, I find that a number of people both in education and in industry share my misgivings. This article, therefore, has two purposes:

1. To examine the conventional performance appraisal plan, which requires the manager to pass judgment on the personal worth of subordinates.
2. To describe an alternative that places on the subordinate the primary responsibility for establishing performance goals and appraising progress toward them.

Current Programs

Formal performance appraisal plans are designed to meet three needs, one for the organization and two for the individual:

1. They provide systematic judgments to back up salary increases, promotions, transfers, and sometimes demotions or terminations.

First published in the May–June 1957 issue. Republished as HBR Classic September–October 1972.

2. They are a means of telling a subordinate how he or she is doing, and suggesting needed changes in behavior, attitudes, skills, or job knowledge; they let the subordinate know "where he or she stands" with the boss.
3. They also are being increasingly used as a basis for the coaching and counseling of the individual by the superior.

PROBLEM OF RESISTANCE

Personnel administrators are aware that appraisal programs tend to run into resistance from the managers who are expected to administer them. Even managers who admit the necessity of such programs frequently balk at the process—especially the interview part. As a result, some companies do not communicate appraisal results to the individual, despite the general conviction that subordinates have a right to know their superior's opinion so they can correct weaknesses.

The boss's resistance is usually attributed to the following causes:

A normal dislike of criticizing a subordinate (and perhaps having to argue about the criticism).

Lack of skill needed to handle the interviews.

Dislike of a new procedure, with its accompanying changes in ways of operating.

Mistrust of the validity of the appraisal instrument.

To meet this problem, formal controls—scheduling, reminders, and so on—are often instituted. It is common experience that without them fewer than half the appraisal interviews are actually held. But even controls do not necessarily work.

Thus, in one company with a well-planned and carefully administered appraisal program, an opinion poll included two questions regarding appraisals. More than 90% of those answering the questionnaire approved the idea of appraisals. They wanted to know how they stood. Some 40% went on to say that they had never had the experience of being told—yet the files showed that over four-fifths of them had signed a form testifying that they had been through an appraisal interview, some of them several times!

The respondents had no reason to lie, nor was there the slightest supposition that their superiors had committed forgery. The probable explanation is that the superiors, being basically resistant to the plan, had conducted the interviews in such a perfunctory manner that many subordinates did not realize what was going on.

Training programs designed to teach the skills of appraising and interviewing do help, but they seldom eliminate managerial resistance entirely. The difficulties connected with "negative appraisals" remain a source of genuine concern. There is always some discomfort involved in telling a subordinate he or she is not doing well. The individual who is "coasting" during the few years prior to retirement after serving the company competently for many years presents a special dilemma to the boss who is preparing for an interview.

Nor does a shift to a form of group appraisal solve the problem. Though the group method tends to have greater validity and, properly administered, can equalize varying standards of judgment, it does not ease the difficulty inherent in the interview. In fact, the superior's discomfort is often intensified when he or she must base the interview on the results of a *group* discussion of the subordinate's worth. Supervisors may make the final judgments, but they are not free to discuss the comments of others that have influenced them.

THE UNDERLYING CAUSE

What should we think about a method—however valuable for meeting organizational needs—that produces such results in a wide range of companies with a variety of appraisal plans? The problem is one that cannot be dismissed lightly.

Perhaps this intuitive managerial reaction to conventional performance appraisal plans shows a deep but unrecognized wisdom. In my view, it does not reflect anything so simple as resistance to change, or dislike for personnel technique, or lack of skill, or mistrust for rating scales. Rather, managers seem to be expressing real misgivings, which they find difficult to put into words.

This could be the underlying cause: the conventional approach, unless handled with consummate skill and delicacy, constitutes something dangerously close to a violation of the integrity of the personality. Managers are uncomfortable when they are put in the position of "playing God." The respect we hold for the inherent value of the individual leaves us distressed when we must take responsibility for judging the personal worth of another person. Yet the conventional approach to performance appraisal forces us not only to make such judgments and to see them acted upon but also to communicate them to those we have judged. Small wonder we resist!

The modern emphasis upon the manager as a leader who strives to *help* subordinates achieve both their own and the company's objectives is hardly consistent with the judicial role demanded by most appraisal plans. If the manager must put on a judicial hat occasionally, he or she does it reluctantly and with understandable qualms. Under such conditions, it is unlikely that subordinates will be any happier with the results than will the boss. It will not be surprising, either, if they fail to recognize that they have been told where they stand.

Of course, managers cannot escape making judgments about subordinates. Without such evaluations, salary and promotion policies cannot be administered sensibly. But are subordinates like products on an assembly line, to be accepted or rejected as a result of an inspection process? The inspection process may be made more objective or more accurate through research on the appraisal instrument, through training of the "inspectors," or through introducing group appraisal; subordinates may be "reworked" by coaching or counseling before the final decision to accept or reject them; but as far as the assumptions of the conventional appraisal process are concerned, we still have what is practically identical with a program for product inspection.

On this interpretation, then, resistance to conventional appraisal programs is eminently sound. It reflects an unwillingness to treat human beings like physical objects. The needs of the organization are obviously important, but when they come into conflict with our convictions about the worth and the dignity of the human personality, one or the other must give.

Indeed, by the fact of their resistance managers are saying that the organization must yield in the face of this fundamental human value. And they are thus being more sensitive than are personnel administrators and social scientists whose business it is to be concerned with the human problems of industry!

A New Approach

If this analysis is correct, the task before us is clear. We must find a new plan—not a compromise to hide the dilemma, but a bold move to resolve the issue.

A number of writers are beginning to approach the whole subject of management from the point of view of basic social values. Peter Drucker's concept of "management by objectives"[1] offers an unusually promising framework within which we can seek a solution. Several companies, notably General Mills, Incorporated, and General Electric Company, have been exploring different methods of appraisal, which rest upon assumptions consistent with Drucker's philosophy.

RESPONSIBILITY ON SUBORDINATE

This approach calls on subordinates to establish short-term performance goals *for themselves*. The superior enters the process actively only *after* subordinates have (a) done a good deal of thinking about their jobs, (b) made a careful assessment of their own strengths and weaknesses, and (c) formulated some specific plans to accomplish their goals. The superior's role is to help employees relate their self-appraisal, their "targets," and their plans for the ensuing period to the realities of the organization.

The first step in this process is to arrive at a clear statement of the major features of the job. Rather than a formal job description, this is a document drawn up *by the subordinate* after studying the company-approved statement. It defines the broad areas of responsibility as they actually work out in practice. The boss and employee discuss the draft jointly and modify it as may be necessary until both of them agree that it is adequate.

Working from this statement of responsibilities, the subordinate then establishes personal goals or "targets" for a period of, say, six months. These targets are *specific* actions to take: e.g., setting up regular staff meetings to improve communication, reorganizing the office, completing or undertaking a certain study. Thus they are explicitly stated and accompanied by a detailed account of the actions he or she proposes to take to reach them. This document is, in turn, discussed with the superior and modified until both are satisfied with it.

At the conclusion of the six-month period, subordinates make *their own* appraisal of what they have accomplished relative to the targets they set earlier. They substantiate it with factual data wherever possible. The "interview" is an examination by superior and subordinate together of the subordinate's self-appraisal, and it culminates in a resetting of targets for the next six months.

Of course, the superior has veto power at each step of this process; in an organizational hierarchy anything else would be unacceptable. However, in practice he or she rarely needs to exercise it. Most subordinates tend to underestimate both their potentialities and their achievements. Moreover, subordinates normally have an understandable wish to satisfy their boss, and are quite willing to adjust their targets or appraisals if the superior feels they are unrealistic. Actually, a much more common problem is to resist the subordinates' tendency to want the boss to tell them what to write down.

ANALYSIS VERSUS APPRAISAL

This approach to performance appraisal differs profoundly from the conventional one, for it shifts the emphasis from *appraisal* to *analysis*. This implies a more positive approach. No longer are subordinates being examined by the superior so that their weaknesses may be determined; rather, they are examining themselves, in order to define not only weaknesses but also strengths and potentials. The importance of this shift of emphasis should not be underestimated. It is basic to each of the specific differences that distinguish this approach from the conventional one.

The first of these differences arises from the subordinate's new role in the process as an active agent, not a passive "object." The subordinate is no longer a pawn in a chess game called management development.

Effective development of managers does not include coercing them (no matter how benevolently) into acceptance of the goals of the enterprise, nor does it mean manipulating their behavior to suit organizational needs. Rather, it calls for creating a relationship within which employees can take responsibility for developing their own potentialities, plan for themselves, and learn from putting their plans into action. In the process, they can gain a genuine sense of satisfaction, for they are utilizing their own capabilities to achieve simultaneously both their objectives and those of the organization. Unless this is the nature of the relationship, "development" becomes a euphemism.

WHO KNOWS BEST?

One of the main differences of this approach is that it rests on the assumption that the individual knows—or can learn—more than anyone else about his or her own capabilities, needs, strengths and weaknesses, and goals. In the end, only the individuals themselves can determine what is best for their development. The conventional approach, on the other hand, makes the assumption that the superior can know enough about subordinates to decide what is best for them.

No available methods can provide the superior with the knowledge needed to make such decisions. Ratings, aptitude and personality tests, and the superior's necessarily limited knowledge of the employee's performance yield at best an imperfect picture. Even the most extensive psychological counseling (assuming the superior possesses the competence for it) would not solve the problem because the product of counseling is self-insight on the part of the *counselee.*

(Psychological tests are not being condemned by this statement. On the contrary, they have genuine value in competent hands. Their use by professionals as part of the process of screening applicants for employment does not raise the same questions as their use to "diagnose" the personal worth of accepted members of a management team. Even in the latter instance, the problem under discussion would not arise if test results and interpretations were given *to the individuals themselves,* to be shared with superiors at their discretion.)

The proper role for superiors, then, is the one that falls naturally to them under the suggested plan: helping subordinates relate their career planning to the needs and realities of the organization. In the discussions, bosses can use their knowledge of the organization to help the subordinate establish targets and methods for achieving them that will (a) lead to increased knowledge and skill, (b) contribute to organizational objectives, and (c) test the subordinates' appraisal of themselves.

This is help that subordinates want. They know well that the rewards and satisfactions they seek from their careers as a manager depend on their contribution to organizational objectives. They are also aware that the superior knows more completely than they what is required for success in this organization and *under this boss.* The superior, then, is the person who can help them test the soundness of their goals and their plans for achieving them. Quite clearly the knowledge and active participation of *both* superior and subordinate are necessary components of this approach.

If superiors accept this role, they need not become a judge of the subordinate's personal worth. They are not telling, deciding, criticizing, or praising—not "playing God." They find themselves listening, using their own knowledge of the organization as a basis for advising, guiding, encouraging subordinates to develop their own potentialities. Incidentally, this often leads superiors themselves to important insights about themselves and their impact on others.

LOOKING TO THE FUTURE

Another significant difference is that the emphasis is on the future rather than the past. The purpose of the plan is to establish realistic targets and to seek the most effective ways of reaching them. Appraisal thus becomes a means to a *constructive* end. The 60-year-old "coaster" can be encouraged to set performance goals and to make a fair appraisal of his or her progress toward them. Even subordinates who have failed can be helped to consider what moves will be best for themselves. The superior rarely faces the uncomfortable prospect of denying a subordinate's personal worth. A transfer or even a demotion can be worked out without the connotation of a "sentence by the judge."

PERFORMANCE VERSUS PERSONALITY

Finally, the accent is on *performance*, on actions relative to goals. There is less tendency for the personality of the subordinate to become an issue. Superiors, instead of finding themselves in the position of a psychologist or a therapist, can become a coach helping the subordinates reach their own decisions on the specific steps that will enable them to reach their targets. Such counseling as may be required demands no deep analysis of the personal motivations or basic adjustment of the subordinate.

To illustrate: consider a subordinate who is hostile, short-tempered, uncooperative, insecure. The superior need not make any psychological diagnosis. The "target-setting" approach naturally directs the subordinate's attention to ways and means of obtaining better interdepartmental collaboration, reducing complaints, winning the confidence of the people under him or her. Rather than facing the troublesome prospect of forcing his or her own psychological diagnosis on the subordinate, the superior can, for example, help the individual plan ways of getting feedback concerning his or her impact on associates and subordinates as a basis for self-appraisal and self-improvement.

There is little chance that individuals involved in a process like this will be in the dark about where they stand, or that they will forget they are the principal participant in their own development and responsible for it.

A New Attitude

As a consequence of these differences we may expect the growth of a different attitude toward appraisal on the part of superior and subordinate alike.

Superiors will gain real satisfaction as they learn to help subordinates integrate their personal goals with the needs of the organization so that both are served. Once the subordinate has worked out a mutually satisfactory plan of action, the superior can delegate to him or her the responsibility for putting it into effect. The manager will see him- or herself in a consistent managerial role rather than being forced to adopt the basically incompatible role of either the judge or the psychologist.

Unless there is a basic personal antagonism between the two people (in which case the relationship should be terminated), the superior can conduct these interviews so that both are actively involved in seeking the right basis for constructive action. The organization, the boss, and the subordinate all stand to gain. Under such circumstances the opportunities for learning and for genuine development of both parties are maximal.

The particular mechanics are of secondary importance. The needs of the organization in the administration of salary and promotion policies can easily be met within the framework of the analysis process. The machinery of the program can be adjusted to the situation. No universal list of rating categories is required. The complications of subjective or prejudiced judgment, of varying standards, of attempts to quantify qualitative data, all can be minimized. In fact, *no* formal machinery is required.

PROBLEMS OF JUDGMENT

I have deliberately slighted the many problems of judgment involved in administering promotions and salaries. These are by no means minor, and this approach will not automatically solve them. However, I believe that if we are prepared to recognize the fundamental problem inherent in the conventional approach, ways can be found to temper our present administrative methods.

And if this approach is accepted, the traditional ingenuity of management will lead to the invention of a variety of methods for its implementation. The mechanics of some conventional plans can be adjusted to be consistent with this point of view. Obviously, a program utilizing ratings of the personal characteristics of subordinates would not be suitable, but one that emphasizes *behavior* might be.

Of course, managerial skill is required. No method will eliminate that. This method can fail as readily as any other in the clumsy hands of insensitive or indifferent or power-seeking managers. But even the limited experience of a few companies with this approach indicates that managerial *resistance* is substantially reduced. As a consequence, it is easier to gain the collaboration of managers in developing the necessary skills.

COST IN TIME

There is one unavoidable cost: the manager must spend considerably more time in implementing a program of this kind. It is not unusual to take a couple of days to work through the initial establishment of responsibilities and goals with each individual. And a periodic appraisal may require several hours rather than the typical 20 minutes.

Reaction to this cost will undoubtedly vary. The management that considers the development of its human resources to be the primary means of achieving the economic objectives of the organization will not be disturbed. It will regard the necessary guidance and coaching as among the most important functions of every superior.

Conclusion

I have sought to show that the conventional approach to performance appraisal stands condemned as a personnel method. It places the manager in the untenable position of judging the personal worth of subordinates, and of acting on these judgments. No manager possesses, or could acquire, the skill necessary to carry out this responsibility effectively. Few would even be willing to accept it if they were fully aware of the implications involved.

It is this unrecognized aspect of conventional appraisal programs that produces the widespread uneasiness and even open resistance of management to appraisals and especially to the appraisal interview.

A sounder approach, which places the major responsibility on the subordinate for establishing performance goals and appraising progress toward them, avoids the major weaknesses of the old plan and benefits the organization by stimulating the development of the subordinate. It is true that more managerial skill and the investment of a considerable amount of time are required, but the greater motivation and the more effective development of subordinates can justify these added costs.

Note

1. See Peter Drucker, *The Practice of Management* (New York: Harper & Brothers, 1954).

2
Split Roles in Performance Appraisal

**Herbert H. Meyer, Emanuel Kay,
and John R. P. French, Jr.**

In management circles, performance appraisal is a highly interesting and provocative topic. And in business literature, too, knowledgeable people write emphatically, pro and con, on the performance appraisal question.[1] In fact, one might almost say that everybody talks and writes about it, but nobody has done any real scientific testing of it.

At the General Electric Company we felt it was important that a truly scientific study be done to test the effectiveness of our traditional performance appraisal program. Why? Simply because our own experience with performance appraisal programs had been both positive and negative. For example:

> Surveys generally show that most people think the idea of performance appraisal is good. They feel that a man should know where he stands and, therefore, the manager should discuss an appraisal of his performance with him periodically.

> In actual practice, however, it is the extremely rare operating manager who will employ such a program on his own initiative. Personnel specialists report that most managers carry out performance appraisal interviews only when strong control procedures are established to ensure that they do so. This is surprising because the managers have been told repeatedly that the system is intended to help them obtain improved performance from their subordinates.

We also found from interviews with employees who have had a good deal of experience with traditional performance appraisal programs that few indeed can cite examples of constructive action taken—or significant improvement achieved—that stem from suggestions received in a performance appraisal interview with their boss.

Traditional Program

Faced with such contradictory evidence, we undertook a study several years ago to determine the effectiveness of our comprehensive performance appraisal process. Special attention was focused on the interview between the subordinate and his manager, because this is the discussion that is supposed to motivate the man to improve his performance. And we found out some very interesting things—among them the following:

Criticism has a negative effect on achievement of goals.

Praise has little effect one way or the other.

Performance improves most when specific goals are established.

Defensiveness resulting from critical appraisal produces inferior performance.

Coaching should be a day-to-day, not a once-a-year, activity.

Mutual goal setting, not criticism, improves performance.

Interviews designed primarily to improve a man's performance should not at the same time weigh his salary or promotion in the balance.

Participation by the employee in the goal-setting procedure helps produce favorable results.

As you can see, the results of this original study indicated that a detailed and comprehensive annual appraisal of a subordinate's performance by his manager is decidedly of questionable value. Furthermore, as is certainly the case when the major objective of such a discussion is to motivate the subordinate to improve his performance, the traditional appraisal interview does not do the job.

In the first part of this article, we will offer readers more than this bird's-eye view of our research into performance appraisal. (We will not, however, burden managers with details of methodology.) We will also describe the one-year follow-up experiment General Electric conducted to validate the conclusions derived from our original study. Here the traditional annual performance appraisal method was tested against a new method we developed, which we called Work Planning and Review (WP&R). As you will see, this approach produced, under actual plant conditions, results that were decidedly superior to those afforded by the traditional performance appraisal method. Finally, we will offer evidence to support our contention that some form of WP&R might well be incorporated into other industrial personnel programs to achieve improvement in work performance.

Appraising Appraisal

In order to assure a fair test of the effectiveness of the traditional performance appraisal method, which had been widely used throughout General Electric, we conducted an intensive study of the process at a large GE plant where the performance appraisal program was judged to be good; that is, in this plant

Appraisals had been based on job responsibilities, rather than on personal characteristics of the individuals involved.

An intensive training program had been carried out for managers in the use of the traditional appraisal method and techniques for conducting appraisal interviews.

The program had been given strong backing by the plant manager and had been policed diligently by the personnel staff so that over 90% of the exempt employees had been appraised and interviewed annually.

This comprehensive annual performance appraisal program, as is typical, was designed to serve two major purposes. The first was to justify recommended salary action. The second, which was motivational in character, was intended to present an opportunity for the manager to review a subordinate's performance and promote discussion on needed improvements. For the latter purpose, the manager was required to draw up a specific program of plans and goals for the subordinate that would help him to improve his job performance and to qualify, hopefully, for future promotion.

INTERVIEW MODIFICATIONS

Preliminary interviews with key managers and subordinates revealed the salary action issue had so dominated the annual comprehensive performance appraisal interview that neither party had been in the right frame of mind to discuss plans for improved performance. To straighten this out, we asked managers to split the traditional appraisal interview into two sessions—discussing appraisal of performance and salary action in one interview and performance improvement plans in another to be held about two weeks later. This split provided us with a better opportunity to conduct our experiment on the effects of participation in goal planning.

To enable us to test the effects of participation, we instructed half the managers to use a *high participation* approach and the other half to use a *low participation* technique.

Thus, each of the "high" managers was instructed to ask his appraisee to prepare a set of goals for achieving improved job performance and to submit them for the manager's review and approval. The manager also was encouraged to permit the subordinate to exert as much influence as possible on the formulation of the final list of job goals agreed on in the performance improvement discussion.

The "low" managers operated in much the same way they had in our traditional appraisal program. They formulated a set of goals for the subordinate, and these goals were then reviewed in the performance improvement session. The manager was instructed to conduct this interview in such a way that his influence in the forming of the final list of job goals would be greater than the subordinate's.

CONDUCTING THE RESEARCH

There were 92 appraisees in the experimental group, representing a cross section of the exempt salaried employees in the plant. This group included engineers; engineering support technicians; foremen; and specialists in manufacturing, customer service, marketing, finance, and purchasing functions. None of the exempt men who participated as appraisees in the experiment had other exempt persons reporting to them; thus they did not serve in conflicting manager-subordinate roles.

The entire group was interviewed and asked to complete questionnaires (a) before and after the salary action interview, and (b) after the delayed second discussion with their managers about performance improvement. These interviews and questionnaires were designed to achieve three objectives:

1. Assess changes in the attitudes of individuals toward their managers and toward the appraisal system after each of the discussions.
2. Get an estimate from the appraisee of the degree to which he usually participated in decisions that affected him. (This was done in order to determine whether or not previous lack of participation affected his response to participation in the experiment.)
3. Obtain a self-appraisal from each subordinate before and after he met with his manager. (This was done in order to determine how discrepancies in these self-appraisals might affect his reaction to the appraisal interview.)

Moreover, each salary action and performance improvement discussion was observed by outsiders trained to record essentially what transpired. (Managers preferred to use neither tape recorders nor unseen observers, feeling that observers unaffiliated with the company—in this case, graduate students in applied psychological disciplines—afforded the best way of obtaining a reasonably close approximation of the normal discussions.) In the appraisal for salary action interviews, for example, the observers recorded the amount of criticism and praise employed by the manager, as well as the reactions of the appraisee to the manager's comments. In the performance improvement discussions, the observers recorded the participation of the subordinate, as well as the amount of influence he seemed to exert in establishing his future success goals.

CRITICISM AND DEFENSIVENESS

In general, the managers completed the performance appraisal forms in a thorough and conscientious manner. Their appraisals were discussed with subordinates in interviews ranging from approximately 30 to 90 minutes in length. On the average, managers covered 32 specific performance items that, when broken down, showed positive (praise) appraisals on 19 items, and negative (criticism) on 13. Typically, praise was more often related to *general* performance characteristics, while criticism was usually focused on *specific* performance items.

The average subordinate reacted defensively to 7 of the manager's criticisms during the appraisal interview (that is, he reacted defensively about 54% of the time when criticized). Denial of shortcomings cited by the manager, blaming others, and various other forms of excuse were recorded by the observers as defensive reactions.

Constructive responses to criticism were *rarely* observed. In fact, the average was less than one per interview. Not too surprising, along with this, was the finding that the more criticism a man received in the performance appraisal discussion, the more defensively he reacted. Men who received an above-average number of criticisms showed more than five times as much defensive behavior as those who received a below-average number of criticisms. Subordinates who received a below-average number of criticisms, for example, reacted defensively only about one time out of three. But those who received an above-average number reacted defensively almost two times out of three.

One explanation for this defensiveness is that it seems to stem from the overrating each man tended to give to his own performance. The average employee's self-estimate of performance *before* appraisal placed him at the 77th percentile. (Only 2 of the 92 participants estimated their performance to be below the average point on the scale.) But when the same men were asked *after* their performance appraisal discussions how they thought their bosses had rated them, the average figure given was at the 65th percentile. The great majority (75 out of 92) saw their manager's evaluation as being less favorable than their self-estimates. Obviously, to these men, the performance appraisal discussion with the manager was a deflating experience. Thus, it was not surprising that the subordinates reacted defensively in their interviews.

CRITICISM AND GOAL ACHIEVEMENT

Even more important is the fact that men who received an above-average number of criticisms in their performance appraisal discussions generally showed *less* goal achievement 10 to 12 weeks later than those who had received fewer criticisms. At first, we thought that this difference might be accounted for by the fact that the subordinates who received more criticisms were probably poorer performers in general. But there was little factual evidence found to support this suspicion.

It was true that those who received an above-average number of criticisms in their appraisal discussions did receive slightly lower summary ratings on overall performance from their managers. But they did not receive proportionally lower salary increases. And the salary increases granted were *supposed* to reflect differences in job performance, according to the salary plan traditionally used in this plant. This argument, admittedly, is something less than perfect.

But it does appear clear that frequent criticism constitutes so strong a threat to self-esteem that it disrupts rather than improves subsequent performance. We expected such a disruptive threat to operate more strongly on those individuals who were already low on self-esteem, just as we expected a man who had confidence in his ability to do his job to react more constructively to criticism. Our group experiment proved these expectations to be correct.

Still further evidence that criticism has a negative effect on performance was found when we investigated areas that had been given special emphasis by the manager in his criticism. Following the appraisal discussion with the manager, each employee was asked to indicate which one aspect of his performance had been most criticized by the manager. Then, when we conducted our follow-up investigation 10 to 12 weeks later, it revealed that improvement in the most-criticized aspects of performance cited was considerably *less* than improvement realized in other areas!

PARTICIPATION EFFECTS

As our original research study had indicated, the effects of a high participation level were also favorable in our group experiment. In general, here is what we found.

Subordinates who received a high participation level in the performance interview reacted more favorably than did those who received a low participation level. The "highs" also, in most cases, achieved a greater percentage of their improvement goals than did their "low" counterparts. For the former, the high participation level was associated with greater mutual understanding between them and their managers, greater acceptance of job goals, a more favorable attitude toward the appraisal system, and a feeling of greater self-realization on the job.

But employees who had traditionally been accustomed to low participation in their daily relationship with the manager did not necessarily perform better under the high-participation treatment. In fact, those men who had received a high level of criticism in their appraisal interviews actually performed better when their managers set goals for them than they did when they set their own goals, as permitted under the high-participation treatment.

In general, our experiment showed that the men who usually worked under high-participation levels performed best on goals they set for themselves. Those who indicated that they usually worked under low levels performed best on goals that the managers set for them. Evidently, the man who usually does not participate in work-planning decisions considers job goals set by the manager to be more important than goals he sets for himself. The man accustomed to a high participation level, on the other hand, may have stronger motivation to achieve goals he sets for himself than to achieve those set by his manager.

GOAL-SETTING IMPORTANCE

While subordinate participation in the goal-setting process had some effect on improved performance, a much more powerful influence was whether goals were set at all. Many times in appraisal discussions, managers mentioned areas of performance where improvement was needed. Quite often these were translated into specific work plans and goals. But this was not always the case. In fact, when we looked at the one performance area that each manager had emphasized in the appraisal interview as most in need of improvement, we found that these items actually were translated into specific work plans and goals for only about 60% of our experiment participants.

When performance was being measured 10 to 12 weeks after the goal-planning sessions, managers were asked to describe what results they hoped for in the way of subordinate on-the-job improvement. They did this for those important performance items that had been mentioned in the interview. Each manager was then asked to estimate on a percentage scale the degree to which his hoped-for changes had actually been observed. The average percent accomplishment estimate for those performance items that *did* get translated into goals was 65, while the percent estimate for those items that *did not* get translated into goals was about 27! Establishing specific plans and goals seemed to ensure that attention would be given to that aspect of job performance.

SUMMATION OF FINDINGS

At the end of this experiment, we were able to draw certain tentative conclusions. These conclusions were the basis of a future research study which we will describe later. In general, we learned that:

COMPREHENSIVE ANNUAL PERFORMANCE APPRAISALS ARE OF QUESTIONABLE VALUE. Certainly a major objective of the manager in traditional appraisal discussions is motivating the subordinate to improve his performance. But the evidence we gathered indicated clearly that praise tended to have no effect, perhaps because it was regarded as the sandwich that surrounded the raw meat of criticism.[2] And criticism itself brought on defensive reactions that were essentially denials of responsibility for a poor performance.

COACHING SHOULD BE A DAY-TO-DAY, NOT A ONCE-A-YEAR, ACTIVITY. There are two main reasons for this:

(1) Employees seem to accept suggestions for improved performance if they are given in a less concentrated form than is the case in comprehensive annual appraisals. As our experiment showed, employees become clearly more prone to reject criticisms as the number of criticisms mount. This indicates that an "overload phenomenon" may be operating. In other words, each individual seems to have a tolerance level for the amount of criticism he can take. And, as this level is approached or passed, it becomes increasingly difficult for him to accept responsibility for the shortcomings pointed out.

(2) Some managers reported that the traditional performance appraisal program tended to cause them to save up items where improvement was needed in order to have enough material to conduct a comprehensive discussion of performance in the annual review. This short-circuited one of the primary purposes of the appraisal program—that of giving feedback to the subordinates as to their performance. Studies of the learning process point out that feedback is less effective if much time is allowed to elapse between the performance and the feedback. This fact alone argues for more frequent discussions between the manager and the subordinate.

GOAL SETTING, NOT CRITICISM, SHOULD BE USED TO IMPROVE PERFORMANCE. One of the most significant findings in our experiment was the fact that far superior results were observed when the manager and the man *together* set specific goals to be achieved, rather than merely discussed needed improvement. Frequent reviews of progress provide natural opportunities for discussing means of improving performance *as needs occur,* and these reviews are far less threatening than the annual appraisal and salary review discussions.

SEPARATE APPRAISALS SHOULD BE HELD FOR DIFFERENT PURPOSES.   Our work demonstrated that it was unrealistic to expect a single performance appraisal program to achieve every conceivable need. It seems foolish to have a manager serving in the self-conflicting role as a counselor (helping a man to improve his performance) when, at the same time, he is presiding as a judge over the same employee's salary action case.

New WP&R Method

This intensive year-long test of the performance appraisal program indicated clearly that work-planning-and-review discussions between a man and his manager appeared to be a far more effective approach in improving job performance than was the concentrated annual performance appraisal program.

For this reason, after the findings had been announced, many GE managers adopted some form of the new WP&R program to motivate performance improvement in employees, especially those at the professional and administrative levels. Briefly described, the WP&R approach calls for periodic meetings between the manager and his subordinate. During these meetings, progress on past goals is reviewed, solutions are sought for job-related problems, and new goals are established. The intent of the method is to create a situation in which manager and subordinate can discuss job performance and needed improvements in detail without the subordinate becoming defensive.

BASIC FEATURES

This WP&R approach differs from the traditional performance appraisal program in that:

There are more frequent discussions of performance.

There are no summary judgments or ratings made.

Salary action discussions are held separately.

The emphasis is on mutual goal planning and problem solving.

As far as frequency is concerned, these WP&R discussions are held more often than traditional performance appraisal interviews, but are not scheduled at rigidly fixed intervals. Usually at the conclusion of one work planning session the subordinate and manager set an approximate date for the next review. Frequency depends both on the nature of the job and on the manager's style of operating. Sometimes these WP&R discussions are held as often as once a month, whereas for other jobs and/or individuals, once every six months is more appropriate.

In these WP&R discussions, the manager and subordinate do not deal in generalities. They consider specific, objectively defined work goals and establish the yardstick for measuring performance. These goals stem, of course, from broader departmental objectives and are defined in relation to the individual's position in the department.

COMPARISON SETTING

After the findings of our experiment were communicated by means of reports and group meetings in the plant where the research was carried out, about half the key managers decided they would abandon the comprehensive annual performance appraisal method and adopt the new WP&R program instead. The other half were hesitant to make such a major change at the time. They decided, consequently, to continue with the traditional performance appraisal program and to try to make it more effective. This provided a natural setting for us to compare the effectiveness of the two approaches. We decided that the comparison should be made in the light of the objectives usually stated for the comprehensive annual performance appraisal program. These objectives were (a) to provide knowledge of results to employees, (b) to justify reasons for salary action, and (c) to motivate and help employees do a better job.

The study design was simple. Before any changes were made, the exempt employees who would be affected by these programs were surveyed to provide baseline data. The WP&R program was then implemented in about half of the exempt group, with the other half continuing to use a modified version of the traditional per-formance appraisal program. One year later, the identical survey questionnaire was again administered in order to compare the changes that had occurred.

ATTITUDES AND ACTIONS

The results of this research study were quite convincing. The group that continued on the traditional performance appraisal showed no change in *any* of the areas measured. The WP&R group, by contrast, expressed significantly more favorable attitudes on al-most all questionnaire items. Specifically, their attitudes changed in a favorable direction over the year that they participated in the new WP&R program with regard to the

amount of help the manager was giving them in improving perfor-mance on the job;

degree to which the manager was receptive to new ideas and suggestions;

ability of the manager to plan;

extent to which the manager made use of their abilities and experience;

degree to which they felt the goals they were shooting for were what they *should* be;

extent to which they received help from the manager in planning for *future* job opportunities;

value of the performance discussions they had with their managers.

In addition to these changes in attitudes, evidence was also found that showed clearly that the members of the WP&R group were much more likely to have taken specific actions to improve per-formance than were those who continued with the traditional per-formance appraisal approach.

Current Observations

Recently we undertook still another intensive study of the WP&R program in order to learn more about the nature of these discussions and how they can be made most effective. While these observations have not been completed, some interesting findings have already come to light—especially in relation to differences between WP&R and traditional performance appraisal discussions.

PERCEIVED DIFFERENCES

For one thing, WP&R interviews are strictly person-to-person in character, rather than having a parent-and-child flavor, as did so many of the traditional performance appraisals. This seems to be due to the fact that it is much more natural under the WP&R program for the subordinate to take the initiative when his or her performance on past goals is being reviewed. Thus, in listening to the subordinate's review of performance, problems, and failings, the manager is automatically cast in the role of *counselor*. This role for the manager, in turn, results naturally in a problem-solving discussion.

In the traditional performance appraisal interview, on the other hand, the manager is automatically cast in the role of *judge*. The subordinate's natural reaction is to assume a defensive posture, and thus all the necessary ingredients for an argument are present.

Since the WP&R approach focuses mainly on immediate, short-term goals, some managers are concerned that longer-range, broader plans and goals might be neglected. Our data show that this concern is unfounded. In almost every case, the discussion of specific work plans and goals seems to lead naturally into a consideration of broader, longer-range plans. In fact, in a substantial percentage of the sessions, even the career plans of the subordinates are reviewed.

In general, the WP&R approach appears to be a better way of defining what is expected of an individual and how he or she is doing on the job. Whereas the traditional performance appraisal often results in resistance to the manager's attempts to help the subordinate, the WP&R approach brings about acceptance of such attempts.

Conclusion

Multiple studies conducted by the Behavioral Research Service at GE reveal that the traditional performance appraisal method contains a number of problems:

1. Appraisal interviews attempt to accomplish the two objectives of providing a written justification for salary action and motivating the employee to improve work performance.
2. The two purposes are in conflict, with the result that the traditional appraisal system essentially becomes a salary discussion in which the manager justifies the action taken.

3. The appraisal discussion has little influence on future job performance.
4. Appreciable improvement is realized only when specified goals and deadlines are mutually established and agreed on by the subordinate and manager in an interview split away from the appraisal interview.

This evidence, coupled with other principles relating to employee motivation, gave rise to the new WP&R program, which is proving to be far more effective in improving job performance than the traditional performance appraisal method. Thus, it appears likely that companies that are currently relying on the comprehensive annual performance appraisal process to achieve improvement in work performance might well consider the advisability of switching to some form of work-planning-and-review in their industrial personnel programs.

Notes

1. Douglas McGregor, "An Uneasy Look at Performance Appraisal," *Harvard Business Review* (May–June 1957), p. 89; Harold Mayfield, "In Defense of Performance Appraisal," *Harvard Business Review* (March–April 1960), p. 81; and Alva F. Kindall and James Gatza, "Positive Program for Performance Appraisal," *Harvard Business Review* (November–December 1963), p. 153.

2. See Richard E. Farson, "Praise Reappraised," *Harvard Business Review* (September–October 1963), p. 61.

3
Appraisal of *What* Performance?

Harry Levinson

A corporate president put a senior executive in charge of a failing operation. His only directive was "Get it in the black." Within two years of that injunction, the new executive moved the operation from a deficit position to one that showed a profit of several million. Fresh from his triumph, the executive announced himself as a candidate for a higher-level position, and indicated that he was already receiving offers from other companies.

The corporate president, however, did not share the executive's positive opinions of his behavior. In fact, the president was not at all pleased with the way the executive had handled things.

Naturally the executive was dismayed, and when he asked what he had done wrong, the corporate president told him that he had indeed accomplished what he had been asked to do, but he had done it singlehandedly, by the sheer force of his own personality. Furthermore, the executive was told, he had replaced people whom the company thought to be good employees with those it regarded as compliant. In effect, by demonstrating his own strength, he had made the organization weaker. Until the executive changed his authoritarian manner, his boss said, it was unlikely that he would be promoted further.

Implicit in this vignette is the major fault in performance appraisal and management by objectives—namely, a fundamental misconception of what is to be appraised.

Performance appraisal has three basic functions: (1) to provide adequate feedback to each person on his or her performance; (2) to serve as a basis for modifying or changing behavior toward more effective working habits; and (3) to provide to managers data with which they may judge future job assignments and compensation. The performance appraisal concept is central to effective management. Much hard and imaginative work has gone into developing and refining it. In fact, there is a great deal of evidence to indicate how useful and effective performance appraisal is. Yet present systems of performance appraisal do not serve any of these functions well.

As it is customarily defined and used, performance appraisal focuses not on behavior but on outcomes of behavior. But even though the executive in the example achieved his objective, he was evaluated on *how* he attained it. Thus, while the system purports to appraise results, in practice, people are really appraised on how they do things—which is not formally described in the setting of objectives, and for which there are rarely data on record.

In my experience, the crucial aspect of any manager's job and the source of most failures, which is practically never described, is the "how." As long as managers appraise the ends yet actually give greater weight to the means, employ a static job description base which does not describe the "how," and do not have support mechanisms for the appraisal process, widespread dissatisfaction with performance appraisal is bound to continue. In fact, one personnel authority speaks of performance appraisal as "the Achilles heel of our profession."[1]

Just how these inadequacies affect performance appraisal systems and how they can be corrected to provide managers with realistic bases for making judgments about employees' performance is the subject of this article.

Inadequacies of Appraisal Systems

It is widely recognized that there are many things inherently wrong with most of the performance appraisal systems in use. The most obvious drawbacks are the following.

No matter how well defined the dimensions for appraising performance on quantitative goals are, judgments on performance are usually subjective and impressionistic.

Because appraisals provide inadequate information about the subtleties of performance, managers using them to compare employees for the purposes of determining salary increases often make arbitrary judgments.

Ratings by different managers, especially those in different units, are usually incomparable. What is excellent work in one unit may be unacceptable in another in the same company.

When salary increases are allocated on the basis of a curve of normal distribution, which is in turn based on rating of results rather than on behavior, competent employees may not only be denied increases, but may also become demotivated.[2]

Trying to base promotion and layoff decisions on appraisal data leaves the decisions open to acrimonious debate. When employees who have been retired early have complained to federal authorities of age discrimination, defendant companies have discovered that there were inadequate data to support the layoff decisions.

Although managers are urged to give feedback freely and often, there are no built-in mechanisms for ensuring that they do so. Delay in feedback creates both frustration, when good performance is not quickly recognized, and anger, when judgment is rendered for inadequacies long past.

There are few effective established mechanisms to cope with either the sense of inadequacy managers have about appraising subordinates, or the paralysis and procrastination that result from guilt about "playing God."

Some people might argue that these problems are deficiencies of managers, not of the system. But even if that were altogether true, managers are part of that system. Performance appraisal needs to be viewed not as a technique but as a process involving both people and data, and as such the whole process is inadequate.

Recognizing that there are many deficiencies in performance appraisals, managers in many companies do not want to do them. In other companies there is a great reluctance to do them straightforwardly. Personnel specialists attribute these problems to the reluctance of managers to adopt new ways and to the fear of irreparably damaging their subordinates' self-esteem. In government, performance appraisal is largely a joke, and in both private and public enterprise, merit ratings are hollow.[3]

One of the main sources of trouble with performance appraisal systems is, as I have already pointed out, that the outcome of behavior rather than the behavior itself is what is evaluated. In fact, most people's jobs are described in terms that are only quantitatively measurable; the job description itself is the root of the problem.

STATIC JOB DESCRIPTION

When people write their own job descriptions (or make statements from which others will write them) essentially they define their responsibilities and basic functions. Then on performance appraisal forms, managers comment on these functions by describing what an individual is supposed to accomplish. Forms in use in many companies today have such directions as:

1. "List the major objectives of this person's job that can be measured qualitatively or quantitatively."
2. "Define the results expected and the standards of performance—money, quantity, quality, time limits, or completion dates."
3. "Describe the action planned as a result of this appraisal, the next steps to be taken—reevaluation, strategy, tactics, and so on."
4. "List the person's strong points—his assets and accomplishments—and his weak points—areas in which improvement is needed. What are the action plans for improvement?"

In most instances the appraiser is asked to do an overall rating with a five-point scale or some similar device. Finally, he is asked to make a statement about the person's potential for the next step or even for higher-level management.

Nowhere in this set of questions or in any of the performance appraisal systems I have examined is anything asked about *how* the person is to attain the ends he or she is charged with reaching.

While some may assert that the ideal way of managing is to give a person a charge and leave him or her alone to accomplish it, this principle is oversimplified in both theory and practice. People need to know the topography of the land they are expected to cross, and the routes as perceived by those to whom they report.

Every manager has multiple obligations, not the least of which are certain kinds of relationships with peers, subordinates, and various consumer, financial, government, supplier, and other publics. Some of these are more important than others, and some need to be handled with much greater skill and aplomb than others. In some situations a manager may be expected to take a vigorous and firm stand, as in labor negotiations; in others he may have to be conciliative; in still others he may even have to be passive. Unless these varied modes of expected behavior are laid out, the job description is static. Because static job descriptions define behavior in gross terms, crucially important differentiated aspects of behavior are lost when performance appraisals are made.

For example, in one of the more progressive performance appraisal systems, which is used by an innovative company, a manager working out his own job description prepares a mission or role statement of what he is supposed to do according to the guide, which specifically directs him to concentrate on the what and the when, not on the why and the how.[4] The guide instructs him to divide his mission into four general areas: (1) innovation, (2) problem solving, (3) ongoing administration, and (4) personal.

In still another company, a manager appraising a subordinate's performance is asked to describe an employee's accomplishments, neglected areas, goals, and objectives. The manager is told that he is to recognize good work, suggest improvement, get agreement on top priority elements of the task, clarify responsibility, verify and correct rumors, and talk about personal and long-range goals.

In another company's outstanding performance appraisal guide, which reflects great detail and careful consideration, the categories are work, effectiveness with others, problem solving, decision making, goal setting, organizing and planning, developing subordinates, attending to self-development, and finding initiatives. Each of these categories is broken down into example statements such as "exhibits high level of independence in work"; "identifies problems and deals with them"; "appropriately subordinates departmental interest to overall company goal"; or "gives people genuine responsibility, holds them accountable, and allows them freedom to act."

Some personnel researchers have advocated role analysis techniques to cope with static job descriptions, and this is a step in the right direction.[5]

But even these techniques are limited because they lean heavily on what other people—supervisors, subordinates, peers—expect of the manager. These expectations are also generalized; they do not specify behavior.

Nowhere in these examples is an individual told what *behavior* is expected of him in a range of contexts. Who are the sensitive people with whom certain kinds of relationships have to be maintained? What are the specific problems and barriers? What have been the historic manufacturing blunders or frictions? How should union relationships and union leaders be dealt with? What are the specific integrative problems to be resolved and what are the historical conflicts? These and many more similar pieces of behavior will be the true bases on which a person will be judged, regardless of the questions an appraisal form asks.

Static job descriptions are catastrophic for managers. Job proficiency and goal achievement usually are necessary but not sufficient conditions for advancement; the key elements in whether one makes it in an organization are political. The collective judgments made about a person, which rarely find their way into performance appraisals, become the social web in which he or she must live. Therefore, when a person is placed in a new situation, whether in a different geographical site, at a different level in the hierarchy, or in a new role, he must be apprised of the subtleties of the relationships he will have with those who will influence his role and his career. Furthermore, he must be helped to differentiate the varied kinds of behavior required to succeed.

Some people develop political diagnostic skill very rapidly; often, however, these are people whose social senses enable them to move beyond their technical and managerial competence. And some may be out-and-out manipulative charlatans who succeed in business without really trying, and whose promotion demoralizes good people. But the great majority of people, those who have concentrated heavily on their professional competence at the expense of acquiring political skill early, will need to have that skill developed, ideally by their own seniors. That development process requires: (1) a dynamic job description, (2) a critical incident process, and (3) a psychological support system.

DYNAMIC JOB DESCRIPTION

If a static job description is at the root of the inadequacies of performance appraisal systems, what is needed is a different kind of job description. What we are looking for is one that amplifies statements of job responsibility and desired outcome by describing the emotional and behavioral topography of the task to be done by the individual in the job.

Psychologists describe behavior in many ways, each having his or her own preferences. I have found four major features of behavior to be fundamentally important in a wide range of managerial settings. These features have to do with how a person characteristically manages what some psychologists call aggression, affection, dependency, and also the nature of the person's ego ideal.[6]

Using one's preferred system, one can begin formulating a dynamic job description by describing the characteristic behavior required by a job. This is what these terms mean with respect to job descriptions:

1. How does this job require the incumbent to handle his aggression, his attacking capacity?

   Must he or she vanquish customers? Must he hold on to his anger in the face of repeated complaints and attacks from others? Will she be the target of hostility and, if so, from whom? Must he give firm direction to others? Must she attack problems vigorously, but handle some areas with great delicacy and finesse? Which problems are to be attacked with vigor and immediacy and which coolly and analytically?

2. How does this job require the incumbent to manage affection, the need to love and to be loved?

   Is the person required to be a socially friendly leader of a close-knit work group? Should the person work closely and supportively with subordinates for task accomplishment? Is the task one in which the person will have to be content with the feeling of a job well done, or is it one that involves more public display and recognition? Will he be obscure and unnoticed, or highly visible? Must she lavish attention on the work, a product, a service, or customers? Must he be cold and distant from others and, if so, from whom?

3. How does this job require the incumbent to manage dependency needs?

   Will the individual be able to lean on others who have skill and competencies, or will he have to do things himself? How much will she be on her own and in what areas? How much support will there be from superiors and staff functions? How well defined is the nature of the work? What kinds of feedback provisions are there? What are the structural and hierarchical relationships? How solid are they and to whom will the person turn and for what? With which people must he interact in order to accomplish what he needs to accomplish, and in what manner?

4. What ego ideal demands does this job fulfill?

If one does the task well, what are the gratifications to be gained? Will the person make a lot of money? Will he achieve considerable organizational and public recognition? Will she be eligible for promotion? Will he feel good about himself and, if so, in what ways? Why? Will she acquire a significant skill, an important element of reputation, or an organizational constituency? Will he acquire power?

Individuals may be described along the same four dynamic dimensions: How does this person characteristically handle aggression? How does he or she characteristically handle affection? How does he or she characteristically handle dependency needs? What is the nature of his or her ego ideal?

Once the subtleties of the task are defined and individuals described, people may be matched to tasks. I am not advocating a return to evaluation of personality traits. I am arguing for a more dynamic conception of the managerial role and a more dynamic assessment of an employee's characteristics. And only when a person's behavior is recognized as basic to how he performs his job will performance appraisal systems be realistic.

CRITICAL INCIDENT PROCESS

Having established a dynamic job description for a person, the next step is to evolve a complementary performance appraisal system that will provide feedback on verifiable behavior, do so in a continuous fashion, and serve coaching-, promotion-, and salary-data needs.

Ideally, a manager and his subordinate will have defined together the objectives to be attained in a certain job, and the criteria by which each will know that those objectives have been attained, including the more qualitative aspects of the job. Then they will have spelled out the subtleties of how various aspects of the job must be performed. They will in this way have elaborated the *behavioral* requirements of the task.

In order for performance appraisal to be effective for coaching, teaching, and changing those aspects of an employee's behavior that are amenable to change, an employee needs to know about each piece of behavior that is good, as well as that which for some reason is not acceptable or needs modification. Such incidents will occur randomly and be judged randomly by his manager.

So that there will be useful data, the manager needs to write down quickly what he has said to the subordinate, describing in a paragraph what the subordinate did or did not do, in what setting, under what circumstances, about what problem. This information forms a *behavioral* record, a critical incident report of which the subordinate already has been informed and which is now in his folder, open to his review.

This critical incident technique is not new.[7] In the past it has been used largely for case illustrations and, in modified forms, has been suggested as a method for first-level supervisors to evaluate line employees. Supervisors already record negative incidents concerning line employees because warnings and disciplinary steps must be documented. However, efforts to develop scales from critical incidents for rating behavior have not worked well.[8] Behavior is too complex to be scaled along a few dimensions and then rated.

But instead of scaling behavior, one might directly record the behavior of those being appraised, and evaluate it at a later date. There are other good reasons for adopting this technique as well. At last, here is a process that provides data to help managers perform the basic functions of performance appraisal systems— namely, provide feedback, coaching, and promotion data. Another plus is that recorded data live longer than the manager recording them.

Here is how behavioral data might be put to use in the critical incident process:

1. *Feedback data:* When there is a semiannual or annual review, an employee will have no surprises and the manager will have on paper what he is using as a basis for making his summary feedback and appraisal. Because the data are on record, an employee cannot deny having heard what was said earlier, nor must the manager try to remember all year what have been the bases of his judgments.

   Also, as each critical incident is recorded, over time there will be data in an individual's folder to be referred to when and if there are suits alleging discrimination. Critical incidents of behavior, which illustrate behavior patterns, will be the only hard evidence acceptable to adjudicating bodies.

2. *Coaching data:* When employees receive feedback information at the time the incident occurs, they may be able to adapt their behavior more easily. With this technique, the employee will receive indications more often on how he is doing, and will be able to correct small problems before they become large ones. Also, if the employee

cannot change his behavior, that fact will become evident to him through the repetitive critical incident notes. If the employee feels unfairly judged or criticized, he may appeal immediately rather than long after the fact. If there are few or no incidents on record, that in itself says something about job behavior, and may be used as a basis for discussion. In any event, both manager and employee will know which behavior is being appraised.

3. *Promotion data:* With such an accumulation of critical incidents, a manager or the personnel department is in a position to evaluate repeatedly how the person characteristically manages aggression, affection, and dependency needs, and the nature of his ego ideal. These successive judgments become cumulative data for better job fit.

When a person is provided continuously with verifiable information, including when he has been passed over for promotion and why, he is able to perceive more accurately the nuances of his behavior and his behavioral patterns. Thus, when offered other opportunities, the employee is in a better position to weigh his own behavioral configurations against those required by the prospective job. A person who knows himself in this way will be more easily able to say about a given job, "That's not for me." He will see that the next job in the pyramid is not necessarily rightfully his. In recognizing his own behavioral limitations he may save himself much grief as well as avoid painful difficulty for his superiors and the organization.

But the most important reason for having such information is to increase the chances of success of those who are chosen for greater responsibility. In most personnel folders there is practically no information about how a manager is likely to do when placed on his own. Data about dependency are noticeably absent, and many a shining prospect dims when there is no one to support him in a higher-level job. Managements need to know early on who can stand alone, and they cannot know that without behavioral information.

4. *Long-term data:* Frequently, new managers do not know their employees and all too often have little information in the folder with which to appraise them. This problem is compounded when managers move quickly from one area to another. For his part, the employee just as frequently has to prove himself to transient bosses who hold his fate in their hands but know nothing of his past performance. With little information, managers feel unqualified to make judgments. With the critical incident process, however, managers can report incidents that can be summarized by someone else.

Some may object to "keeping book" on their people or resist a program of constant reviews and endless reports—both extreme views. Some may argue that supervisors will not follow the method. But if managers cannot get raises for or transfer employees without adequate documentation, they will soon learn the need to follow through. The critical incident process compels superiors to face subordinates, a responsibility too many shirk.

While it might seem difficult to analyze performance in terms of aggression, affection, dependency, the ego ideal, or other psychological concepts, to do so is no different from learning to use economic, financial, or accounting concepts. Many managers already talk about these same issues in other words, for example: "taking charge" versus "being a nice guy"; "needing to be stroked" versus the "self-starter"; "fast track" versus the "shelf-sitter." A little practice, together with support mechanisms, can go a long way.

SUPPORT MECHANISMS

Performance appraisal cannot be limited to a yearly downward reward-punishment judgment. Ideally, appraisal should be a part of a continuing process by which both manager and employee may be guided. In addition, it should enhance an effective superior-subordinate relationship.

To accomplish these aims, performance appraisal must be supported by mechanisms that enable the manager to master his inadequacies and to cope with his feelings of guilt; have a record of that part of his work that occurs outside the purview of his own boss (e.g., task force assignments that require someone to appraise a whole group); and modify those aspects of his superior's behavior that hamper his performance. All of this requires an upward appraisal process.

1. *Managing the guilt.* The manager's guilt about appraising subordinates appears when managers complain about "playing God," about destroying people. A great crippler of effective performance appraisal is the feeling of guilt, much of which is irrational, but which most people have when they criticize others.[9] Guilt is what leads to the fear of doing appraisals. It is the root of procrastination, of the failure to appraise honestly, and of the overreaction which can demolish subordinates.

Fortunately, there are group methods for relieving guilt and for helping managers and supervisors understand the critical importance, indeed the necessity, of accurate behavioral evaluations. One way is by having people together at the same peer level discuss their problems in appraisal and talk about their feelings in undertaking the appraisal task. In addition, rehearsals of role playing increase a manager's sense of familiarity and competence and ease his anxiety.

In fact, a five-step process, one step per week for five weeks, can be extremely helpful:

Week one: Group discussion among peers (no more than 12) about their feelings about appraising subordinates.

Week two: Group discussions resulting in advice from each other on the specific problems that each anticipates in appraising individuals.

Week three: Role playing appraisal interviews.

Week four: Actual appraisals.

Week five: Group discussion to review the appraisals, problems encountered, both anticipated and unanticipated, lessons learned, and skill needs that may have surfaced.

2. *Group appraisal:* By group appraisal, I do not mean peer approval of each other, which usually fails; rather, I mean appraisal of a group's accomplishment. When people work together in a group, whether reporting to the same person or not, they need to establish criteria by which they and those to whom they report will know how well the task force or the group has done—in terms of behavior as well as results. Group appraisals provide information that is helpful both in establishing criteria and in providing each individual with feedback.

At the end of a given task, a group may do a group appraisal or be appraised by the manager to whom they report, and that appraisal may be entered into folders of each of the people who are involved. It will then serve as another basis for managerial and self-judgment.

3. *Upward appraisal:* Finally, there should be upward appraisal. Some beginning voluntary steps in this direction are being taken in the Sun Oil Company, and by individual executives in other companies. Upward appraisal is a very difficult process because most managers do not want to be evaluated by their subordinates. As a matter of fact, however, most managers *are* evaluated indirectly by their employees, and these evaluations are frequently behavioral.

The employees' work itself is a kind of evaluation. Their work may be done erratically or irresponsibly. Or they may be poorly motivated. Negative behavior is a form of appraisal, and one from which a manager gains little. A manager cannot be quite sure what precipitated the behavior he sees, let alone be sure what to do about it.

If, however, the manager is getting dynamic behavioral appraisal from his employees, then he, too, may correct his course. But if he asks his subordinates for upward appraisal without warning, he is likely to be greeted with dead silence and great caution. A helpful way to deal with this situation is to ask one's employees to define the criteria by which they would appraise the manager's job, not to judge his actual performance.

This process of definition may require a manager to meet with employees weekly for months to define the criteria. By the end of three months, say, the employees should be much more comfortable working with their manager on this issue. And if the manager can be trusted at all, then when he or she finally asks them to evaluate the performance, including specific behaviors, along the dimensions they have worked out together, they are likely to be more willing to do so. Of course, if there is not trust, there is no possibility of upward appraisal. In any event, the upward performance appraisal should go to the manager's superior so that people do not jeopardize themselves by speaking directly.

Under present performance appraisal systems, it is difficult to compensate managers for developing people because the criteria are elusive. With a developing file of upward appraisals, however, executives can judge how well a manager has done in developing his people. The employees cannot evaluate the whole of their manager's job, but they can say a great deal about how well he or she has facilitated their work, increased their proficiency, cleared barriers, protected them against political forces, and raised their level of competence—in short, how the manager has met their ministration, maturation, and mastery needs.[10] A top executive can then quantify such upward evaluations and use the outcome as a basis for compensating a manager for his effectiveness in developing his employees.

When a group of manager peers experiments with upward appraisal and works it out to their own comfort, as well as to that of their employees, then it might be tried at the next lower level. When several successive levels have worked out their own systems, the process might be formalized throughout the organization. Acceptance of the upward appraisal concept is likely to be greater if it has been tested and modeled by the very people who must use it, and if it has not been imposed on them by the personnel department. With appropriate experience, the managers involved in the process would ultimately evolve suitable appraisal forms.

What about Results?

What does adopting the critical incident technique and the dynamic job description mean for judging a person's ability to obtain results? Does quantitative performance lose its importance?

My answer is an unqualified no. There will always be other issues that managers will have to determine, such as level of compensation or promotability—issues that should be dealt with in other sessions after the basic behavioral performance appraisal.[11]

Some of the performance appraisal information may be helpful in making such determinations, but neither of these two functions should contaminate the performance appraisal feedback process. There can still be an annual compensation evaluation, based not only on behavior, which is the basis for coaching, but also on outcome. Did an employee make money? Did he reach quantitative goals? Did she resolve problems in the organization that were her responsibility?

No doubt, there will be some overlapping between behavior and outcome, but the two are qualitatively different. One might behave as it was expected he should, but at the same time not do what had to be done to handle the vagaries of the marketplace. He might not have responded with enough speed or flexibility to a problem, even though his behavior corresponded to all that originally was asked of him in the job description and goal-setting process.

Both behavior and outcome are important, and neither should be overlooked. It is most important, however, that they not be confused.

Notes

1. Herbert Heneman, "Research Roundup," *The Personnel Administrator* (June 1975), p. 61.

2. Paul H. Thompson and Gene W. Dalton, "Performance Appraisal: Managers Beware," *Harvard Business Review* (January–February 1970), p. 149.

3. Herbert S. Meyer, "The Pay for Performance Dilemma," *Organizational Dynamics* (Winter 1975), p. 39.

4. John B. Lasagna, "Make Your MBO Pragmatic," *Harvard Business Review* (November–December 1971), p. 64.

5. Ishwar Dayal, "Role Analysis Techniques in Job Descriptions," *California Management Review* (Summer 1969), p. 47.

6. Harry Levinson, *The Great Jackass Fallacy* (Boston: Division of Research, Harvard Business School, 1973), ch. 3.

7. John C. Flanagan, "The Critical Incident Technique," *Psychological Bulletin* 51 (1954), pp. 327; and John C. Flanagan and Robert K. Burns, "The Employee Performance Record: A New Appraisal and Development Tool," *Harvard Business Review* (September–October 1955), p. 95.

8. Donald P. Schwab, Herbert Heneman, and Thomas DeCotis, "Behaviorally Anchored Rating Scales: A Review of the Literature," *Personnel Psychology* 28 (1975), p. 549.

9. Harry Levinson, "Management by Whose Objectives?" *Harvard Business Review* (July–August 1970), p. 125.

10. Harry Levinson, *The Exceptional Executive* (Cambridge, Mass.: Harvard University Press, 1968).

11. Herbert H. Meyer, Emanuel Kay, and John R. P. French, Jr., "Split Roles in Performance Appraisal," *Harvard Business Review* (January–February 1965), p. 123.

4
Management by Whose Objectives?

Harry Levinson

Despite the fact that the concept of management by objectives (MBO) has by this time become an integral part of the managerial process, the typical MBO effort perpetuates and intensifies hostility, resentment, and distrust between a manager and subordinates. As currently practiced, it is really just industrial engineering with a new name, applied to higher managerial levels, and with the same resistances.

Obviously, somewhere between the concept of MBO and its implementation, something has seriously gone wrong. Coupled with performance appraisal, the intent is to follow the Frederick Taylor tradition of a more rational management process. That is, which people are to do what, who is to have effective control over it, and how compensation is to be related directly to individual achievement. The MBO process, in its essence, is an effort to be fair and reasonable, to predict performance and judge it more carefully, and presumably to provide individuals with an opportunity to be self-motivating by setting their own objectives.

The intent of clarifying job obligations and measuring performance against an individual's own goals seems reasonable enough. The concern for having both superior and subordinate consider the same matters in reviewing the performance of the latter is eminently sensible. The effort to come to common agreement on what constitutes the subordinate's job is highly desirable.

Yet, like most rationalizations in the Taylor tradition, MBO as a process is one of the greatest of managerial illusions because it fails to take adequately into account the deeper emotional components of motivation.

In this article, I shall indicate how I think management by objectives, as currently practiced in most organizations, is self-defeating, and serves simply to increase pressure on the individual. By doing so, I do not reject either MBO or performance appraisal out of hand.

Rather, by raising the basic question "Whose objectives?" I propose to suggest how they might be made more constructive devices for effective management. The issues I shall raise have largely to do with psychological considerations, and particularly with the assumptions about motivation that underlie these techniques.

The "Ideal" Process

Since management by objectives is closely related to performance appraisal and review, I shall consider these together as one practice, which is intended:

To measure and judge performance.

To relate individual performance to organizational goals.

To clarify both the job to be done and the expectations of accomplishment.

To foster the increasing competence and growth of the subordinate.

To enhance communications between superior and subordinate.

To serve as a basis for judgments about salary and promotion.

To stimulate the subordinate's motivation.

To serve as a device for organizational control and integration.

MAJOR PROBLEMS

According to contemporary thinking, the "ideal" process should proceed in five steps: (1) individual discussion with the superior of the subordinate's description of his or her own job, (2) establishment of short-term performance targets, (3) meetings with the superior to discuss progress toward targets, (4) establishment of checkpoints to measure progress, and (5) discussion between superior and subordinate at the end of a defined period to assess the results of the subordinate's efforts. In *ideal* practice, this process occurs against a background of more frequent, even day-to-day, contacts and is separate from salary review. But, in *actual* practice, there are many problems. Consider:

No matter how detailed the job description, it is essentially static—that is, a series of statements.

However, the more complex the task and the more flexible a subordinate must be in it, the less any fixed statement of job elements will fit what he or she does. Thus, the higher an individual rises in an organization and the more varied and subtle the work performed, the more difficult it is to pin down objectives that represent more than a fraction of that person's effort.

With preestablished goals and descriptions, little weight can be given to the areas of discretion open to the individual, but not incorporated into his or her job description or objectives.

I am referring here to those spontaneously creative activities an innovative executive might choose to do, or those tasks a responsible executive sees that need to be done. As we move more toward a service society, in which tasks are less well defined but spontaneity of service and self-assumed responsibility are crucial, this becomes pressing.

Most job descriptions are limited to what people do by themselves in their work.

They do not adequately take into account the increasing interdependence of managerial work in organizations. This limitation becomes more important as the impact of social and organizational factors on individual performance becomes better understood. The more an individual's effectiveness depends on what other people do, the less that person alone can be held responsible for the outcome of his or her efforts.

If a primary concern in performance review is counseling the subordinate, appraisal should consider and take into account the total situation in which the superior and subordinate are operating.

In addition, it should take into account the relationship of the subordinate's job to other jobs. In counseling, much of the focus is on helping the subordinate learn to negotiate the system. There is no provision in most reviews and, on appraisal forms with which I am familiar, no place to report and record such discussion.

The setting and evolution of objectives is done over too brief a period of time to provide for adequate interaction among different levels of an organization.

This militates against opportunity for peers, both in the same work unit and in complementary units, to develop objectives together for maximum integration. Thus both the setting of objectives and the appraisal of performance make little contribution toward the development of teamwork and more effective organizational self-control.

Coupled with these problems is the difficulty superiors experience when they undertake appraisals.

Douglas McGregor complained that the major reason appraisal failed was that superiors disliked "playing God" by making judgments about another individual's worth.[1] He likened the superior's experience to inspection of assembly line products and contended that the superior's revulsion was against being inhuman. To cope with this problem, McGregor recommended that an individual should set his or her own goals, checking them out with the superior, and should use the appraisal session as a counseling device. Thus the superior would become one who helped the subordinate achieve his or her own goals instead of a dehumanized inspector of products.

Parenthetically, I doubt very much that the failure of appraisal stems from playing God or feeling inhuman. My own observation leads me to believe that managers experience their appraisal of others as a hostile, aggressive act that unconsciously is felt to be hurting or destroying the other person. The appraisal situation, therefore, gives rise to powerful, paralyzing feelings of guilt that make it extremely difficult for most executives to be constructively critical of subordinates.

OBJECTIVITY PLEA

Be that as it may, the more complex and difficult the appraisal process and the setting and evaluation of objectives, the more pressing the cry for objectivity. This is a vain plea. Every organization is a social system, a network of interpersonal relationships. A person may do an excellent job by objective standards of measurement, but may fail miserably as a partner, subordinate, superior, or colleague. It is a commonplace that more people fail to be promoted for personal reasons than for technical inadequacy.

Furthermore, since every subordinate is a part of his or her superior's efforts to achieve certain goals, the subordinate will inevitably be appraised on how well he or she works with the superior and helps the latter meet those goals. A heavy subjective element necessarily enters into every appraisal and goal-setting experience.

The plea for objectivity is vain for another reason. The greater the emphasis on measurement and quantification, the more likely the subtle, nonmeasurable elements of the task will be sacrificed. Quality of performance frequently, therefore, loses out to quantification.

A CASE EXAMPLE: A manufacturing plant that produces high-quality, high-prestige products, backed by a reputation for customer consideration and service, has instituted an MBO program. It is well worked out and has done much to clarify both individual goals and organizational performance. It is an important component of the professional management style of the company that has resulted in commendable growth.

But an interesting, and ultimately destructive, process has been set in motion. The managers are beginning to worry because when they now ask why something has not been done, they hear from each other, "That isn't in my goals." They complain that customer service is deteriorating. The vague goal, "improve customer service," is almost impossible to measure. There is therefore heavy concentration on those subgoals that can be measured. Thus time per customer, number of customer calls, and similar measures are used as guides in judging performance. The *less* time per customer and the *fewer* the calls, the better the customer service manager meets company objectives: cutting costs, increasing profit—and killing the business.

Most of the managers in that organization joined it because of its reputation for high quality and good service. They want to make good products and earn the continued admiration of their customers, as well as the envy of their industry. When they are not operating at that high level, they feel guilty. They become angry with themselves and the company. They feel that they might just as well be working for someone else who admittedly does a sloppy job of quality control and could hardly care less about service.

The same problem exists with respect to the development of personnel, which is another vague goal that is hard to measure in comparison with subgoals that are measurable. If asked, all managers can name a younger person as a potential successor, particularly if their promotion depends on doing so; but no one has the time, or indeed feels that they are being paid, to train the younger person thoroughly. Nor can one have the time or be paid, for there is no way in that organization to measure how well a manager does in developing another.

The Missed Point

All of the problems with objectives and appraisals outlined in the example discussed in the foregoing section indicate that MBO is not working well despite what some companies think about their programs. The underlying reason it is not working well is that it misses the whole human point.

To see how the point is being missed, let us follow the typical MBO process. Characteristically, top management sets its corporate goal for the coming year. This may be in terms of return on investment, sales, production, growth, or other measurable factors.

Within this frame of reference, reporting managers may then be asked how much their units intend to contribute toward meeting that goal, or they may be asked to set their own goals relatively independent of the corporate goal. If they are left free to set their own goals, these in any case are expected to be higher than those they had the previous year. Usually, each reporting manager's range of choices is limited to her option for a piece of the organizational action, or improvement of specific statistics. In some cases, it may also include obtaining specific training or skills.

Once a reporting manager decides on the unit's goals and has them approved by his or her superior, those become the manager's goals. Presumably, he or she is committed to and responsible for achieving them; thereafter subject to being hoist by his or her own petard.

Now, let us reexamine this process closely: the whole method is based on a short-term, egocentrically oriented perspective and an underlying reward-punishment psychology. The typical MBO process puts the reporting manager in much the same position as a rat in a maze, who has choices between only two alternatives. The experimenter who puts the rat in the maze assumes that the rat wants the food reward; if the experimenter cannot presume that, the rat is starved to make sure it wants the food.

Management by objectives differs only in that it permits the subordinate to determine his or her own bait from a limited range of choices. Having done so, the MBO process assumes that the subordinate will (a) work hard to get it, (b) be pushed internally by reason of personal commitment, and (c) make himself or herself responsible to the organization for doing so.

In fairness to most managers, they certainly try, but not without increasing resentment and complaint for feeling like rats in a maze, guilt for not paying attention to those parts of the job not in their objectives, and passive resistance to the mounting pressure for ever-higher goals.

PERSONAL GOALS

The MBO process leaves out the answers to such questions as: What are managers' personal objectives? What do they need and want out of their work? How do their needs and wants change from year to year? What relevance do organizational objectives and their part in them have to such needs and wants?

Obviously, no objectives will have significant incentive power if they are forced choices unrelated to an individual's underlying dreams, wishes, and personal aspirations.

For example: if a salesperson relishes the pleasure of relationships with hard-earned but low-volume customers, this is a powerful need. Suppose the boss, who is concerned about increasing the volume of sales, urges the salesperson to concentrate on the larger-quantity customers rather than the smaller ones, which will provide the necessary increase in volume, and then asks how much of an increase can be achieved.

To work with the larger-quantity customers means that the salesperson will be less likely to sell to the individuals with whom relationships have been well established and be more likely to deal with purchasing agents, technical people, and staff specialists who will demand knowledge and information that salesperson may not have in sophisticated detail. Moreover, as a single salesperson, he or she may fail to be supported by the organization with technical help to meet these demands.

When this happens, not only may the salesperson lose a favorite way of operating, which has well served his or her own needs, but also feel inadequate. If compelled to make a choice about the percentage of sales volume increase he or she expects to attain, a salesperson may well do that, but under great psychological pressure. No one has recognized the psychological realities the person faces, let alone helped him or her to work with them. It is simply assumed that since a sales goal is a rational one, it will be pursued rationally.

The problem may be further compounded if, as is not unusual, formal changes are made in the organizational structure. If sales territories are shifted, if modes of compensation are changed, if problems of delivery occur, or whatever, all of these are factors beyond the salesperson's control. Nevertheless, even with certain allowances, the salesperson is still held responsible for meeting the sales goal.

PSYCHOLOGICAL NEEDS

Lest the reader think the example we have just seen is overdrawn or irrelevant, I know of a young sales manager who is about to resign his job, despite his success in it, because he chooses not to be expendable in an organization that he feels regards him only as an instrument for reaching a goal. Many young people are refusing to enter large organizations for just this reason.

Some may argue that my criticism is unfair, that many organizations start their planning and setting of objectives from below. Therefore, the company cannot be accused of putting its subordinates in a maze. But it does so. In almost all cases, the only legitimate objectives to be set are those having to do with measurable increases in performance. This highlights, again, the question "Whose objectives?" This question becomes more pressing in those circumstances where lower-level people set their objectives, only to be questioned by higher-level managers and told their targets are not high enough.

Here you may well ask, "What's the matter with that? Aren't we in business, and isn't the purpose of employees' work to serve the requirements of the business?" The answer to both questions is "Obviously." But that is only part of the story.

If people's most powerful driving force comprises their needs, wishes, and personal aspirations, combined with the compelling wish to look good in their own eyes for meeting those deeply held personal goals, then management by objectives should begin with *their* objectives. What do they want to do with their lives? Where do they want to go? What will make them feel good about themselves? What do they want to be able to look back on when they have expended their unrecoverable years?

At this point, some may say that those concerns are their business. The company has other business, and it must assume that people are interested in working in the company's business rather than their own. That kind of differentiation is impossible. Everyone is always working toward meeting his or her psychological needs. Those who think otherwise, and believe such powerful internal forces can be successfully disregarded or bought off for long, are deluding themselves.

The Mutual Task

The organizational task becomes one of first understanding subordinates' needs, and then, with them, assessing how well they can be met in the organization, doing what the organization needs to have done. Thus the highest point of self-motivation arises when there is a complementary conjunction of the subordinate's needs and the organization's requirements. The requirements of both mesh, interrelate, and become synergistic. The energies of individual and organization are pooled for mutual advantage.

If the two sets of needs do not mesh, then a person has to fight himself or herself and the organization, in addition to achieving the work that must be done and the targets that have been defined. In such a case, the subordinate and the superior must evaluate together where the subordinate wants to go, where the organization is going, and how significant the discrepancy is. The subordinate might well be better off somewhere else, and the organization would be better with someone else whose needs mesh better with organization requirements.

LONG-RUN COSTS

The issue of meshed interests is particularly relevant for middle-aged, senior-level managers.[2] As people come into middle age, their values often begin to change, and they feel anew the pressure to accomplish many long-deferred dreams. When such wishes begin to stir, they begin to experience severe conflict.

Up to this point, they have committed themselves to the organization and have done sufficiently well in it to attain high rank. Usually, they are slated for even higher levels of responsibility. The organization has been good to them, and their superiors are depending on them to provide its leadership. They have been models for the younger managers, whom they have urged to aspire to organizational heights. To think of leaving is to desert both their superiors and their subordinates.

Since there are few avenues within the organization to talk about such conflict, they try to suppress their wishes. The internal pressure continues to mount until they finally make an impulsive break, surprising and dismaying both themselves and their colleagues. I can think of three vice presidents who have done just that.

The issue is not so much that they decide to leave, but the cost of the way they depart. Early discussion with superiors of their personal goals would have enabled both to examine possible relocation alternatives within the organization. If there were none, then both the managers and their superiors might have come to an earlier, more comfortable decision about separation. The organizations would have had more time to make satisfactory alternative plans, as well as to have taken steps to compensate for the managers' lagging enthusiasm. Lower-level managers would then have seen each company as humane in its enlightened self-interest and would not have had to create fearful fantasies about what the top management conflicts were that had caused good people to leave.

To place consideration of the managers' personal objectives first does not minimize the importance of the organization's goals. It does not mean there is anything wrong with the organization's need to increase its return on investment, its size, its productivity, or its other goals. However, I contend that it is ridiculous to make assumptions about the motivations of individuals, and then to set up means of increasing the pressures on people based on these often questionable assumptions. While there may be certain demonstrable short-run statistical gains, what are the long-run costs?

One cost is that people may leave; another, that they may fall back from competitive positions to plateaus. Why should people be expendable for others and sacrifice themselves for something that is not part of their own cherished dreams? Still another cost may be the loss of the essence of the business, as happened in the case example we saw earlier of the manufacturing plant that had the problem of deteriorating customer service.

In that example, initially there was no dialogue. Nobody heard what the managers said, what they wanted, where they wanted to go, where they wanted the organization to go, and how they felt about the supposedly rational procedures that had been initiated. The underlying psychological assumption that management unconsciously made was that the managers *had to be made* more efficient; ergo, management by objectives.

Top management typically assumes that it alone has the prerogative to (a) set the objectives, (b) provide the rewards and targets, and (c) drive anyone who works for the organization. As long as this reward-punishment psychology exists in any organization, the MBO appraisal process is certain to fail.

Many organizations are making this issue worse by promising young people they will have challenges, since they assume these people will be challenged by management's objectives. Managements are having difficulty, even when they have high turnover rates, hearing these youngsters say they could hardly care less for management's unilaterally determined objectives. Managements then become angry, complain that the young people do not want to work, or that they want to become presidents overnight.

What the young people are asking is: What about me and my needs? Who will listen? How much will management help me meet my own requirements while also meeting its objectives?

The power of this force is reflected in the finding that the more subordinates participate in the appraisal interview by presenting their own ideas and beliefs, the more likely they are to feel that (a) the superior is helpful and constructive, (b) some current job problems are being cleared up, and (c) reasonable future goals are being set.[3]

The Suggested Steps

Given the validity of all the MBO problems I have been discussing to this point, there are a number of possibilities for coping with them. Here, I suggest three beginning steps to consider.

MOTIVATIONAL ASSESSMENT. Every management by objectives program and its accompanying performance appraisal system should be examined as to the extent to which it (1) expresses the conviction that people are patsies to be driven, urged, and manipulated, and (2) fosters a genuine partnership between people and organization, in which each has some influence over the other, as contrasted with a rat-in-maze relationship.

It is not easy for the nonpsychologist to answer such questions, but there are clues to the answers. One clue is how decisions about compensation, particularly bonuses, are made. For example:

A sales manager asked my judgment about an incentive plan for highly motivated salespeople who were in a seller's market. I asked why one was needed, and he responded, "To give them an incentive." When I pointed out that they were already highly motivated and apparently needed no incentive, he changed his rationale and said that the company wanted to share its success to keep the salespeople identified with it, and to express its recognition of their contribution.

I asked, "Why not let them establish the reward related to performance?" The question startled him; obviously, if they were going to decide, who needed him? A fundamental aspect of his role, as he saw it, was to drive them ever onward, whether they needed it or not.

A middle-management bonus plan tied to performance proved to be highly unsatisfactory in a plastic-fabricating company. Frustrated that its well-intentioned efforts were not working and determined to follow precepts of participative management, ranking executives involved many people in formulating a new one—personnel, control, marketing executives, and others—in fact, everyone but the managers who were to receive the bonuses. Top management is now dismayed that the new plan is as unsatisfactory as the old and is bitter that participation failed to work.

Another clue is the focus of company meetings. Some are devoted to intensifying the competition between units. Others lean heavily to exhortation and inspiration. Contrast these orientations with meetings in which people are apprised of problems and plan to cope with them.

GROUP ACTION.   Every objectives and appraisal program should include group goal setting, group definition of both individual and group tasks, group appraisal of its accomplishments, group appraisal of each individual member's contribution to the group effort (without basing compensation on that appraisal), and shared compensation based on the relative success with which group goals are achieved. Objectives should include long-term as well as short-term goals.

The rationale is simple. Every managerial job is an interdependent task. Managers have responsibilities to each other as well as to their superiors. The reason for having an organization is to achieve more together than each could alone. Why, then, emphasize and reward individual performance alone, based on static job descriptions? That can only orient people to both incorrect and self-centered goals.

Therefore, where people are in complementary relationships, whether they report to the same superior or not, both horizontal and vertical goal formulation should be formalized, with regular, frequent opportunity for review of problems and progress. They should help each other define and describe their respective jobs, enhancing control and integration at the point of action.

In my judgment, for example, a group of managers (sales, promotion, advertising) reporting to a vice president of marketing should formulate their collective goals, and define ways both of helping each other and of assessing each others' effectiveness in the common task. The group assessment of each manager's work should be a means of providing each with constructive feedback, not for determining pay. However, in addition to salary, each should receive, as part of whatever additional compensation is offered, a return based on the group effort.

The group's discussion within itself and with its superior should include examination of organizational and environmental obstacles to goal achievement, and particularly of what organizational and leadership supports are required to attain objectives. One important reason for this is that often people think there are barriers where none would exist if they initiated action. ("You mean the president really wants us to get together and solve this problem?")

Another reason is that frequently when higher management sets goals, it is unaware of significant barriers to achievement, leaving managers cynical. For example, if there is no comprehensive orientation and support program to help new employees adapt, then pressure on lower-level managers to employ disadvantaged minority group members and to reduce their turnover can be experienced by those managers only as hollow mockery.

APPRAISAL OF APPRAISERS. Every management by objectives and appraisal program should include regular appraisals of managers by subordinates, and be reviewed by the manager's superior. Every manager should be specifically compensated for how well he or she develops people, based on such appraisals. The very phrase *reporting to* reflects the fact that although a manager has a responsibility, the superior also has a responsibility for what the manager does and how he or she does it.

In fact, both common sense and research indicate that the single most significant influence outside themselves on how managers do their jobs is their superior. If that is the case, then the key environmental factor in task accomplishment and managerial growth is the relationship between manager and superior.

Therefore, objectives should include not only the individual manager's personal and occupational goals, but also the corporate goals the manager and the superior share in common. They should together appraise their relationship vis-à-vis both the manager's individual goals and their joint objectives, review what they have done together, and discuss its implications for their next joint steps.

Managers rarely are in a position to judge their superiors' overall performance, but they can appraise them on the basis of how well they have helped them to do their jobs, how well they are helping them to increase their proficiency and visibility, what problems the supervisor poses for the manager, and what kinds of support the manager can use. Such feedback serves several purposes.

Most important, it offers superiors some guidance on their own managerial performance. In addition, and particularly when managers are protected by higher-level review of their appraisals, it provides supervisors with direct feedback on their own behavior. This is much more constructive than behind-the-back complaint and vituperative terminal interviews, in which cases superiors have no opportunity either to defend themselves or correct their behavior. Every professional counselor has had recently fired executive clients who did not know why they had been discharged for being poor superiors when, according to their information, their subordinates thought so much of them. As a matter of self-interest, every manager should want appraisal by subordinates.

The Basic Consideration

When the three organizational conditions we have just seen do in fact exist, then it is appropriate to think of starting management by objectives with a consideration of each individual's personal objectives; if the underlying attitude in the organization is that people are objects, there is certainly no point in starting with the individual. Nor is there any point in trying to establish confidence in superiors when subordinates are not protected from superiors' rivalry with them, or when they are playing people off against their peers. Anyone who expressed fears and innermost wishes under these circumstances would be a damned fool.

For reasons I have already indicated, it should be entirely legitimate in every business for these concerns to be the basis for individual objectives-setting. This is because the fundamental managerial consideration necessarily must be focused on the question "How do we meet both individual and organizational purposes?" If a major intention of management by objectives is to enlist the self-motivated commitment of the individual, then that commitment must derive from the individual's powerful wishes to support the organization's goals; otherwise, the commitment will be merely incidental to any personal wishes.

That having been said, the real difficulty begins. How can any superior know what a subordinate's personal goals and wishes are if the subordinate—like most of us—is not clear about them? How ethical is it for a superior to pry into someone's personal life? How can a superior avoid forming a negative judgment about someone who apparently is losing interest in the work, or is not altogether identified with the company? How can the superior keep that knowledge from interfering with judgments he or she might otherwise make, and opportunities he or she might otherwise offer? How often are the personal goals, particularly in middle age, temporary fantasies that are better not discussed? Can superiors who are untrained in psychology handle such information constructively? Will they perhaps do more harm than good?

These are critically important questions. They deserve careful thought. My answers should be taken as no more than beginning steps.

EGO CONCEPTS

Living is a process of constant adaptation. An individual's personal goals, wishes, and aspirations are continuously evolving, and being continuously modified by experience. That is one reason why it is so difficult for an individual to specify concrete personal objectives.

Nevertheless, each of us has a built-in road map, a picture of ourself at our future best. Psychologists speak of this as an *ego ideal,* which is comprised of a person's values, the expectations held by parents and others, competences and skills, and favorite ways of behaving. Our ego ideal is essentially the way we think we ought to be. Much of a person's ego ideal is unconscious, which is another reason why it is not clear to that person.

SUBORDINATE'S SELF-EXAMINATION.   Although we cannot usually spell out our ego ideal, we can talk about those experiences that have been highly gratifying, even exhilarating. We can specify those rare peak experiences that made us feel very good about ourselves. When we have an opportunity to talk about what we have found especially gratifying and also what we think would be gratifying, we are touching on central elements of our ego ideal.

Given the opportunity to talk about such experiences and wishes on successive occasions, we can begin to spell out for ourselves the central thrust of our lives. Reviewing all of the occupational choices we have made and the reasons for making them, we can begin to see the common threads in those choices and therefore the momentum of our personality. As these become clearer, we are in a better position to weigh alternatives against the mainstream of our personality.

For example, people who have successively chosen occupational alternatives in which they were individually competitive, and whose most exhilarating experiences have come from defeating an opponent or single-handedly vanquishing a problem, would be unlikely to find a staff position exhilarating, no matter what it paid or what it was called. The ideal for them is that of a vanquishing, competitive person.

The important concept here is that it is not necessary that people spell out concrete goals at any one point; rather, it is helpful to individuals and the organization if they are able to examine and review aloud on a continuing basis their thoughts and feelings about themselves in relation to their work. Such a process makes it legitimate for them to bring their own feelings to consciousness and talk about them in the business context as the basis for their relationship to the organization.

By listening, and helping subordinates to spell out how and what they feel, the superior does not *do* anything to the subordinate, and therefore by that self-appraisal process cannot hurt him or her. The information serves both the subordinate and the superior as a criterion for examining the relationship of the subordinate's feelings and, however dimly perceived, personal goals to organizational goals. Even if some wishes and aspirations are mere fantasy and

HARVARD BUSINESS SCHOOL PRESS, BOSTON, MA 02163

THANK YOU FOR YOUR INTEREST IN THIS BOOK

We would like to know more about our readers. Please complete and return this card:

Book Title/Author _____

Purchased at _____

Comments _____

_____

☐ **Please send me the Harvard Business School Press book catalog.**

☐ **Please send me information on forthcoming books in:**

☐ Accounting/Control   ☐ General Management/Business Policy
☐ Finance   ☐ International Business
☐ Manufacturing/Operations Mgt.   ☐ Business & the Public Sector
☐ Marketing   ☐ Business History
☐ Human Resource Management   ☐ Industry Studies – please specify:

_____

☐ **I am interested in course adoption materials from Harvard Business School.**

☐ **My Job Title/Industry** _____

Your Name _____

Address _____

City _____ State _____ Zip _____

Quantity discounts are available on corporate and institutional orders of HBS Press books.
For further information, call (617) 495-6700.

RRC4

HBS
PRESS

Harvard Business School Press
Boston, Massachusetts 02163

BUSINESS REPLY MAIL
FIRST CLASS PERMIT NO. 2725 BOSTON, MA

POSTAGE WILL BE PAID BY ADDRESSEE:

Harvard Business School Press
Morgan 41
Harvard Business School
Boston, Massachusetts 02163

impossible to gratify, if it is legitimate to talk about them without being laughed at, the subordinate can compare them with the realities of his or her life and make more reasonable choices.

Even in the safest organizational atmosphere, for reasons already mentioned, it will not be easy for managers to talk about their goals. The best-intentioned supervisor is likely to be something less than a highly skilled interviewer. These two facts suggest that any effort to ascertain a subordinate's personal goals is futile; but I think not.

The important point is not the specificity of the statement that a person can make, but the nature of a superior-subordinate relationship that makes it safe to explore such feelings and gives first consideration to the individual. In such a context, both subordinate and superior may come closer to evolving an individual-organization fit than they might otherwise.

SUPERIOR'S INTROSPECTION.　An individual-organization relationship requires the superior to do some introspection, too. Suppose she has prided herself on bringing along a bright young woman who, she now learns, is thinking of moving into a different field. How can she keep from being angry and disappointed? How can she cope with the conflict she now has when it is time to make recommendations for advancement or a raise?

The superior cannot keep from being angry and disappointed. Such feelings are natural in that circumstance. She can express her feelings of disappointment to her protégé without being critical of the latter. But, if she continues to feel angry, then she needs to ask herself why another person's assertion of independence irritates her so. The issues of advancement and raises should continue to be based on the same realistic premises as they would have been before.

Of course, it now becomes appropriate to consider with the woman whether—in view of her feelings—she wants to take on the burden of added responsibility and can reasonably discharge it. If she thinks she does, and can, she is likely to pursue the new responsibility with added determination. With her occupational choice conflict no longer hidden, and with fewer feelings of guilt about it, her commitment to her chosen alternative is likely to be more intense.

And if she has earned a raise, she should get it. To withhold it is to punish her, which puts the relationship back on a reward-punishment basis.

The question of how ethical it is to conduct such discussions as part of a business situation hinges on both the climate of the organization and on the sense of personal responsibility of each executive. Where the organization ethos is one of building trust and keeping confidences, there is no reason why executives cannot be as ethical as lawyers or physicians.

If individual executives cannot be trusted in their relationships with subordinates, then they cannot have their respect or confidence in any case, and the ordinary MBO appraisal process simply serves as a management pressure device. If the organization ethos is one of rapacious internal competition, backbiting, and distrust, there is little point in talking about self-motivation, human needs, or commitment.

Conclusion

Management by objectives and performance appraisal processes, as typically practiced, are inherently self-defeating over the long run because they are based on a reward-punishment psychology that serves to intensify the pressure on the individual while really providing a very limited choice of objectives. Such processes can be improved by examining the psychological assumptions underlying them, by extending them to include group appraisal and appraisal of superiors by subordinates, and by considering the personal goals of the individual first. These practices require a high level of ethical standards and personal responsibility in the organization.

Such appraisal processes would diminish the feeling on the part of the superior that appraisal is a hostile, destructive act. While a superior would still have to judge the subordinate's individual performance, this judgment would occur in a context of continuing consideration for personal needs and reappraisal of organizational and environmental realities.

Not having to be continuously on the defensive, and aware of the organization's genuine interest in having managers meet personal goals as well as organizational goals, managers would be freer to evaluate themselves against what has to be done. Since they would have many additional frames of reference in both horizontal and vertical goal setting, they would need no longer to see themselves under appraisal (attack, judgment) as an isolated individual against the system. Furthermore, they would have multiple modes for contributing their own ideas and a varied method for exerting influence upward and horizontally.

In these contexts, too, they could raise questions and concerns about qualitative aspects of performance. Then managers, colleagues, and superiors could together act to cope with such issues without the barrier of having to consider only statistics. Thus a continuing process of interchange would counteract the problem of the static job description and provide multiple avenues for feedback on performance and joint action.

In such an organizational climate, work relationships would then become dynamic networks for both personal and organizational achievements. No incidental gain from such arrangements is that problems would more likely be solved spontaneously at the lowest possible levels, and free superiors simultaneously from the burden of the passed buck and the onus of being the purveyors of hostility.

Notes

1. Douglas McGregor, "An Uneasy Look at Performance Appraisal," *Harvard Business Review* (May–June 1957), p. 89.
2. Harry Levinson, "On Being a Middle-aged Manager," *Harvard Business Review* (July–August 1969), p. 51.
3. Ronald J. Burke and Douglas S. Wilcox, "Characteristics of Effective Employee Performance Reviews and Developmental Interviews," *Personal Psychology,* vol. 22, no. 3 (1969), p. 291.

5
Employee Growth through Performance Management

Michael Beer and Robert A. Ruh

In recent years, management by objectives (MBO) has enjoyed a good deal of popularity. Both personnel specialists and line managers have responded enthusiastically to the emphasis that MBO places on subordinates' results and accountability rather than on their personal qualities. MBO's popularity is easy to understand.

First, many, if not most, managers feel quite uncomfortable judging the means by which their subordinates accomplish their goals. There are, of course, many reasons for this discomfort. Some managers find evaluating people incompatible with the egalitarian ideals of our society. Others shy away from the role of providing feedback because they fear emotionally laden interpersonal situations. Still others are simply so results-oriented that they have no time for such "personnel stuff."

Second, MBO has proved to be a useful vehicle for increasing the quantity and quality of communication between line managers and subordinates concerning responsibilities, objectives, plans, and results. In addition, research has shown that the setting of specific objectives generally increases the individual's motivation to do certain tasks well.

Despite its usefulness, many managers have found that MBO also has its limitations. In fact, its major strength is its major weakness: MBO focuses the attention of the boss and the subordinate exclusively on task results. For example, a manufacturing manager reviewed the objectives of his plant manager and found that objectives for cost reduction as well as for gross margins had been exceeded. He was pleased. He was not so pleased when he learned sometime later that the MBO process had failed to uncover crucial information: the plant manager had not developed a cohesive plant staff and was not getting along well with managers in other functional areas. MBO does not, therefore, help the manager to observe and evaluate the behavior of his or her subordinates; yet such observation and evaluation are vital to making intelligent promotion decisions and helping employees improve their performance.

Take, for example, the case of a hypothetical sales manager whose job is to improve the performance of his sales force. Suppose that this manager has two salesmen performing substantially below standard; both are achieving only 80% of their revenue budgets. How is the manager to help these people improve? Clearly, his first step must be to analyze why each salesman is doing so poorly. It's possible that one salesman lacks the forcefulness and aggressiveness needed to overcome objections and "close" sales, while the other salesman may be alienating customers with his aggressiveness and overconfidence. Obviously, different approaches are called for to help these two people improve, even though their results are about the same.

The dilemma the vice president of sales would have in the same hypothetical organization illustrates the deficiency of MBO as far as making promotion decisions goes. Let's suppose that the vice president has one sales management position to fill and that the two most logical candidates both consistently achieve 150% of their quotas. In order to pick the better of the two, the vice president must analyze their behavior patterns.

Imagine that one salesman achieves his outstanding results through sheer strength of drive. Fiercely competitive, he is effective because he is a hard worker and persistent. Unfortunately, this salesman is not very well organized. Indeed, he is rather sloppy with paperwork, and most of his colleagues find him quite difficult to work with. In contrast, imagine that the other salesman performs so well primarily because he does a good job at analyzing his territory and customers and because he plans and organizes effective selling strategies. In addition, he is particularly adept at gaining the help and cooperation he needs from others on the sales force and the marketing staff. Clearly, which of these two people would make the better sales manager cannot be determined by results alone.

For a number of years, managers at Corning Glass Works have used MBO. But because of its shortcomings, staff psychologists and personnel specialists began to look for a system that would incorporate its strengths with a better way to help managers observe, evaluate, and aid in improving the performance of subordinates. After several years of research and development, we produced what we call the performance management system. The PMS is the formal vehicle now used by Corning to manage, measure, and improve the performance and potential for advancement of approximately 3,800 managerial and professional employees.

Our purpose in this article is to describe and analyze this system. It is working at Corning, and we think it can work in other companies. But because a system is only as good as the commitment and skill of people who must use it, we shall also discuss the strategy and tactics used to introduce it as a corporate program and then its strengths and deficiencies. First, however, we would like to share with you the thinking behind the system and why we thought it would be effective.

Managing, Judging, and Helping

One of the most critical problems facing corporations is management development. A central thesis underlying Corning's PMS is that, while classroom learning has its place, effective managerial performance is best developed through practical challenges and experiences on the job with guidance and feedback from superiors. Analysis of current organizational life indicates that the element most frequently missing or deficient in this equation is accurate and objective performance feedback.

PMS was developed to help managers give such feedback in a helpful and constructive manner and to aid the supervisor and subordinate in creating a developmental plan. It is distinguished from other performance appraisal systems by the following characteristics: (1) its formal recognition of the manager's triple role in dealing with subordinates, (2) its emphasis on both development and evaluation, (3) its use of a profile displaying the individual's strengths and developmental needs relative to himself rather than to others, and (4) its integration of the results achieved (MBO) with the means by which they have been achieved.

The development of Corning's PMS was triggered by several problems normally encountered by managers because of their triple role as *managers* responsible for the achievement of organization goals, *judges* who must evaluate performance and make decisions about salary and promotability, and *helpers* who must develop subordinates into more effective and promotable employees. Experience has shown that these functions are not always carried out successfully because they are confused by the manager and they interfere with one another when the manager attempts to communicate with a subordinate.

For example, if you ask a manager who uses only MBO if he reviews his subordinates' performance and helps them develop and improve, he will probably answer yes. Yet, while managing by objectives can play a critical part in ensuring individual and group results, it fails to help subordinates understand what behavior they must modify or adopt to improve those results.

Another typical problem arises from the conflict between the manager's role as judge and his role as helper. To fulfill his responsibilities to the organization, the manager must submit evaluations to the personnel department, make recommendations about subordinates' promotions, and make salary judgments. Research has shown that his role as judge interferes with his ability to develop a helping relationship with subordinates.[1] A subordinate often begins to feel so defensive that he or she does not hear what the boss is saying, especially when the boss is trying to be a judge and a helper at the same time. Management at Corning developed PMS to help managers differentiate between these roles and to perform each of them effectively.

Designing the System

Essentially, PMS has three parts—MBO, performance development and review, and evaluation and salary review. Exhibit I indicates how the first two parts, independent and parallel to each other, feed into the third.

What makes the system unusual is a combination of two factors— a careful separation of each part from the other two (that is, each part is carried out separately from the other parts in meetings held at different times between manager and subordinate) and a step-by-step process for company managers to use in performance development and review.

Exhibit I. *Managing Performance*

Management by objectives	Performance development and review
Agree on objectives	Observe behavior
▼	▼
Set criteria	Describe incidents typical of the person
▼	▼
Make plans	Analyze data
▼	▼
Execute plans	Discuss problems and goals
▼	▼
Measure results	Make plans
▼	▼
Review results	Review progress
▼	▼
Begin new cycle	Begin new cycle
▼	▼

Performance results evaluation

Make salary decisions

▼

Make placement decisions

HOW A SUBORDINATE PERFORMS

While MBO seemed to be a process better designed by each manager to fit his own situation than by the corporation, and the evaluation and salary review process in itself presented few problems, performance development and review was another matter entirely. There were elements of performance common to the various functions and units of the organization, and, as we said before, many managers were encountering difficulty in helping subordinates improve their performance. Consequently, to fill this gap, we developed a step-by-step approach.

Using a *performance description questionnaire,* the manager first observes and describes his subordinates' behavior. Then, using a *performance profile,* he analyzes their strengths and weaknesses. Finally, through one or more *developmental interviews,* he attempts to help his subordinates see what changes in behavior are needed and plan for them. In these interviews, boss and subordinate jointly identify areas for improvement and establish plans to develop the abilities needed.

CRITICAL QUESTIONS.   The performance description questionnaire contains 76 items on which the performance of an exempt salaried person is evaluated by his immediate supervisor. Each item describes a specific type of behavior that has been identified as an important component of effective performance. Exhibit II lists eight items from the questionnaire. The supervisor is asked to indicate on a six-point rating scale the extent to which he agrees that his subordinate behaves in ways similar to those described in the questionnaire. Space below each item provides the superior a chance to add comments or examples that substantiate the descriptive rating—"critical incidents" he has actually observed.

Taken together, the behavioral statements represent a comprehensive picture of effective performance within Corning Glass Works. They were identified through extensive research throughout the company and thus reflect the nature of the business environment as well as the company's culture and values and the nature of the tasks to be performed. What this means, of course, is that, while some of the performance items are common to many organizations, others are of significance only to Corning. It also implies that periodic research to update the list is needed as Corning's business, strategy, culture, and tasks change.

Exhibit II.   Items from Performance Descriptions Questionnaire

Individual performance

1. Objects to ideas before they are explained.

2. Takes the initiative in group meetings.

3. Is unable to distinguish between important and un-important problems.

4. Has difficulty in meeting project deadlines.

5. Gives sufficient attention to detail when seeking so-lutions to problems.

6. Gives poor presentations.

7. Sees his problems in light of the problems of others (that is, does not limit his thinking to his own position or organization unit).

8. Offers constructive ideas both within and outside his own job.

At Corning, the first step in the research was to pool what supervisors considered the critical incidents in the job performance of their exempt employees. We asked 50 supervisors, representing a cross section of levels, functions, and divisions within the company, to describe subordinates' specific actions that had led to either significant improvements or significant decrements in their departments' performance. The supervisors identified approximately 300 critical incidents, which we then translated into 150 general behavioral descriptions.

After further research to test the validity of these general descriptions on 300 employees (selected at random), we arrived at 76 items having a statistically significant correlation with performance and management potential throughout the company.

INDIVIDUALIZED PROFILES.   While a supervisor can easily evaluate each of his subordinates on all 76 items, it would be extremely time-consuming to review all 76 with each of his subordinates. So we had

Exhibit III. Performance Profile

Individual performance	Subordinate A		Subordinate B		Subordinate C	
	Weakness	Strength	Weakness	Strength	Weakness	Strength
Openness to influence	●●		●●●●			●
Constructive initiative		●●				●●●●●
Priority setting		●●		●●		●●●●●
Work accomplishment	●●		●●●●●●●●		●●	
Thoroughness and accuracy		●●		●		●
Formal communications	●●			●	●●●●●	
Organizational perspective		●●	●			●●●●
Credibility	●●			●●●	●●	
Cooperation		●●	●		●●	
Decisiveness	●●			●●	●●	
Flexibility	●					

Performance					
Delegation/participation	••	••	•••••	••	
Support for company	••	••	••	••••••••	
Communication and positive motivation	••	••	•••••		••
Follow-up and control	••	••	•••••		••
Unit improvement	••	••	••	••	•••••
Selection, placement, and instruction	••	••	••••		••
Unit productivity	••	••	••	••	
Conflict resolution	••	••	•••	••	

to invent some "shorthand" he could use to transmit to his subordinates the complex information obtained in the questionnaire.

First, we summarized the 76 items along 19 performance dimensions, 8 relating to supervision and 11 to individual performance, which are listed on the left-hand side of Exhibit III. We will not describe here the statistical methods used to arrive at these dimensions; suffice it to say that problems were encountered.

The most troublesome problem was that the supervisors tended to rate items quite similarly for a particular subordinate depending on whether they saw him as a good performer or a poor one in the first place. This tendency of the rater to allow his initial impressions to influence all subsequent descriptions is known as the "halo error." The good performer would not receive feedback that would help him better himself for promotion, and the poor performer would feel "dumped on" and be unable to marshal his energies to work on anything.

We felt that everyone has developmental needs, even the best performers in the corporation. Thus everyone could gain from working on the few performance dimensions for which he had received the lowest ratings.

To break the halo effect, we next developed the performance profile, a tool to help managers discriminate among a subordinate's strengths and developmental needs. For each subordinate, the supervisor receives a performance profile like the three samples shown in Exhibit III. The center line indicates the person's own average. The dimensions extending to the left are the subordinate's weaknesses; the dimensions extending to the right are the subordinate's strengths. The number of dots indicate specific degrees of weakness or strength. Note that these three profiles should not be compared with each other, since each is structured to reflect only the individual's performance.

We have found that managers are surprised when they receive the profile because they are not used to thinking about their subordinates as having negative qualities, or perhaps at least not the particular ones listed. To us, their surprise indicates that the profile is breaking the halo effect. In fact, the profile has four distinct advantages:

1. It helps both the supervisor and the subordinate to be analytical and discriminating in their evaluation of performance.
2. It, therefore, helps ensure individuals fair recognition for their strengths and constructive criticism for their shortcomings.

3. It reduces the supervisor's defensiveness and his need to "prove" the validity of his judgments.
4. It reduces the subordinate's defensiveness and his need to enhance his superior's judgment of him in relation to his "competitors."

THE INTERVIEW.   A subordinate's performance profile is developed by computer after his supervisor has filled out and sent in his performance description questionnaire. After receiving the profile, the manager is urged to use it to analyze his subordinate's performance in preparation for the developmental interview. Often the supervisor will want to identify the specific behavioral ratings that have caused a dimension to come out as a developmental need. In the interview, the specific behavior that needs attention can be discussed.

Some supervisors have found that asking subordinates to fill out questionnaires on themselves encourages open and nondefensive discussion of their performance. Each dimension can be reviewed and discrepancies between superiors' and subordinates' impressions discussed.

It is not our intent here to describe the ground rules for effective developmental interviews; much has been written about this elsewhere.[2] We do wish to point out that in the PMS the developmental interview is a meeting distinct and separate from an MBO session or an evaluation session. The questionnaire and the profile are tools that help the manager differentiate development from MBO and evaluation and that reduce the anxiety associated with the developmental interview.

Finally, it is our belief that developmental plans and objectives are needed if change is actually to occur. The manager needs tools to help him form a developmental plan with his subordinates. These come in the form of (a) an interview guide, for translating explicit developmental needs into specific areas for which training programs have been identified, and (b) a matrix framework as shown in Exhibit IV, for translating broad needs into general strategies for development.

HOW A SUBORDINATE IS EVALUATED

As we mentioned earlier, evaluation interviews of a subordinate's current performance, potential, promotability, and salary increase

Exhibit IV.   Developmental Matrix (an initial guide to alternative approaches to personal development)

Strategies for Improvement

General areas where improvement is needed	Training — Job-related skills or knowledge	In the laboratory or on the job	Counseling — Professional consulting, counseling	Supervision — Coaching	Observing boss's managerial style	Job enrichment — Job redesign	Job rotation
Understanding of role				●●		●●	
Effort, motivation, attitude		●●		●●	●●●	●●	●●●
Knowledge of job or ability	●●●			●●●		●●	●●
Interpersonal skills		●●	●●●	●●●			
Personality traits		●●	●●	●●			

are distinct from MBO and appraisal sessions. It is best to make these evaluations when the subordinate is due for a salary increase. The manager rates each subordinate's overall performance and potential. The ratings, which are shared with subordinates and endorsed by the supervisor at the next level, reflect both the whats and the hows of performance.

Seeking Commitment

Since the effectiveness of any personnel system, no matter how well designed, is largely determined by the understanding, commitment, and skills of the line managers who must actually implement the program, we introduced PMS with these managers in mind.

The best way for a staff function to engender resentment or apathy toward a program is to "cram it down the throats" of the people who must implement it, so we did not attempt to introduce the system throughout the corporation all at once. Instead, we gained the approval and support of top corporate management first and then introduced the system to one division at a time on a quasi-voluntary basis. In essence, we sold each division vice president on the program with no pressure from top corporate management. In accordance with what is known about effective change, we started with the divisions that seemed the most receptive and the most likely to succeed in using the program.

After selling the program to corporate and divisional managers on an individual basis, our primary vehicle for introducing the program within each division was a workshop training session. These sessions, which lasted either two full days or one very long day, covered the following points:

The need for and importance of effective performance appraisal.

The rationale for a program that integrates behavior with results-centered approaches to appraisal.

The research that led to performance development and review.

The MBO approach to performance appraisal and how it is implemented.

The use of the questionnaire and the profile.

The way to conduct a developmental interview in a constructive, problem-solving manner.

In addition to the traditional lecture-and-discussion format, we used a variety of instructional techniques including informal discussion groups, films, and role playing.

Gaining Acceptance and Making Refinements

To investigate the extent to which PMS was being used and its effectiveness, we conducted a study in the four divisions having the most experience with the program, ranging from approximately two years to less than one year.[3] We found that 230 of the 351 supervisory personnel in seven plants and four division staff groups had participated in a performance development and review interview, either as bosses or subordinates or as both. Mobility was the primary reason why not all of the managers had participated; an employee or his supervisor very often changed jobs before they had worked together six months. Another reason appeared to be cases of little or no perceived encouragement to use the system.

Through a questionnaire we sent out, however, more than 90% of those who had participated in an interview provided us with detailed feedback on their impressions of the program. In addition, we checked our interpretations with the division management staffs during subsequent meetings we held with them. They confirmed and often elaborated on our interpretations.

Of course there are bound to be some complaints with any new, complex system involving a large number of people. Our data, however, indicated a generally high acceptance of PMS among those who had used it. First of all, all supervisors accepted some form of performance feedback as part of their jobs. Second, PMS in general and the questionnaire and profile in particular were seen as greatly helpful in the performance appraisal and development process.

REDUCTION OF ANXIETY

It is interesting that the person who found PMS the most helpful was the interviewer. Apparently, the active role of the supervisor placed more responsibility and pressure on him than on the subordinate.

For some, simply having the more formal, scientific-looking results of the questionnaire and profile rather than depending solely on their less systematized observations and conclusions helped set an easygoing tone. For most people, the profile appeared to function as an agenda that furthermore helped stimulate discussion of all aspects of a subordinate's performance. Despite these advances, the supervisors we sampled still seemed to feel that they greatly needed to improve their skills in conducting developmental interviews, and a related study on the effectiveness of the PMS workshop confirmed this finding.

IMPORTANT LINE RELATIONSHIPS

One would think a highly accepted system like PMS would spread itself by word of mouth, at least within a single plant. Our results do not confirm this optimistic notion. In fact, it seems that few people communicate their positive views to others in the company. The availability of a good system is not enough to spread its use; a vigorously active program is necessary.

For instance, we found a couple of chains of supervisor-subordinate relationships that had not used the PMS. These people reported that although they hadn't been told *not* to use it, they did not feel that they should until the man at the top of the chain told them to or at least had used it with his own subordinates. Other people seemed to want PMS and indicated that they were "waiting for follow-up," that is, pressure from someone in authority.

ORGANIZATIONAL ASSET

If we accept the premise that the manager's most important task is managing the performance of his subordinates and that constructive performance feedback is a key element in developing managers, then PMS is definitely an organizational asset.

In order to use PMS most effectively, significant resources are needed to follow the introductory workshop with on-the-spot consultation in planning and conducting developmental interviews. Too often, training is thought of as the final step in the introductory process. We recommend instead that personnel specialists help managers go through the PMS process at least once. In order to ensure that a performance management system will be used in the first place, key managers at all levels must state their commitment to it and model its use.

At Corning, many managers have found that just identifying the performance dimensions that are important to organizational effectiveness helps develop a common language for discussing performance and making decisions about people, something that is absent in most organizations. Thus, a performance management system can increase the objectivity and enhance the validity of personnel decisions.

Notes

1. Herbert H. Meyer, Emanuel Kay, and John R. P. French, Jr., "Split Roles in Performance Appraisal," *Harvard Business Review* (January–February 1965), p. 123.
2. Norman R. F. Maier, *The Appraisal Interview: Gestures, Methods, and Skills* (New York: John Wiley, 1958).
3. Jack E. Dawson and B. B. (Steve) McCaa, "Performance Development and Review: An Evaluation of Its Utilization," a paper presented at *Performance Management System: Research, Design, Introduction and Evaluation,* a symposium of the American Psychological Association Convention, New Orleans, 1974.

6
Make Performance Appraisal Relevant

Winston Oberg

These frequently voiced goals of performance appraisal programs underscore the importance of such programs to any ongoing business organization:

Help or prod supervisors to observe their subordinates more closely and to do a better coaching job.

Motivate employees by providing feedback on how they are doing.

Provide backup data for management decisions concerning merit increases, transfers, dismissals, and so on.

Improve organization development by identifying people with promotion potential and pinpointing development needs.

Establish a research and reference base for personnel decisions.

It has been estimated that over three-fourths of U.S. companies now have performance appraisal programs.[1]

In actual practice, however, formal performance appraisal programs have often yielded unsatisfactory and disappointing results, as the growing body of critical literature attests.[2] Some critics even suggest that we abandon performance appraisal as a lost hope, and they point to scores of problems and pitfalls as evidence.

But considering the potential of appraisal programs, the issue should not be whether to scrap them; rather, it should be how to make them better. I have found that one reason for failures is that companies often select indiscriminately from the wide battery of available performance appraisal techniques without really thinking about which particular technique is best suited to a particular appraisal objective.

For example, the most commonly used appraisal techniques include

1. Essay appraisal.
2. Graphic rating scale.
3. Field review.
4. Forced-choice rating.
5. Critical incident appraisal.
6. Management-by-objectives approach.
7. Work-standards approach.
8. Ranking methods.
9. Assessment centers.

Each of these has its own combination of strengths and weaknesses, and none is able to achieve all of the purposes for which management institutes performance appraisal systems. Nor is any one technique able to evade all of the pitfalls. The best anyone can hope to do is to match an appropriate appraisal method to a particular performance appraisal goal.

In this article, I shall attempt to lay the groundwork for such a matching effort. First, I shall review some familiar pitfalls in appraisal programs; then, against this background, I shall assess the strengths and weaknesses of the nine commonly used appraisal techniques. In the last section, I shall match the organizational objectives listed at the outset of this article with the techniques best suited to achieving them.

Some Common Pitfalls

Obstacles to the success of formal performance appraisal programs should be familiar to most managers, either from painful personal experience or from the growing body of critical literature. Here are the most troublesome and frequently cited drawbacks:

Performance appraisal programs demand too much from supervisors. Formal performance appraisals obviously require at least periodic supervisor observation of subordinates' performance.

However, the typical first-line supervisor can hardly know, in a very adequate way, just what each of 20, 30, or more subordinates is doing.

Standards and ratings tend to vary widely and, often, unfairly. Some raters are tough, others are lenient. Some departments have highly competent people; others have less competent people. Consequently, employees subject to less competition or lenient ratings can receive higher appraisals than equally competent or superior associates.

Personal values and bias can replace organizational standards. An appraiser may not lack standards, but the standards he uses are sometimes the wrong ones. For example, unfairly low ratings may be given to valued subordinates so they will not be promoted out of the rater's department. More often, however, outright bias dictates favored treatment for some employees.

Because of lack of communication, employees may not know how they are rated. The standards by which employees think they are being judged are sometimes different from those their superiors actually use. No performance appraisal system can be very effective for management decisions, organization development, or any other purpose until the people being appraised know what is expected of them and by what criteria they are being judged.

Appraisal techniques tend to be used as performance panaceas. If a worker lacks the basic ability or has not been given the necessary training for his job, it is neither reasonable to try to stimulate adequate performance through performance appraisals, nor fair to base salary, dismissal, or other negative decisions on such an appraisal. No appraisal program can substitute for sound selection, placement, and training programs. Poor performance represents someone else's failure.

In many cases, the validity of ratings is reduced by supervisory resistance to making the ratings. Rather than confront their less effective subordinates with negative ratings, negative feedback in appraisal interviews, and below-average salary increases, supervisors often take the more comfortable way out and give average or above-average ratings to inferior performers.

Performance appraisal ratings can boomerang when communicated to employees. Negative feedback (i.e., criticism) not only fails to motivate the typical employee, but also can cause him to perform worse.[3] Only those employees who have a high degree of self-esteem appear to be stimulated by criticism to improve their performance.

Performance appraisals interfere with the more constructive coaching relationship that should exist between a superior and his subordinates. Performance appraisal interviews tend to emphasize the superior position of the supervisor by placing him in the role of judge, thus countering his equally important role of teacher and coach. This is particularly damaging in organizations that are attempting to maintain a more participative organizational climate.

A Look at Methods

The foregoing list of major program pitfalls represents a formidable challenge, even considering the available battery of appraisal techniques. But attempting to avoid these pitfalls by doing away with appraisals themselves is like trying to solve the problems of life by committing suicide. The more logical task is to identify those appraisal practices that are (a) most likely to achieve a particular objective and (b) least vulnerable to the obstacles already discussed.

Before relating the specific techniques to the goals of performance appraisal stated at the outset of the article, I shall briefly review each, taking them more or less in an order of increasing complexity. The best-known techniques will be treated most briefly.

ESSAY APPRAISAL

In its simplest form, this technique asks the rater to write a paragraph or more covering an individual's strengths, weaknesses, potential, and so on. In most selection situations, particularly those involving professional, sales, or managerial positions, essay appraisals from former employers, teachers, or associates carry significant weight. The assumption seems to be that an honest and informed statement—either by word of mouth or in writing—from someone who knows a man well, is fully as valid as more formal and more complicated methods.

The biggest drawback to essay appraisals is their variability in length and content. Moreover, since different essays touch on different aspects of a man's performance or personal qualifications, essay ratings are difficult to combine or compare. For comparability, some type of more formal method, like the graphic rating scale, is desirable.

GRAPHIC RATING SCALE

This technique may not yield the depth of an essay appraisal, but it is more consistent and reliable. Typically, a graphic scale assesses a person on the quality and quantity of his work (is he outstanding, above average, average, or unsatisfactory?) and on a variety of other factors that vary with the job but usually include personal traits like reliability and cooperation. It may also include specific performance items like oral and written communication.

The graphic scale has come under frequent attack, but remains the most widely used rating method. In a classic comparison between the "old-fashioned" graphic scale and the much more sophisticated forced-choice technique, the former proved to be fully as valid as the best of the forced-choice forms, and better than most of them.[4] It is also cheaper to develop and more acceptable to raters than the forced-choice form. For many purposes there is no need to use anything more complicated than a graphic scale supplemented by a few essay questions.

FIELD REVIEW

When there is reason to suspect rater bias, when some raters appear to be using higher standards than others, or when comparability of ratings is essential, essay or graphic ratings are often combined with a systematic review process. The field review is one of several techniques for doing this. A member of the personnel or central administrative staff meets with small groups of raters from each supervisory unit and goes over each employee's rating with them to (a) identify areas of inter-rater disagreement, (b) help the group arrive at a consensus, and (c) determine that each rater conceives the standards similarly.

This group-judgment technique tends to be more fair and more valid than individual ratings and permits the central staff to develop an awareness of the varying degrees of leniency or severity—as well as bias—exhibited by raters in different departments. On the negative side, the process is very time-consuming.

FORCED-CHOICE RATING

Like the field review, this technique was developed to reduce bias and establish objective standards of comparison between individuals, but it does not involve the intervention of a third party. Although there are many variations of this method, the most common one asks raters to choose from among groups of statements those that *best* fit the individual being rated and those that *least* fit him. The statements are then weighted or scored, very much the way a psychological test is scored. People with high scores are, by definition, the better employees; those with low scores are the poorer ones. Since the rater does not know what the scoring weights for each statement are, in theory at least, he cannot play favorites. He simply describes his people, and someone in the personnel department applies the scoring weights to determine who gets the best rating.

The rationale behind this technique is difficult to fault. It is the same rationale used in developing selection test batteries. In practice, however, the forced-choice method tends to irritate raters, who feel they are not being trusted. They want to say openly how they rate someone and not be second-guessed or tricked into making "honest" appraisals.

A few clever raters have even found ways to beat the system. When they want to give average employee Harry Smith a high rating, they simply describe the best employee they know. If the best employee is Elliott Jones, they describe Jones on Smith's forced-choice form. Thus, Smith gets a good rating and, hopefully, a raise.

An additional drawback is the difficulty and cost of developing forms. Consequently, the technique is usually limited to middle- and lower-management levels where the jobs are sufficiently similar to make standard or common forms feasible.

Finally, forced-choice forms tend to be of little value—and probably have a negative effect—when used in performance appraisal interviews.

CRITICAL INCIDENT APPRAISAL

The discussion of ratings with employees has, in many companies, proved to be a traumatic experience for supervisors. Some have learned from bitter experience what General Electric later documented: people who receive honest but negative feedback are typically not motivated to do better—and often do worse—after the appraisal interview.[5] Consequently, supervisors tend to avoid such interviews or, if forced to hold them, avoid giving negative ratings when the ratings have to be shown to the employee.

One stumbling block has no doubt been the unsatisfactory rating form used. Typically, these are graphic scales that often include rather vague traits like initiative, cooperativeness, reliability, and even personality. Discussing these with an employee can be difficult.

The critical incident technique looks like a natural to some people for performance review interviews, because it gives a supervisor actual, factual incidents to discuss with an employee. Supervisors are asked to keep a record, a "little black book," on each employee and to record actual incidents of positive or negative behavior. For example:

Bob Mitchell, who has been rated as somewhat unreliable, fails to meet several deadlines during the appraisal period. His supervisor makes a note of these incidents and is now prepared with hard, factual data:

"Bob, I rated you down on reliability because, on three different occasions over the last two months, you told me you would do something and you didn't do it. You remember six weeks ago when I . . ."

Instead of arguing over traits, the discussion now deals with actual behavior. Possibly, Bob has misunderstood the supervisor or has good reasons for his apparent "unreliability." If so, he now has an opportunity to respond. His performance, not his personality, is being criticized. He knows specifically how to perform differently if he wants to be rated higher the next time. Of course, Bob might feel the supervisor was using unfairly high standards in evaluating his performance. But at least he would know just what those standards are.

There are, however, several drawbacks to this approach. It requires that supervisors jot down incidents on a daily or, at the very least, a weekly basis. This can become a chore. Furthermore, the critical incident rating technique need not, but may, cause a supervisor to delay feedback to employees. And it is hardly desirable to wait six months or a year to confront an employee with a misdeed or mistake.

Finally, the supervisor sets the standards. If they seem unfair to a subordinate, might he not be more motivated if he at least has some say in setting, or at least agreeing to, the standards against which he is judged?

MANAGEMENT BY OBJECTIVES

To avoid, or to deal with, the feeling that they are being judged by unfairly high standards, employees in some organizations are being asked to set—or help set—their own performance goals. Within the past five or six years, MBO has become something of a fad and is so familiar to most managers that I will not dwell on it here.

It should be noted, however, that when MBO is applied at lower organizational levels, employees do not always want to be involved in their own goal setting. As Arthur N. Turner and Paul R. Lawrence discovered, many do not want self-direction or autonomy.[6] As a result, more coercive variations of MBO are becoming increasingly common, and some critics see MBO drifting into a kind of manipulative form of management in which pseudo-participation substitutes for the real thing. Employees are consulted, but management ends up imposing its standards and its objectives.[7]

Some organizations, therefore, are introducing a work-standards approach to goal setting in which the goals are openly set by management. In fact, there appears to be something of a vogue in the setting of such work standards in white-collar and service areas.

WORK-STANDARDS APPROACH

Instead of asking employees to set their own performance goals, many organizations set measured daily work standards. In short, the work-standards technique establishes work and staffing targets aimed at improving productivity. When realistically used, it can make possible an objective and accurate appraisal of the work of employees and supervisors.

To be effective, the standards must be visible and fair. Hence a good deal of time is spent observing employees on the job, simplifying and improving the job where possible, and attempting to arrive at realistic output standards.

It is not clear, in every case, that work standards have been integrated with an organization's performance appraisal program. However, since the work-standards program provides each employee with a more or less complete set of his job duties, it would seem only natural that supervisors will eventually relate performance appraisal and interview comments to these duties. I would expect this to happen increasingly where work standards exist. The use of work standards should make performance interviews less threatening than the use of personal, more subjective standards alone.

The most serious drawback appears to be the problem of comparability. If people are evaluated on different standards, how can the ratings be brought together for comparison purposes when decisions have to be made on promotions or on salary increases? For these purposes some form of ranking is necessary.

RANKING METHODS

For comparative purposes, particularly when it is necessary to compare people who work for different supervisors, individual statements, ratings, or appraisal forms are not particularly useful. Instead, it is necessary to recognize that comparisons involve an overall subjective judgment to which a host of additional facts and impressions must somehow be added. There is no single form or way to do this.

Comparing people in different units for the purpose of, say, choosing a service supervisor or determining the relative size of salary increases for different supervisors, requires subjective judgment, not statistics. The best approach appears to be a ranking technique involving pooled judgment. The two most effective methods are alternation ranking and paired-comparison ranking.

ALTERNATION RANKING. In this method, the names of employees are listed on the left-hand side of a sheet of paper—preferably in random order. If the rankings are for salary purposes, a supervisor is asked to choose the "most valuable" employee on the list, cross his name off, and put it at the top of the column on the right-hand side of the sheet. Next, he selects the "least valuable" employee on the list, crosses his name off, and puts it at the bottom of the right-hand column. The ranker then selects the "most valuable" person from the remaining list, crosses his name off and enters it below the top name on the right-hand list, and so on.

PAIRED-COMPARISON RANKING. This technique is probably just as accurate as alternation ranking and might be more so. But with large numbers of employees it becomes extremely time-consuming and cumbersome.

To illustrate the method, let us say we have five employees: Mr. Abbott, Mr. Barnes, Mr. Cox, Mr. Drew, and Mr. Eliot. We list their names on the left-hand side of the sheet. We compare Abbott with Barnes on whatever criterion we have chosen, say, present value to the organization. If we feel Abbott is more valuable than Barnes, we put a tally beside Abbott's name. We then compare Abbott with Cox, with Drew, and with Eliot. The process is repeated for each individual. The man with the most tallies is the most valuable person, at least in the eyes of the rater; the man with no tallies at all is regarded as the least valuable person.

Both ranking techniques, particularly when combined with multiple rankings (i.e., when two or more people are asked to make independent rankings of the same work group and their lists are averaged), are among the best available for generating valid order-of-merit rankings for salary administration purposes.

ASSESSMENT CENTERS

So far, we have been talking about assessing past performance. What about the assessment of future performance or potential? In any placement decision and even more so in promotion decisions, some prediction of future performance is necessary. How can this kind of prediction be made most validly and most fairly?

One widely used rule of thumb is that "what a man has done is the best predictor of what he will do in the future." But suppose you are picking a man to be a supervisor and this person has never held supervisory responsibility? Or suppose you are selecting a man for a job from among a group of candidates, none of whom has done the job or one like it? In these situations, many organizations use assessment centers to predict future performance more accurately.

Typically, individuals from different departments are brought together to spend two or three days working on individual and group assignments similar to the ones they will be handling if they are promoted. The pooled judgment of observers—sometimes derived by paired comparison or alternation ranking—leads to an order-of-merit ranking for each participant. Less structured, subjective judgments are also made.

There is a good deal of evidence that people chosen by assessment center methods work out better than those not chosen by these methods.[8] The center also makes it possible for people who are working for departments of low status or low visibility in an organization to become visible and, in the competitive situation of an assessment center, show how they stack up against people from more well-known departments. This has the effect of equalizing opportunity, improving morale, and enlarging the pool of possible promotion candidates.

Fitting Practice to Purpose

In the foregoing analysis, I have tried to show that each performance appraisal technique has its own combination of strengths and weaknesses. The success of any program that makes use of these techniques will largely depend on how they are used relative to the goals of that program.

For example, goal-setting and work-standards methods will be most effective for objective coaching, counseling, and motivational purposes, but some form of critical incident appraisal is better when a supervisor's personal judgment and criticism are necessary.

Comparisons of individuals, especially in win-lose situations when only one person can be promoted or only a limited number can be given large salary increases, necessitate a still different approach. Each person should be rated on the same form, which must be as simple as possible, probably involving essay and graphic responses. Then order-of-merit rankings and final averaging should follow. To be more explicit, here are the appraisal goals listed at the outset of this article and the techniques best suited to them.

1. Help or prod supervisors to observe their subordinates more closely and to do a better coaching job.

    The critical incident appraisal appears to be ideal for this purpose, if supervisors can be convinced they should take the time to look for, and record, significant events. Time delays, however, are a major drawback to this technique and should be kept as short as possible. Still, over the longer term, a supervisor will gain a better knowledge of his own performance standards, including his possible biases, as he reviews the incidents he has recorded. He may even decide to change or reweight his own criteria.

    Another technique that is useful for coaching purposes is, of course, MBO. Like the critical incident method, it focuses on actual behavior and actual results, which can be discussed objectively and constructively, with little or no need for a supervisor to "play God."

2. Motivate employees by providing feedback on how they are doing.

The MBO approach, if it involves real participation, appears to be most likely to lead to an inner commitment to improved performance. However, the work-standards approach can also motivate, although in a more coercive way. If organizations staff to meet their work standards, the work force is reduced and people are compelled to work harder.

The former technique is more "democratic," while the latter technique is more "autocratic." Both can be effective; both make use of specific work goals or targets, and both provide for knowledge of results.

If performance appraisal information is to be communicated to subordinates, either in writing or in an interview, the two most effective techniques are the management-by-objectives approach and the critical incident method. The latter, by communicating not only factual data but also the flavor of a supervisor's own values and biases, can be effective in an area where objective work standards or quantitative goals are not available.

3. Provide backup data for management decisions concerning merit increases, promotions, transfers, dismissals, and so on.

Most decisions involving employees require a comparison of people doing very different kinds of work. In this respect, the more specifically job-related techniques like management by objectives or work standards are not appropriate, or, if used, must be supplemented by less restricted methods.

For promotion to supervisory positions, the forced-choice rating form, if carefully developed and validated, could prove best. But the difficulty and cost of developing such a form and the resistance of raters to its use render it impractical except in large organizations.

Companies faced with the problem of selecting promotable men from a number of departments or divisions might consider using an assessment center. This minimizes the bias resulting from differences in departmental "visibility" and enlarges the pool of potential promotables.

The best appraisal method for most other management decisions will probably involve a very simple kind of graphic form or a combined graphic and essay form. If this is supplemented by the use of field reviews, it will be measurably strengthened. Following the individual appraisals, groups of supervisors should then be asked to rank the people they have rated, using a technique like alternation ranking or paired comparison. Pooled or averaged rankings will then tend to cancel out the most extreme forms of bias and should yield fair and valid order-of-merit lists.

4. Improve organization development by identifying people with promotion potential and pinpointing development needs.

 Comparison of people for promotion purposes has already been discussed. However, identification of training and development needs will probably best—and most simply—come from the essay part of the combined graphic/essay rating form recommended for the previous goal.

5. Establish a reference and research base for personnel decisions.

 For this goal, the simplest form is the best form. A graphic/essay combination is adequate for most reference purposes. But order-of-merit salary rankings should be used to develop criterion groups of good and poor performers.

Conclusion

Formal systems for appraising performance are neither worthless nor evil, as some critics have implied. Nor are they panaceas, as many managers might wish. A formal appraisal system is, at the very least, a commendable attempt to make visible, and hence improvable, a set of essential organization activities. Personal judgments about employee performance are inescapable, and subjective values and fallible human perception are always involved. Formal appraisal systems, to the degree that they bring these perceptions and values into the open, make it possible for at least some of the inherent bias and error to be recognized and remedied.

By improving the probability that good performance will be recognized and rewarded and poor performance corrected, a sound appraisal system can contribute both to organizational morale and organizational performance. Moreover, the alternative to a bad appraisal program need not be no appraisal program at all, as some critics have suggested. It can and ought to be a better appraisal program. And the first step in that direction is a thoughtful matching of practice to purpose.

Notes

[1.] See W. R. Spriegel and Edwin W. Mumma, *Merit Rating of Supervisors and Executives* (Austin: Bureau of Business Research, University of Texas, 1961); and Richard V. Miller, "Merit Rating in

Industry: A Survey of Current Practices and Problems," *ILR Research* (Fall 1959).

2. See, for example, Douglas McGregor, "An Uneasy Look at Performance Appraisal," *Harvard Business Review* (May–June 1957), p. 89; Paul H. Thompson and Gene W. Dalton, "Performance Appraisal: Managers Beware," *Harvard Business Review* (January–February 1970), p. 149; and Albert W. Schrader, "Let's Abolish the Annual Performance Review," *Management of Personnel Quarterly* (Fall 1969), p. 293.

3. See Herbert H. Meyer, Emanuel Kay, and John R. P. French, Jr., "Split Roles in Performance Appraisal," *Harvard Business Review* (January–February 1965), p. 123.

4. James Berkshire and Richard Highland, "Forced-Choice Performance Rating on a Methodological Study," *Personnel Psychology* (Autumn 1953), p. 355.

5. Meyer, Kay, and French, "Split Roles in Performance Appraisal," p. 123.

6. Arthur N. Turner and Paul R. Lawrence, *Industrial Jobs and the Worker* (Boston: Division of Research, Harvard Business School, 1965).

7. See, for example, Harry Levinson, "Management by Whose Objectives?" *Harvard Business Review* (July–August 1970), p. 125.

8. See, for example, Robert C. Albrook, "Spot Executives Early," *Fortune* (July 1968), p. 106; and William C. Byham, "Assessment Centers for Spotting Future Managers," *Harvard Business Review* (July–August 1970), p. 150.

7
Cyanamid's New Take on Performance Appraisal

**Saul W. Gellerman and
William G. Hodgson**

In one form or another, performance appraisals have been with us more than 50 years. Few would quarrel with the notion of linking pay to performance, thus rewarding good work and (the employer hopes) giving mediocre performers an incentive or a goad to do better next year. If those who fail to perform quit, the organization benefits.

Still, performance appraisal systems remain endlessly controversial. For one thing, many (if not most) achievers are motivated at least as much by pride or the desire to excel as they are by the hope of better pay. Critics also claim that poor ratings tend to demotivate inferior performers rather than to spur their improvement. Moreover, these poor performers often don't quit; many hang on for years and years. Then there's the sometimes thorny question of how to measure performance. Finally, many managers regard with distaste the obligatory, one-to-one meetings with subordinates to talk about results versus expectations.

At American Cyanamid Company, a performance appraisal system called "progress reviews" had been in operation for more than a decade when, in 1984, the company decided to take a hard look at it. The reviews were part of the merit-based salary administration procedure.

The evaluation grew out of an effort launched by CEO George J. Sella, Jr. to change the company's culture. In a survey, its executives had used these words to describe Cyanamid: conservative, bureaucratic, and not sufficiently people-oriented. While giving it high ratings for integrity and dedication to research and development, they had wished it had "a looser structure," stirred "more creativity," and exhibited more "willingness to take risks."

In response, Sella set $1 million aside for an "innovation fund" to support projects that might improve the quality of life for the company's employees.

A project that got under way at the same time was a different approach to the much-criticized performance appraisal scheme. Undertaken in the Medical Research Division, it was adjudged a success, and a similar plan has been adopted for all 11,500 salaried Cyanamid employees in the United States.

In effect companywide only since 1986, the new tack is still on trial. But there's no question of its success among the knowledge workers in the Medical Research Division.

This alone may have great significance in view of the growing numbers and importance in organizations of workers who make their living mainly by interpreting information. (About one out of eight people in the labor force is now in that category, and their proportion is growing fast.) Satisfying the desire for recognition and advancement of these professional or quasi-professional employees often conflicts with the preference of the organization's bureaucracy for uniform and easily administered procedures, like the performance appraisal.

Acute Dissatisfaction

At Cyanamid, under the old system, salaried people whose performance was judged to be best received an *O* (for "outstanding"), which entitled them to the highest raises. Most others received one or the other of two rankings: *X* ("excellent in several major areas"), or *R* ("achieves expected results"). Approximately 20% of the employees in a given unit were supposed to be rated *O;* 40%, *X;* and 40%, *R*. Subdividing these categories were plus and minus qualifiers, for example, *X+* and *X−* on either side of *X*. There was also a fourth rating, *N* (for "needs improvement"), rarely given. Thus there were ten possible ratings.

Division administrators of the plan customarily awarded ratings more or less in keeping with the 20-40-40 guideline. This also affected salary increases, which were set according to a range in each category. The biggest raises went to employees who won O ratings but who stood low in their salary ranges. The fixed distribution of rewards tended to flatten out the pay raises of those who had earned the same ratings for a period of time.

Scientists in Cyanamid's Medical Research Division, asked for their reactions to the system, offered acid comments, including these:

"The progress reviews do illustrate some aspects of how my superior rates me, but I know damned well that it's also influenced by quotas."

"My work could be outstanding year in and year out, but if one other person in my group was outstanding, I would be denied such a rating."

"Until it's my turn, I can't get a better rating no matter what I do."

"I don't take it seriously. It's a Mickey Mouse numbers game. My superior and I just laugh at it, and we get through it as quickly as we can."

"Evidently there is an effort to fit the people within a section to a bell curve so they can dole out raises and not go over the budget. But as a scientist I know that a bell curve should be applied only when a population is large enough, and these departments are very small."

Among Cyanamid managers, the procedure had advocates and detractors. The advocates held that although it suffered from many of the usual flaws inherent in performance appraisal, its central purpose—to reward and encourage excellence—was simply too important to be sacrificed. Others thought that too often rewards seemed correlated with education and length of service. And further, that the system created apathy and a sense of futility among employees receiving lower ratings whose performance, if measured against their job descriptions rather than against each other, was entirely satisfactory. To the critics, the worst aspect was the demotivating effect of an R rating, which was generally regarded as a stigma.

Cyanamid's personnel department often heard complaints from managers who felt uncomfortable handling the progress reviews. Supervisors were required to identify and discuss aspects of an employee's performance that needed improvement. They dreaded this task. They often felt forced to dwell on trivial shortcomings that ordinarily would be overlooked or on habits that were unlikely to change. And managers shrank from the duty of comparing an employee's performance with that of others in the same department. Many complained of having to face the resentment of employees who got R's.

Clearly, the company was ready for a change.

Divisional Trial

The Medical Research Division carried out the experiment in two of its sections, each employing roughly 70 people, over a two-year period. These sections were chosen because they were the most comparable in the division with respect to size, mission, job characteristics, demographics (especially education and length of employment), and salary distribution. Both sections do experiments and laboratory analysis; both include employees in about the same proportions at the bachelor's, master's, and Ph.D. levels, as well as managers at these levels.

The first step was to establish a baseline of attitudes and perceptions for both groups by means of a questionnaire. This survey found that the two groups were comparable in their almost uniform dislike of the progress reviews, particularly in their antipathy toward the predetermined distribution of ratings. One section now became a control group and the other an experimental group.

While the control group continued under the old system, the experimental group was introduced to a new plan that had these features:

It had only three possible performance ratings.

It assumed that most employees, most of the time, perform somewhere within a broad range of acceptability, and that while fine distinctions within this range are possible (like above or below normal expectations), making them is neither necessary administratively nor desirable motivationally. This broad range of expected performance levels was designated G (for "good").

It assumed that occasionally, but not inevitably, someone's contribution so greatly surpasses the usual range of performance that no reasonable observer would include it within the normal expectations for the particular function. This is not simply a matter of improving on the performance of one's peers but of exceeding the demands of the job itself. Such performance is often a matter of both luck and pluck, of not only being in the right place at the right time but also of seizing opportunities and exploiting them creatively. This category of performance was called *E* (for "exceptional").

Finally, it assumed that performance is sometimes unacceptable and that unless an employee makes a prompt, pronounced, and lasting improvement, he or she should no longer be considered qualified to hold the job. This is not a mere matter of being the poorest performer in one's group but of failing to fill the requirements of the job. This category of performance was designated *U* (for "unacceptable").

It called for no recommended distribution. Since the *E* and *U* categories had narrow, stringent definitions, few (or even, occasionally, no) employees would get either rating. By far the greatest number would ordinarily be rated *G*. The distribution depended on how many employees' work fit the three descriptions.

The system simplified the salary procedure. All employees rated *G* and *E* were awarded raises based only on their positions in the salary range. The *E*'s also received lump-sum bonuses equal to fixed percentages of their salaries. Those rated *U* received no raises.

In the revised progress review interviews, supervisors were expected to compliment subordinates on their strengths and accomplishments, and refer to shortcomings only if they were serious (as in the case of the *U*'s) or were clearly within the employees' power to change through improved effort or attention. The purpose was to make the meeting an ego-supporting instead of ego-damaging experience. The theory was that workers who felt good about themselves would perform better, or at least view their circumstances in a more favorable light, than those who had to defend themselves against what they might see as attacks.

The new system simplified the managers' task. Determining ratings was easier and, more important, the communication of the rating decision was easier. No longer were some employees stigmatized when their work was actually acceptable.

But the program also had its costs. The better performers among the *G*'s (and for that matter the worse performers) were lumped with the others in that big group. Moreover, employees who excelled were not necessarily rewarded differently from their peers. Division officers feared that these features would cause those whose work had been superior to lose their drive to excel. One purpose of the experiment was to determine if this would occur.

HAPPY RESULTS

Following expectations, the vast majority of the members of the experimental group scored *G* in the appraisals. The distribution of performance ratings in two years was this:

	1985	1986
Exceptional	10%	13%
Good	87	87
Unacceptable	3	0

In measuring the reactions of the two groups over one- and two-year intervals, the division used the same survey as the one that established baseline attitudes toward the progress reviews. The results showed a much more favorable attitude developing toward the experimental procedure. Supervisors noted that their subordinates were complaining less.

The responses of the experimental group to a series of statements, four of which are shown in Exhibit I, indicate a growing perception of the performance review system as being less arbitrary. This contrasts sharply with the control group's attitude.

Can the responses of the experimental group be attributed to a "Hawthorne effect"—the brief surge in favorable attitudes that often follows changes in long-standing procedures? We doubt it. Such an attitude would not last two years. The experimental group became more favorably disposed later in the trial period. Nor is it likely that the negative trend in the control group reflected envy of the experimental group, since the existence of the study was not widely known outside the experimental group.

These results imply that views about compensation among comparably paid groups of professional workers depend less on salary levels than on the perceived fairness of the system for determining pay. They may also be a reaction to a simpler, more easily understood way of assigning salary increases.

A happy benefit for managers was a reduction in time spent preparing for the interviews with subordinates: an average of about six hours each under the old review system compared with about three hours for the experimental group's supervisors. One reason, no doubt, was the change from sessions full of negative comments to anticipation of more pleasant meetings. Whereas, for instance, some 80% of subordinates were reported by their superior in 1984 to be critical of the matching of performance ratings to the recommended

Exhibit I. **Encouraging Results from Surveys of the Two Groups**

Statement: Under the progress review system, the factors on which the overall evaluation of my work is based are clearly defined and relevant to my job. (Percentages of "undecided" responses are omitted for all four statements.)

	Experimental Group		Control Group	
	Yes	No	Yes	No
1984	16%	34%	28%	38%
1985	37	24	28	34
1986	55	18	21	35

Statement: On balance, the progress review gives a fair appraisal of my overall performance.

	Yes	No	Yes	No
1984	41%	33%	31%	28%
1985	43	21	22	33
1986	63	18	24	32

Statement: Under the progress review system, the relationship between my performance appraisal and my salary increase is clear and logical.

	Yes	No	Yes	No
1984	29%	42%	34%	51%
1985	30	39	17	61
1986	36	26	17	65

Statement: As far as I can tell, the advancement of other employees in my department during the past year has been primarily on the basis of ability and accomplishment. (This question was inadvertently omitted in 1985.)

	Yes	No	Yes	No
1984	26%	21%	31%	44%
1986	51	26	32	32

distribution, the experimental group's supervisors reported that 85% of their subordinates expressed satisfaction about the *absence* of such distributions.

After two years of exposure to the new system, the most favorable views toward it came from the Ph.D.'s—despite the advantages they had enjoyed under the previous system. This reinforced their claim that they were motivated more by professional pride than by money. One of them wrote in response to a survey question: "For me, the work ethic, my professional pride, and drive are stronger motivating factors than salary increases. But a poor salary increase could be a demotivator."

The Medical Research Division groups were small and unrepresentative of the company as a whole, so it is necessary to interpret the results cautiously. But they are internally consistent. They imply that, at least with highly educated workers, performance appraisal systems that are designed to support rather than deflate egos bolster motivation and promote acceptance of a salary administration system, at no greater financial cost whatever.

Cyanamid Buys It

Without waiting for the end of the experiment in the Medical Research Division, and in a sense anticipating its results, Cyanamid introduced in 1986 new progress review systems for all its salaried workers domestically. The new systems have these characteristics:

There is no recommended distribution.

There are three possible ratings, S ("superior"), Q ("quality"), and N ("needs improvement").

Specific objectives are emphasized, with sign-off by both employee and supervisor on annual performance objectives.

The employee is involved in the performance planning process, particularly in setting up a training and development plan.

The experiment in the medical group confirmed management's judgment in designing those features. But in fairness it must be said that the company would have made these moves even if the trial had not confirmed their worth.

Cyanamid's experience with its new system has been largely positive, but of course it is still new. Early reactions indicate it is considerably more effective and helpful for supervisors and subordinates than the previous system. Some personnel managers have expressed a preference for further differentiation within the broad Q rating; but for the present, top management has decided to keep the system intact while acquiring more experience with it. So far, available evidence indicates that it is broadly applicable to salaried workers of all kinds, not just scientists, and that it represents an improvement over the previous system for all such groups.

The new performance appraisal system has not been without its critics, either in its trial mode or now. Some thought that the Medical Research Division program, however popular with employees and supervisors, was overly egalitarian and would ultimately discourage the most capable people from striving to excel. Others feared that the lack of emphasis on employee shortcomings during progress review interviews would gradually entrench sloppy or inefficient habits. The experiment furnished no evidence to support these fears; but if they would eventually prove to be true, they would have to be reckoned as costs to be weighed against the benefits of the system.

At first glance, the different method of administering salaries may seem to have broken the link between pay and performance (and to have done so without damage to the organization): within the broad group of G's—87% or more of the total, as we noted—raises were based not on performance differences but on the position of one's salary within a range.

The traditional system, however, may actually have broken that link more than the new one has, by rating workers' performance against each other rather than against the expectations implied in their job descriptions, and by making finer distinctions between acceptably performing people than can be justified.

The experiment recognized that in companies that hire selectively, promote on the basis of superior performance, and reassign or dismiss on the basis of inadequate performance, the distribution of performance does not follow a bell curve but is skewed disproportionately toward superior performance. Therefore, expectations must be similarly skewed; presumably, most people will turn in results that fall within a broad range of acceptability, and only a few will either exceed or come up short of that range.

By eliminating the implied stigma of inferiority that inevitably follows when most others are rated superior, the new system has restored the perception of a link between pay and performance for those whose performance had in fact been quite acceptable. It has not created a new stigma for those formerly rated as superior because they too preferred being rated against the expectations for their jobs rather than against other workers in jobs not necessarily similar to theirs.

Two main lessons have emerged thus far from the Cyanamid experience. First, motivation is more important than administrative convenience. Second, professional pride can be a powerful motivator and should not be discounted in considering how changes in performance appraisal and compensation systems will affect the productivity of knowledge workers.

About the Contributors

Michael Beer is professor of business administration, Harvard Business School. A specialist in organizational behavior, he has written numerous articles for management and professional journals, including *Harvard Business Review*. Most recently, he has written a book tentatively titled *Rediscovering Competitiveness: How to Develop an Adaptive Organization*, with Russell A. Eisenstadt and Bert Spector (Harvard Business School Press, forthcoming).

David H. Burnham is president, David H. Burnham and Associates, an organizational development and training consulting firm with offices in Cohasset, Massachusetts, and London.

John R. P. French, Jr., was program director at the Research Center for Group Dynamics, Institute for Social Research, University of Michigan, when the article in this book was published in *Harvard Business Review*.

Saul W. Gellerman is dean of the Graduate School of Management, University of Dallas. An industrial psychologist, he formerly headed his own consulting firm. He is the author of *Problems and Cases for Decisions in Management* (Random House, 1984).

Frederick Herzberg, Distinguished Professor of Management, University of Utah, was head of the Department of Psychology when he wrote his article, now a *Harvard Business Review* Classic. His writings include *The Managerial Choice: To Be Efficient and to Be Human* (Olympus, 1982).

William G. Hodgson is director of research services for the Medical Research Division of American Cyanamid Company.

Rosabeth Moss Kanter is Class of 1960 Professor of Business Administration, Harvard Business School. She has received many national honors and written numerous articles and books—among them, *The Change Masters: Innovation and Entrepreneurship in the American Corporation* (Simon & Schuster, 1983) and, most recently, *When Giants Learn to Dance: Mastering the Challenges of Strategy, Management, and Careers in the 1990s* (Simon & Schuster, 1989). The Harvard Business Review Video program *The Middle Manager as Innovator* is based on one of her *Harvard Business Review* articles.

Emanuel Kay, a psychologist, was a research specialist for General Electric Company, Behavioral Research Service, when the article in this book was published in *Harvard Business Review*.

Harry Levinson is president of the Levinson Institute, a consulting firm in Cambridge, Massachusetts, specializing in the psychological aspects of leadership and the management of stress and change. He is clinical professor of psychology, Department of Psychiatry, Harvard Medical School, and has been a visiting professor at Harvard Business School. The author of several books, he recently edited *Designing and Managing Your Career*, Harvard Business Review Book Series (Harvard Business School Press, 1988).

Jay W. Lorsch is Louis E. Kirsten Professor of Human Relations, Harvard Business School. He is also senior associate dean and a director of research. A specialist in organizational behavior, he has been a consultant on management problems to many firms. He is the author of numerous articles and books, including *Organization and Environment*, with Paul R. Lawrence (Harvard Business School Press, 1986), and, most recently, *Pawns or Potentates: The Reality of America's Corporate Boards* (Harvard Business School Press, 1989).

David C. McClelland is professor emeritus of psychology, Harvard University, and Distinguished Research Professor of Psychology, Boston University. He is also senior research associate, Center for Applied Social Science, Boston University. His article, written with David H. Burnham, won the 1976 McKinsey Award. He has published many other articles and books, including, most recently, *Human Motivation* (Cambridge University Press, 1988).

Douglas McGregor was professor of management, School of Industrial Management, Massachusetts Institute of Technology. Previously he had been active in the field of industrial relations and served as president of Antioch College. He died in 1964.

Herbert H. Meyer was a consultant for General Electric Company, Behavioral Research Service, before his retirement in 1979.

Winston Oberg was professor of management, Graduate School of Business Administration, Michigan State University, when he wrote the article included in this book.

Robert A. Ruh is vice president—human resources, Medical Specialty Devices Division, Baxter Health Care Corporation. He is the author of several articles and coauthor of *The Scanlon Plan for Organization Development: Identity, Participation, and Equity* (Michigan State University Press, 1974).

Wickham Skinner is professor of business administration, emeritus, Harvard Business School. An authority on focused factories, he has written many articles in *Harvard Business Review*, one of which won the 1986 McKinsey Award. He is also the author of several books, including *Manufacturing: The Formidable Competitive Weapon* (second edition, Wiley, 1985).

Haruo Takagi is associate professor, Keio University, Tokyo, and the author of *The Flaw in Japanese Management* (UMI Research Press, 1985).

R. Roosevelt Thomas, Jr., was assistant professor, Harvard Business School, when he wrote the Harvard Business School Note included in the collection.

Victor H. Vroom is John G. Searle Professor of Organization and Management and professor of psychology at Yale University, where he has taught since 1972. He is an expert on leadership. He has published eight books—most recently, with A. G. Jago, *The New Leadership: Managing Participation in Organizations* (Prentice Hall, 1988)—and many journal articles. He currently serves on the editorial board of the *Journal of Conflict Resolution*.

Richard E. Walton is Jesse Isidor Straus Professor of Business Administration, Harvard Business School. He is an authority on work-force management issues and a pioneer in the development of high-commitment organizations. His books include *Innovating to Compete: Lessons for Diffusing and Managing Change in the Workplace* (Jossey-Bass, 1987) and, most recently, *Up and Running: Integrating Technology and the Organization* (Harvard Business School Press, 1989).

INDEX